Life Matters is the Mr. Rogers bible for adults. The Merrills' stories, wisdom, and navigational tools will help you achieve your greatest goals and make your life's journey more enjoyable.

 —Pat Croce, former President of the Philadelphia 76ers
 and the author of *I Feel Great!* and *110%*

Read this book, *Life Matters*—it's the fourth "Gotta Do." This book clearly articulates and demonstrates that balance in work, time, and money is not only achievable but critical to winning in the game of life.

 —Pete Beaudrault, former President and CEO of Hard Rock
 Café Intl., President and CEO of RLE Intl Consultants

Congratulations! You have discovered how to control and maximize one's full potential and not lose but gain quality of life. The world needs alignment and this book!

 —Stedman Graham, entrepreneur, author, speaker

At last, a way to "sync" what matters most with what we actually do! And with an approach that helps people understand, simplify, and incorporate the power of technology in resolving life balance issues. The Merrills present the ideal solution for knowledge workers who want to have quality family life.

 —Curt Allen, former President and CEO, MyFamily.com,
 President and CEO, Agilix Labs

Roger and Becky Merrill understand that life balance isn't a static condition that you obtain, but a dynamic skill that you learn. From the opening self-quiz to the last insightful conclusion, this book gives personal and individualized help in developing true balance.

 —Richard and Linda Eyre, authors of *Lifebalance* and
 The Book of Nurturing

One of the reasons *Life Matters* is unique is because it recognizes what a huge factor money plays in life balance issues. As well as dealing with work, family, and time, this book provides a positive, practical, integrated approach to creating financial balance and solving money problems.

 —Marci Redding, Chief Operating Officer,
 themoneyplanner.com

OTHER BOOKS BY THE AUTHORS

*First Things First: to Live, to Love, to Learn,
to Leave a Legacy*
(with Stephen R. Covey)

The Nature of Leadership
(with Stephen R. Covey and Dewitt Jones)

Connections: Quadrant II Time Management

Life matters

CREATING A DYNAMIC
BALANCE OF WORK, FAMILY,
TIME, AND MONEY

A. ROGER MERRILL
REBECCA R. MERRILL

McGraw-Hill

New York / Chicago / San Francisco / Lisbon / London
Madrid / Mexico City / Milan / New Delhi / San Juan
Seoul / Singapore / Sydney / Toronto

The *McGraw·Hill* Companies

1 2 3 4 5 6 7 8 9 0 DOC/DOC 0 9 8 7 6 5 4 3

ISBN 0-07-142213-7

McGraw-Hill books are available at special discounts to use as premiums and sales promotions, or for use in corporate training programs. For more information, please write to the Director of Special Sales, Professional Publishing, McGraw-Hill, Two Penn Plaza, New York, NY 10121-2298. Or contact your local bookstore.

 This book is printed on recycled, acid-free paper containing a minimum of 50% recycled de-inked paper.

Library of Congress Cataloging-in-Publication Data

Merrill, A. Roger.
    Life matters : creating a dynamic balance of
work, family, time, and money / by A. Roger Merrill and Rebecca
Merrill.— 1st ed.
    p. cm.
Includes bibliographical references and index.
    ISBN 0-07-142213-7 (hardcover : alk. paper)
    1. Conduct of life. 2. Work and family. 3. Married people—Time
management. 4. Married people—Finance, Personal. I. Merrill, Rebecca
    R. II. Title.
    BJ1581.2.M47 2003
    158—dc21

                                     2003007675

CONTENTS

To our parents, children and grandchildren—
the roots that give us strength
and the fruits that bring us joy;
and to all
who sincerely believe
that "life matters!"

ACKNOWLEDGMENTS

We would like to express our deep appreciation to:

- Stephen R. Covey and to many others whose modeling, mentoring, research, and writing have had a significant impact on our thoughts and in our lives.

- Greg Link for his valuable insights, friendship, help, and constant support.

- Ken and Marci Redding of themoneyplanner.com for their collaboration in the area of personal finance.

- Kathleen Bahr and Cheri Loveless for their scholarly insights in the area of family work in the modern world.

- Nancy Hancock and her associates at McGraw-Hill for all their help—especially for input that has pushed us to new levels of organization and communication.

- Jan Miller and her associates at Dupree-Miller.

Annie Oswald, Sean Covey, Debra Lund, Boyd Craig, Toni Harris, and others who have been helpful and supportive in many ways throughout this effort.

Most importantly, we would like to express gratitude to our parents and to our incredible children and their spouses. Not only have they provided tremendous help in reviewing and contributing to this manuscript, but—along with our wonderful grandchildren and our marvelous work opportunities—they have provided the rich, meaningful life experience that has given us something to write about.

FOREWORD

"Profound knowledge." These are the words of the late Edwards Deming—the management/quality guru who helped bring America back to economic prominence in the 1970s and '80s. He used this phrase to describe the deeper knowledge of human nature and principles needed to understand and make practical knowledge work.

Profound knowledge is literally what this book is. In fact, what I would say is "profound wisdom," because it interweaves timeless, universal, self-evident principles into all of the knowledge that is given. The great educator Alfred North Whitehead differentiated knowledge from wisdom in this way:

> *In a sense, knowledge shrinks as wisdom grows; for details are swallowed up in principles. The details of knowledge which are important will be picked up ad hoc in each avocation of life, but the habit of the active utilization of well-understood principles is the final possession of wisdom.*

Rebecca and Roger Merrill are not only truly marvelous people, they are a remarkable couple. As will become wonderfully obvious to you, they practice and live what they teach. They didn't just learn these things; they *earned* them, often the hard way, as they clearly, humbly acknowledge.

I hope you share my passion for this remarkable book. I would like to share with you my experience with both Roger and Rebecca. I believe the more you understand them and my experiences with them both, the better you will understand the material in this book.

I have known Roger almost my entire adult life. We have been involved together in many enterprises and projects, and I can honestly say that he is one of the finest people I have ever known—a beautiful blending of heart, mind, and spirit. I also esteem him to be one of the finest and wisest teachers I have ever seen. He has been teaching material like this in his professional work all over the world for over 35 years.

Rebecca has been a godsend to me. Her faithful editing and contributions to *The 7 Habits of Highly Effective People*, from my point of view, were absolutely indispensable to the success of that book. Her editing and writing contributions together with her husband, Roger, to our book *First Things First* were core to it becoming, to my knowledge, the best-selling, hardcover time management book ever written. Rebecca also helped enormously in editing and creatively producing *The 7 Habits of Highly Effective Families*, which also, to my understanding, is the best-selling, hardcover family book ever published. There is no one I have worked with who is more diligent, more conscientious, more second-mile, or more empathic and supportive than Rebecca. You will come to "feel" what I'm saying as you read her personal stories, learnings, and "earnings."

After working with Roger and Rebecca on *First Things First*, I learned so much about technology and tools in managing time. I've always thought of Roger as a techno nut. He pays such a price in analyzing all the different alternatives before purchasing technology tools to optimize effectiveness and efficiency that I simply give my confidence to his conclusions and save my time in the research and analysis. The way that Roger brings to Rebecca all this amazing technology has wonderfully leveraged her special gifts.

You will find, as you read this material, the spirit of good teachers, because they always start with the student's mind, understanding, concerns, needs, and hopes. For instance, they softly but powerfully expose popular myths and misconceptions in order to give a platform for sharing insights—myths that most people have unconsciously come to believe such as:

"Balance means equalizing the scale."

"Faster is better."

"Work and family are natural enemies."

The Merrills quote Oliver Wendell Holmes, who once said, "I wouldn't give a fig for the simplicity on this side of complexity, but I would give my right arm for the simplicity on the far side of complexity." When, in this book, you get into the four fields of work, family, time, and money, you will come to see and feel that you are learning the simplicity on the far side of complexity. And what they call the three "gotta do's" organizes the material excellently.

Another very unique contribution of this book is their insights on money and personal finance. You will see how well the principles presented in the first three sections are applied to this vital and often painful area of our lives. It will give you a great cumulative sense of confidence in the underlying principles, in yourself, and in your ability to apply the principles personally and in your family.

Organizations will also find great value in teaching these principles of effectiveness to their people. Our research has shown a direct—and I feel obvious—connection between how well harmonized people's personal lives are and their effectiveness at work. Ultimately, organizational productivity comes from each individual's ability to focus on and execute around the top strategic priorities of their work group and organization. By implementing the "optimizers" described in "Work Matters" and creating this dynamic life balance that the Merrills describe, people will significantly increase their value to their organizations.

HOW TO GET THE MOST FROM THIS BOOK

I would like to offer two ideas on how to get the very most from this book:

First, *teach* or share each of the seven chapters with your loved ones, friends, or professional associates. Almost everyone knows that it is when you teach something that you really learn it. I would do it slowly and carefully.

Second, *discuss and apply* the ideas step by step. Start with baby steps, if you wish.

I will tell you what will happen if you do these two things: you will make the positive changes in your life legitimate with others because you will be sharing what you, yourself, are learning. When you share with others what you are learning in the spirit of humility, it will cause them to see you in a new light. This will tend to break down old labels. It will literally make change legitimate in your family and professional culture. It will also enroll those with whom you share and discuss your learnings to become part of your support team. One of the things that we've learned in the field of personal change is that a nurturing support team is almost essential, particularly if you seek change that is real and sustainable.

To learn and not to do is really not to learn. To know and not to do is really not to know. As you come to understand and then share this material with others—not with the intent of shaping them up, but with the intent to sincerely share what you, yourself, are genuinely learning—you will be on your way in all four of these areas, particularly if you make internal commitments and begin making the necessary changes. If you "fall off the wagon" from time to time, reread the last chapter on wisdom and get inspired by the various ideas and quotes. You might also go back to the first two chapters so that you have a burning sense of purpose and fire that come from understanding the "why" of things.

Even though I have worked with the Merrills for over 20 years and have seen them in many different contexts, I was both surprised and delighted with all of their new material, new insights, and new learnings. Seriously, this is profound stuff. It is deep and enormously practical.

This material is anything but trite, success-formula blather. You will discover fresh new angles in every subject. Look for them. You will see the larger context given and principles introduced before the practical side is approached. Illustrations are abundant. The reading flows.

How many couples do you know that could synergistically produce such a magnificent book? Synergy means "one plus one equals three or more." In other words, the whole is greater than the sum of the parts. This book is a synergistic product wherein the differences between Roger and Rebecca become strengths. The fruit of their synergy will enable people in all situations and walks of life to identify with practical common sense in the four fields of work, family, time, and money. The significance of this approach? Common sense is not common practice.

But it could be.

Stephen R. Covey

CHAPTER

1

WHAT MATTERS?

Balance is beautiful.
Miyoko Ohno

One of the profound impacts of events such as the war on terrorism, corporate scandal, the struggling stock market, and 9/11 is that they bring us dramatically and undeniably face-to-face with some of the things that matter most in our lives.

ROGER

For the past three decades I've taught corporate and public programs on time management and life leadership. Nearly always, it's taken a little time up front to break through people's comfort zone enough to get them to really consider their lives on a deeper basis.

Sure, people were frustrated with their lack of life balance. In fact, FranklinCovey surveys of more than 300,000 participants show that the increasing pulse of life balance frustration had even reached the point of the number one challenge for most.[1]

Sure, they were frustrated with increasing corporate demands and family disintegration. Nobody liked the fact that corporate

1

"success" seemed to demand increasing hours on the job . . . or that social statistics were showing that the divorce rate had more than doubled, teen suicide had nearly tripled, and out-of-wedlock births had more than quadrupled in the past 30 years[2]—particularly when some of those statistics reflected what was going on in their own homes.

Still, the overwhelming need people felt to somehow justify their self-worth through "busyness" had led to an urgency addiction that made being "too busy" to do what really mattered most at home or at work, something of an accepted necessary evil—at least on the surface.

But events of the recent past have changed that mind-set for many. When I approach a group now, there's a much more immediate, unified resonance with the need to focus our lives on "importance" instead of "urgency." There's an increased focus on spending time with the family. There's an increased focus on improving job performance.

But the burning question in everyone's mind now is HOW? HOW can I have the best of both worlds?

HOW can I prioritize the family and also do a great job at work?

And HOW can I do it in the midst of today's challenges, including job insecurity, family issues, and economic stress?

REBECCA

For women, the challenge is particularly intense. The pendulum has swung dramatically from the pre–World War II era when women were essentially wives, mothers, and homemakers . . . to the '70s, when many became convinced there was no real fulfillment except in the "glittering" corporate world . . . to the '90s, when some began to feel they'd literally thrown the baby out with the bathwater and tried to become "superwomen" and do it all . . . to the 21st century, when even though women have more choices than ever before, many feel successful in the workplace but inadequate as mothers, or resentful of or unappreciated in their work, and/or compelled to work because of economic pressure or social expectation.

How many women today really find joy in their work?

How many genuinely feel good about the quantity and quality of the time they're giving to their families?

How many make job choices that are not primarily economically driven?

How many feel they're really making a significant contribution in the workplace or in the world?

Women have unique talents and abilities that enable us to excel, both in the home and in the workplace. But our very uniqueness—including the ability to give and nurture life—provides intensified challenges when it comes to creating work/family balance. There are issues that every woman has to address, and one woman's life balance answers are not necessarily another's.

For decades, life balance has been a huge issue in our society. Even now, in a time when most of us are quicker to connect with what matters most, there's still a gap—sometimes an enormous gap—between what we say matters most and the way we actually spend our time and money.

If you want to get an idea of how significant this gap may be in your own life, just take a minute and pull out your planner or calendar. Pull out your checkbook or credit card statement. Look at where you've spent your time and money over the past few weeks. Do those spending decisions really reflect the things that matter most to you?

For many people—unfortunately—the answer to that question is "No." And the consequences are evident in their lives.

In our work, we've seen immensely successful executives who have climbed the ladder of success, only to leave behind them broken marriages and children who won't even give them the time of day, and others who see themselves as family focused, but are trapped in mediocrity at work. We've seen parents who feel guilty because they miss their children's ball games to attend meetings at work ... and others who feel guilty because they miss meetings to be at their children's ball games.

We've seen women who have left home to pursue careers and feel guilty about not being with their children . . . and others who have left the workplace to be with their children and feel that their inherent talent and capacity are unrecognized, unappreciated, and unused. We've seen working husbands and wives who are very much like two ships passing in the night, experiencing pain in their relationship as they struggle to figure out who does the dishes, carries out the garbage, and changes the diapers in this new two-working-parent society.

We've seen couples moving from excitement about the birth of a child to enormous distress at the realization that they both have to keep working in order to maintain their current standard of living. We've seen single parents who feel they're drowning in the struggle to be Mom, Dad, bread winner, and rational human being all at once. We've seen people whose hearts yearn to spend more time with their families or contribute to society in more meaningful ways, but whose time and energy are held hostage by huge debt loads, habits, and lifestyles that keep them from doing it. We've seen others who give "lip service" to values such as family strength and financial independence, but then go out and spend in unplanned ways that create huge indebtedness and strain relationships in the process.

And we've seen all of these things play out on the sands of a shifting economy. In recent years, for example, organizations were almost forced to become more "family friendly" in order to attract and retain the brightest and most productive employees. But as we're writing this book in a "down" economy, companies that are on the "family friendly" path are essentially there by value and choice, and many people are happy to simply have a job.

As we have explored these intense and often poignant life balance issues over the years, it has become more and more apparent that work, family, money, and time are not simply isolated arenas in which people can make incremental improvements and reap huge success. They are the essential elements of a highly interrelated and complex system. And while events such as the downturn in the economy or the threat of war may cause the pendulum to swing, drawing our attention to one element or another, the bigger picture of history and our own experience affirm the truth that over time, work, family, money, and time are *all* important and you simply can't sustain quality of life without reasonable success in each of these vital areas.

BOTTOM LINE:

Work matters. Work is far more than a job or career. It is a fundamental, ennobling principle of quality life. It's how we sustain ourselves and our families. It is also how we express our love, how we contribute, and how we nurture the divine and creative within.

Family matters. Family is the fundamental principle of personal happiness and of a regenerating, renewing society. The most important "success" is success at home, and making each generation better is the way we best contribute to society as a whole.

Time matters. Time is the language of value, the commerce of life balance. We can talk and dream all we want, but in the final analysis, it's what we do or don't do as we live each day that makes the difference. The way we spend our time reflects our ability to consistently focus on and achieve our highest priorities. It is the measure of our ability to translate what matters most into the decision moments of our daily lives.

Money matters. Money is also a language of value and is integrally related to almost every issue surrounding the relationship between work, family, and time. It is a concrete manifestation of the value others place on our time and life energy, and also a manifestation of the value we place on the "things" money can buy. To spend money is to exchange the results of past effort or commit future time to try to improve the quality of present and future moments for ourselves and/or others. The challenge of managing money is one of our most potentially helpful tools in building discipline and character in our lives.

Wisdom matters. Because life is dynamic, the real issue is not "balance," it's balanc*ing*. It's creating the *capacity* to balance—day in, day out—in the unique and ever-changing circumstances of our lives. Thus, wisdom is vital, not only in long-range planning and goal setting, but also and especially in daily "decision moments"— moments that test our integrity, expand our awareness, challenge our thinking, threaten to divert us from our predetermined path, or open doors of unanticipated opportunity. Consequently, in any decision moment, we cannot "not" decide. Indecision *is* decision. Life moves on. Consequences happen. Having the judgment to make good decisions daily is what empowers us with the ongoing capacity to weave work, family, money, and time into a satisfying balance.

The challenge, then, is to succeed in each of these four life areas—work, family, time, and money—and to develop the wisdom to synergistically balance the four in the ever-changing kaleidoscope of circumstances in which we live.

A PERSONAL EVALUATION

Before you read further, we suggest that you take a few minutes and assess how you feel about each of these vital elements in your own life. You may find it helpful to answer the questions below. As you read each set of statements, circle the number that best represents where you are: *0* means you feel best described by the statement on the left; *4* means you feel best described by the statement on the right; *1*, *2*, or *3* means that you identify with some position in between. If you prefer, you can answer this questionnaire electronically and have it automatically scored at www.franklincovey.com/lifematters.

WORK

I really don't like my work. Maybe:	**0 1 2 3 4**	I really love my work. I feel a sense of joy and contribution in doing it.

- My work environment (my boss, the people I work with, the lack of freedom or opportunity, etc.) is terrible.
- I feel like my job is meaningless and boring, but I don't have the education or skill to do something I'd like better.
- I only work because I have to.

I'm a fairly good employee, but I don't think either my boss or I would say I'm really great. I don't get the ratings, raises, or promotions I'd like.	**0 1 2 3 4**	I feel I am a good worker. I do my job well, and I believe my employer would rate my performance on the job as "excellent."
If I lost my job, I have no idea what I'd do.	**0 1 2 3 4**	My employability is not an issue. I have enough education and skill to get another good job should the one I currently have fall through.
My family has little or no idea of what I do on the job. We rarely talk about my work (except when I complain about it), and I never take family members to my workplace. All they know is that when I'm at work, I'm not meeting their needs at home.	**0 1 2 3 4**	My family knows about and appreciates the work I do. They're familiar with my workplace. They see my work as a positive contribution to the welfare of the family, and also to those who use the product or service I help create.
I feel like I work too many hours and neglect my family.	**0 1 2 3 4**	I feel comfortable with the amount and quality of time I spend on the job and with the results.

Total work score: (0-20): ____

FAMILY

I know family is important, but it feels like a lot of work. There are too many demands, too many arguments, too many people to please.	**0 1 2 3 4**	I love my family. I really enjoy spending time with them on a daily basis, and they enjoy spending time with me.

I don't know how to make my family better. I feel so tired when I get home, I just want to be by myself and "crash."	0 1 2 3 4	I try to be—and believe I am—a good family member (husband, wife, parent, etc.). I find joy and satisfaction in really investing in my family role.
The only things we really enjoy as a family are recreational—going on vacations, going to movies or sports events, etc.	0 1 2 3 4	As a family, we know how to work and learn together as well as play together, and we enjoy doing it and getting the results.
We live in the same house, but it feels like we're individuals going in different directions. We don't have a shared vision, open communication, or enough trust in each other to pull together as a team.	0 1 2 3 4	We have a sense of shared vision, and we generally have open communication and shared problem-solving. Together, we feel we have strength and resilience to face the issues and handle the tough challenges of life.
I'm not satisfied with the amount of time I spend at home. Work and/or other things keep me away from the family too much.	0 1 2 3 4	I feel good about the amount and quality of time I spend with my family and with the results.

Total family score: (0-20): ____

TIME

I nearly always feel like I'm running fast, "putting out fires," and trying to get everything done. But if I were to stop and ask myself if what I'm doing really matters, much of the time the answer would be "No."	0 1 2 3 4	I focus on achieving my highest priorities. I feel satisfied that I generally spend my time on what matters most.

I feel constantly torn between work and home. I'm always busy, but I feel like I'm not meeting the needs in either arena.	**0 1 2 3 4**	I feel comfortable with the way I balance my time between work and family and with the results.
I rarely have time to invest in personal development or building relationships. I know it's important to exercise and eat right, but I don't do it. I'm so busy . . . it feels like there's never time.	**0 1 2 3 4**	I take time on a regular basis to invest in personal development and quality relationships. I also invest time in maintaining personal well-being so that health and energy are not limiting factors in my life.
To me, technology feels like: • A jungle—confusing, overwhelming . . . I have no idea how to get through it. • A "necessary evil"—a "have to know" I struggle with on the job. • A "black hole" that sucks up my time and money with little positive return.	**0 1 2 3 4**	I appreciate technology. I invest appropriate time in keeping up on new developments, and I'm able to use technology effectively to help me accomplish what matters most.
What are my children learning about "time" from living in our home? Probably that you have to spend it working like crazy (often at unpleasant tasks) and worrying like crazy (usually about money) . . . and the best relief from working and worrying is to go on vacations, buy things, or watch TV.	**0 1 2 3 4**	In our home, we try to maintain an environment of positive, peaceful interaction and growth. We try to teach our children the principles of time management and life leadership that will empower them to live happy, balanced lives when they're adults.

Total time score: (0-20): ____

MONEY

	0 1 2 3 4	
I don't know where the money goes. It feels like there are always unmet needs and we're always behind. The economic factor is a driving concern in our lives.	0 1 2 3 4	I feel satisfied that we have enough money to meet our needs and that we're spending our money on what matters most.
Either: • I have ongoing credit card debt and I'm paying interest every month. • Even if I get a raise, the money disappears, and it seems like I'm no better off than I was before. • I do not have adequate reserves set aside for retirement, children's education, or other future needs. • Me living a budget? You've got to be kidding!	0 1 2 3 4	I feel that I've developed a significant degree of financial competence. My affairs are in order, I am not in major debt, I regularly live within my means and contribute to a reasonable retirement plan and other savings goals.
Finances are basically a major pain in our family. We usually don't talk about it; we argue about it. We're not in agreement on earning or spending priorities, and our spending is not coordinated.	0 1 2 3 4	Finances are one of our family's strengths. Dealing with money issues has helped us develop shared vision and values, effective systems, character strength, communication and trust.
We basically live from paycheck to paycheck and have few or no financial reserves. If one of us were to lose our job, we'd be in a terrible pinch.	0 1 2 3 4	Our family's welfare is not completely at the mercy of circumstance. We have sufficient resources set aside to weather some of the storms of economic fluctuation and temporary unemployment.

Either:	0 1 2 3 4	We regularly take the

Either:
- We just buy our kids the stuff they want or need.
- We've tried to give our kids earning jobs or allowances and encourage them to be careful with their money.

In either case, we haven't sat down and taught our children the basic principles of financial well-being. (In fact, we're not even sure we know them!)

0 1 2 3 4

We regularly take the opportunity to teach and give our children experience in living principles of financial management that will empower them to be effective money managers in their own families someday.

Total money score: (0-20): ____

WISDOM

I tend to get lost in the "busyness" of each day. It's difficult for me to maintain an ongoing sense of purpose and direction. I don't know how to recognize the inner promptings of conscience. I often feel confused and torn.

0 1 2 3 4

I feel a sense of overall meaning and purpose in my life and that I live each day true to my own inner promptings.

Decisions are hard for me. I have difficulty sorting through issues and knowing what matters most at the time.

0 1 2 3 4

I am comfortable making day-to-day decisions and feel they contribute positively to my overall direction and life balance.

I get frustrated when unexpected things come up that threaten to alter my plan for the day.

0 1 2 3 4

I'm able to respond to unanticipated work and family needs with confidence and peace.

I'm inspired by good thoughts, but I rarely have time to read. If I do, it's usually job-related "have to" reading or "escape" reading. I hardly ever take time to draw from the more uplifting, ennobling thoughts and literature that nurture the soul.	0 1 2 3 4	I take time to regularly replenish my store of wisdom, judgment, and perspective.
Our family rarely or never spends time together reading and discussing great thoughts.	0 1 2 3 4	We regularly take time as a family to read and discuss some of the major wisdom literature of the world.

Total wisdom score: (0-20): ____
Total overall score: (0 to 100): _____ .

Your total score will give you a holistic picture of how you feel about work, family, money, time, and the degree to which you feel you integrate them into a satisfying, balanced whole. The section scores will highlight areas of greatest potential for improvement. We recommend you retake this survey periodically to help index your improvement.

Because life is moving at an increasingly fast pace, the consequence of having one or more of these essential life elements out of order is becoming more and more severe. If you aren't highly employable and good at your work . . . if you don't have the character and competence to be a good spouse, parent, son, daughter or sibling . . . if you're in debt over your head and constantly pressed by economic concerns . . . if you're stressed and feel as if you never have enough time and that important things in your life aren't getting done . . . these things are going to negatively, significantly, and increasingly impact on the quality of your life.

But the good news—actually, the *great* news—is that when you do get work, family, money, and time aligned and working together, they not only provide a sense of competence and fulfillment in each individual area, they create a powerful synergy and a driving engine that keeps you moving forward with increased energy and overall life satisfaction. They also transform daily challenges into the "resistance training weights" that build enduring wisdom, character, and life balance capacity.

WHAT YOU CAN EXPECT FROM THIS BOOK

So how do you do it? How do you achieve competence in handling each of these four areas and also blend them into a synergistic life system that creates this capacity and positive momentum?

That's what *Life Matters* is all about.

Thirty-five years of personal and professional experience have convinced us that there are three focused, high-leverage Gotta Do's that are absolutely essential in order for any individual to create effective life balance. In Chapter 2, we'll explore these essential Gotta Do's. In Chapters 3 through 6, we'll use them as a framework to show you how to create positive change in the way you deal specifically with work, family, money, and time. In Chapter 7, we'll show you how you can develop the wisdom to blend these four life elements into an effective and satisfying whole.

As we explore these essential elements of life balance, we're going to ask you to ask yourself some hard questions about your deepest values, attitudes, motives, and habits. The greatest asset you can bring to this experience is a deep inner honesty that will enable you to face these questions—and the answers—head-on.

We'll also make specific, practical suggestions as to how you can implement your answers. These suggestions, though simple, are not simplistic. In the spirit of Oliver Wendell Holmes—"I wouldn't give a fig for the simplicity on this side of complexity; I would give my right arm for the simplicity on the far side of complexity"—we have gone through literal mountains of material and tried to boil it down into simple, high-impact, high-leverage ideas and applications. The practical *to do's* "on the far side" have reason, research, and experience behind them. And as people worldwide attest, they work. They're doable. They grow out of timeless principles. They can be adapted in any situation. We've also included a categorized bibliography of selected works for those who are interested in further study.

As you read, though, we ask you to always keep in mind that *you* are in the driver's seat. An application that's perfect for somebody else might not be right for you. We'll share our experience and hope it provides insight. But always remember: you are unique. Your situation is unique. Your family, your relationships, your work, and your challenges are all unique. That's why you're the only one who can make the choices regarding how these principles will best apply in your situation.

The resources we've brought to this book will most likely challenge your thinking. But we assure you that with a genuine willingness to question your deepest paradigms and work through the issues, you have the capacity to create a sense of balance in your life that will radiate from your deepest inner core to your major decisions to the smallest details of your everyday life.

Our own struggles and our work with people worldwide have convinced us that if you approach the material in this book openly and with sincere desire and commitment, you'll be able to create a personalized, principle-based approach robust enough to handle the challenges and opportunities of effectively balancing work, family, money, and time in an increasingly whitewater world.

CHAPTER

2

THE THREE
GOTTA DO'S

You can do anything you want, but not everything.
—William Ray Rippy

We live in a world that is filled and running over with books, television programs, seminars, tapes, CDs, articles, and Web sites that contain thousands of ideas about what we can do to make life better. These ideas range from little things, like keeping track of the water you drink during the day by only using one container, to huge things, such as listening with empathy to improve a strained relationship.

Many of these are good ideas. Some of them are great ideas. But there are a few key *do's* in life that make such an enormous difference—their impact is so huge, their implications so far-reaching, that they truly are in a class by themselves.

In the area of life balance, these pivotal "Gotta Do's" are:

1. Validate expectations.

2. Optimize effort.

3. Develop "navigational intelligence."

To tap into the power of these Gotta Do's is the key to the building a momentum-generating life balance capacity.

GOTTA DO 1: VALIDATE EXPECTATIONS

When you're operating out of assumptions and paradigms that are incomplete, inaccurate, or distorted, there's no way you're going to get maximum quality results. Align your expectations with reality—with the way things really are—and with the timeless and universal principles that create the positive results you want to achieve.

Years ago, an associate shared with us the following experience:

While a woman was waiting for her plane at London's Heathrow Airport, she purchased a package of English shortbread cookies. Making her way to a seating area, she carefully arranged her luggage and was getting settled when a man approached and indicated by pleasant gesture that he would like to occupy the seat next to her. She nodded and he sat down.

After a few moments, the woman decided to eat some of the cookies she had purchased, and she reached down to get them. As she opened the package, she noticed the man beside her watching with great interest. She took the first cookie and began to eat when, to her great surprise, the man reached over, smiling, and took the second cookie.

The woman ate her cookie in stunned silence, astonished at the audacity of the man. After a moment she determinedly reached for the third cookie, but no sooner had she taken it out of the package than he, again smiling and without a word, reached over and took the fourth. Her indignation rose as back and forth they went in total silence, she taking a cookie, he taking a cookie, until they reached the bottom of the package where the final cookie remained.

Without hesitation, the man reached over and took it, broke it in half, and cheerfully handed her one of the pieces. The woman took her half of the cookie with an icy glare. After finishing his half, the man stood, still smiling. With a polite bow, he turned and walked away.

The woman could not believe that anyone could be so arrogant and rude. She was extremely flustered, her stomach churning. Making her way back to the airport gift shop, she picked up a package of antacid. As she opened her purse to get the money to pay for it, she stopped short.

There in the bag was her *unopened package of shortbread cookies!*[1]

Can you even begin to imagine the embarrassment, the chagrin, this woman felt when she discovered her mistake? Think of her attitudes and her behavior—inappropriate, rude, potentially destructive—and all stemming from the way she *saw* the situation. If she had seen things as they really were, how different her experience would have been! Instead of wasting all that time and energy struggling with shock, anger, suspicion, and embarrassment, she could have enjoyed a pleasant conversation with a man of obvious manners, character, charm, and a great sense of humor.

As observers, it's easy for us to laugh at the situation. But most of the time we're not the observers; we are the participants in real-life situations in which our own attitudes and behaviors are the result of some unrecognized, incorrect, or incomplete thinking pattern. In these situations, we don't find it so easy to laugh. We live with the pain, the frustration, the misjudgment, often never making it to that final scene where we discover that the basic assumptions causing the pain were wrong all along.

Just take a minute and imagine what your own possible involvement in this experience might have been. Suppose, for example, that you had watched this interaction but you hadn't been in on that final discovery that the cookies were really his. Suppose you were to board the plane and find that the man involved had the seat next to you. What would your reaction be when they brought your meal? Do you think you might eat with your fork poised in defense, watching him warily out of the corner of your eye?

Now suppose you were aware of that final discovery. Would that affect how you saw the man as he took the seat next to you? A little . . . or a lot?

The point is, because the way we see so dramatically affects our thoughts and behaviors, it's absolutely vital that we *see* clearly. And this is especially true when it comes to expectations, because our expectations create the basis of our decisions and actions and of the results we get in our lives.

They also create most of our frustration. As our friend and colleague Stephen Covey has observed, "Frustration is a function of expectation." When our expectations are based on illusion or wishful thinking, or when they don't take into honest consideration the realities of our own situation, we'll likely be disappointed and frustrated most of the time.

In our previous book, *First Things First*, we explained the importance of the way we *see* in terms of the "See-Do-Get" cycle pictured below.

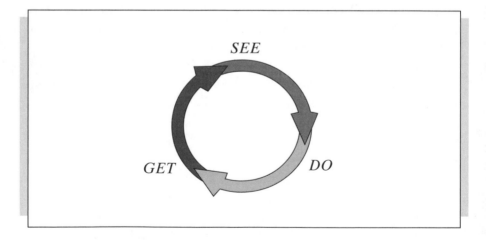

The idea is that what we *see* determines what we *do*. And what we *do* determines the results we *get*. So if we really want to change the results we're getting in our lives, the most effective place to begin is to work on the way we *see*.

ALIGNING WITH "REAL" AND "REALISTIC"

The most effective way we can intervene at the *see* level is to validate our expectations in two vital ways:

* With what is *real*: the timeless, universal "true north" principles that govern in all of life

* With what is *realistic*: what you can reasonably hope to achieve or become in your own situation

To align expectations in these two ways is to create the foundation out of which life balance capacity naturally grows.

So what is "real"?

Principles are real. They are those timeless, universal truths that govern all of life. They are a sure foundation—one that will not disintegrate over time or fade with passing philosophies and fads. To understand and align our expectations with principles will generally lead to thought patterns and actions that bring long-term success.

Consider "trust," for example. Trust is a timeless principle. It operates in our lives and relationships whether we're aware of it or not, whether we respect it or not. If we personally *value* trust and we *see* relationships in terms of building trust, we're going to *do* things that are trustworthy. We're going to treat people with consideration. We're going to respect confidences. We're going to keep our word. We're going to act in ways that reflect our concern for the well-being of others. And generally, the results we get will be high trust relationships that will weather life's storms.

On the other hand, if we *don't* value trust and instead see life and relationships in terms of immediate self-gratification—"What's in it for me now?"—we're more likely to *do* things that may maximize some short-term return but do not build long-term trusting relationships. We may make promises we don't intend to keep. We may befriend people today and "stab them in the back" tomorrow. We may engage in unethical business practices that create immediate profit. But, long-term, what are the results? Such actions will never build lasting quality relationships or long-term success.

ROGER

At one time when I was facilitating a management seminar and brought up the issue of trust, a participant shared a very sad story.

He said that the CEO of his company had recently retired. This man was arrogant and almost brutal when it came to the way he dealt with people. Evidently, he thought that his hard line and tough decision-making approach were of great benefit to the company and that people appreciated it.

The day following his retirement party, he came to the office to pick up some things he'd left. He no longer had any authority; his ID was not recognized in the security system. When he asked the security guard to let him in, the guard wouldn't do it. After years of being treated rudely, this guard was finally in a position to give back a little of what he'd been dished . . . and he did!

After quite an ordeal, the ex-CEO was finally admitted inside the building. But when he went to his office, nobody spoke to him. Nobody helped him. They just looked at him with disdain. There was obviously no respect for this man. And without his authority, nobody had to treat him well, so they didn't.

The realization of the consequences of his behavior hit him like a ton of bricks. He realized that all the "respect" he thought he'd had was nothing more than a required response to his authority and his hand on the purse strings. There was no real respect because there was no character there to respect.

The point is, while incorrect paradigms may appear to bring temporary results, truly *seeing* life in terms of timeless principles—such as trust—is clearly and absolutely foundational to any genuine whole-life success.

So, too, is *seeing* life in terms of what is realistic.

Suppose, for example, that you've become convinced that trust is a principle of effectiveness, and you determine that you want to embrace it as a guiding principle in your life. But for years you've been operating out of a different paradigm, and you've done things that created rifts in your relationships with other people. Is it reasonable to expect that just because you've had a major paradigm shift, suddenly all the problems created by your previous operational paradigm will suddenly disappear?

No, it's not. But it *is* reasonable to expect that there are things you can do that will make a big difference over time. You can sincerely apologize. You can make efforts to rectify problems and restore losses created by your actions. You can begin to interact with integrity in every situation. You can begin to build trust and heal broken relationships. Even if those you're trying to work with choose not to respond in positive ways, you will still be making a powerful positive difference. By valuing trust, you're building your own character and significantly enhancing your ability to handle future relationships in more effective ways.

This *will* improve the quality of your life. But it isn't necessarily a "quick fix." And if you *expect* it to be, it's likely that you'll be disappointed.

As you begin to think about life in terms of what is realistic, keep in mind that this does *not* mean you cannot dream. In fact, the opposite is true. As long as your dreams are in harmony with principles, being realistic is what empowers you to fulfill them.

Erik Weihenmayer had a dream—to climb Mount Everest. Many people have had that dream. Less than a hundred ever accomplished it, and Erik was one of those.

But what made Erik's accomplishment so incredible is that Erik is blind.

In a speech at a recent FranklinCovey Symposium, Erik told how, encouraged by the example of Helen Keller—who "took the world's perceptions about the disabled and shattered them into a million pieces"—he set his goal to climb the mountain. But he had no illusions about the difficulties he faced. It was with realistic expectations that he dealt with his own limitations. He paid the price to be in excellent physical condition. He spent years becoming a world-class climber and made many ascents before attempting Everest. He worked hard to earn the trust of his climbing team. He discovered ways to compensate for the sight he didn't have, such as putting tiny bells on the climbers in front of him.

Erik was not only a dreamer; he was a realist. One of the reasons he was able to fulfill such a fantastic dream was because he faced the reality of where he was, and he developed ways—in his unique situation—to reach his goal.[2]

So, too, did Admiral James B. Stockdale.

ROGER

*Some time ago I presented at a program for CEOs in Arizona. Leadership and management expert Jim Collins was on the program just before me. He was speaking on his book that would soon be out—*Good to Great*—in which he shares research identifying the characteristics of good companies that have "made the leap" to greatness and enduring success. Having arrived early, I was excited to sit in on his presentation.*

As he spoke, Jim told of an interview he'd had with Admiral James Stockdale, the highest ranking military officer in a prisoner-of-war camp during the Vietnam War. During the eight years of his internment, Admiral Stockdale was subject to terrible conditions. He was personally tortured over 20 times. Nevertheless, he managed to lead and inspire his men and help them develop ways to communicate and endure.

When Jim asked him how he managed to survive, he replied, "I never doubted not only that I would get out, but also that I would prevail in the end and turn the experience into the defining event of my life . . . " He also observed, though, that the "optimists"—those who expected to be out by Christmas, and weren't . . . or Easter, and weren't . . . or Thanksgiving. and weren't . . . or the next Christmas, and weren't . . . eventually did not survive. They "died of a broken heart."

Admiral Stockdale concluded: "You must never confuse faith that you will prevail in the end—which you can never afford to lose—with the discipline to confront the most brutal facts of your current reality, whatever they might be."

Jim came to call this the "Stockdale Paradox," and said he'd been surprised to discover it was a common characteristic of all the successful companies he and his team researched. In his book, he observed that the "Stockdale Paradox is a signature of all those who create greatness, be it in leading their own lives or in leading others."[3]

To us, this "Stockdale Paradox" unforgettably illustrates the power of validating both our unfailing confidence in the overarching, long-term principles that govern in life and also the sometimes harsh or brutal realities of "now."

MYTHS AND MISCONCEPTIONS

To illustrate how expectations affect our ability to create life balance, let's look at some myths and misconceptions: expectations that are *not* aligned with what is real and realistic. As you read, consider whether one or more of these reflects the way you think and impacts the things you do and the results you get. Consider the difference it would make if your expectations were more fully aligned.

MYTH 1: THE IDEAL LIFE IS WORRY FREE

Though we may not realize it, many of us live with the underlying assumption that the ideal life is problem-free. When things are difficult or they don't work out the way we plan, we're surprised. We live with the illusion that others—usually those whose lives we envy—don't have difficulties, and we think we're somehow lacking or marked by fate because we do. As a result, we see problems and challenges as "curve balls" that leave us scrambling to recover.

But think about it. Looking beyond the tabloids and media-created images, how many people do you personally know—really *know*—who don't have problems or challenges in their lives? Have you had the experience of thinking someone was problem-free from a distance, but when you got to know that person, discovering that he or she had challenges of which you were unaware? Looking back over thousands of years of recorded human history, do you see any evidence that life on this earth has been "a breeze" for most people, or that challenge is not an inherent part of life?

As the noted author and psychologist Dr. M. Scott Peck has observed:

Life is difficult. This is a great truth, one of the greatest truths. It is a great truth because once we truly see this truth, we transcend it. Once we know that life is difficult—then life is no longer difficult. Because once it is accepted, the fact that life is difficult no longer matters.[4]

Once we align our expectations and accept the reality that life, by nature, is both unpredictable and challenging, we remove much of the frustration we live with day by day. In fact, we can then find satisfaction—even joy—in facing the unknown and overcoming challenge.

Think about some of the great literature or profound thoughts you may have read over the years, or some of the classic movies you've seen. Do they not reflect this more realistic view of life? Don't they make it clear that real satisfaction comes as we face difficulty and come to recognize or develop the character and capacity to solve problems and transcend challenge?

Again, M. Scott Peck has said:

Problems call forth our courage and our wisdom; indeed, they create our courage and our wisdom. It is only because of problems that we grow mentally or spiritually. When we desire to encourage the growth of the human spirit, we challenge and encourage the human capacity to solve problems.[5]

Validating our expectations concerning the nature of life can free us of much of our frustration. It also empowers us to transform problems and challenges into opportunities to grow—and to find satisfaction and joy in the journey.

MYTH 2: "BALANCE" MEANS EQUALIZING THE SCALE

Some of us labor under the 18th-century notion that everything can be reduced to mechanical, mathematical terms. We see "balance" as allocating the same amount of time and energy to both sides of a scale to keep them even. We live with the expectation that there is some point at which we ought to be able to create this kind of "balance," and that life ever after will be easier and more satisfying as a result. But we don't ever seem to reach that point, so we're frustrated most of the time.

Is life really like that—mechanical, static, sterile, cold?

Try another view.

Balance is staying upright on your surfboard when the waves are high and the ocean spray is in your face.

Balance is successfully maneuvering your kayak through whitewater rapids.

Balance is maintaining the grace and agility of an Olympic ice skater or the steadiness of a tai chi master as you execute intricate moves with precision.

Considering what we know of human experience, how can we possibly think we can feel "balanced" by simply equalizing the time and energy we spend on work and family—especially during seasons of natural focus, such as when we're starting a new business or we have a new baby or elderly parents who need care.

Life is not static—it's dynamic. Balance in one season is not the same as balance in another. Balance for one person or family is not the same as balance for another. And there are times when seasonal *imbalance* contributes best to life balance as a whole.

The mechanical, equal-sides-of-the-scale notion of balance works in a mechanical situation. But life is not mechanical. And if we're operating out of the expectation that "balance" is an event and that someday we'll be able to allocate our time appropriately to achieve it once and for all, it's likely that we'll be sorely disappointed.

More aligned with what's real and realistic is the view that life balance is a constantly changing, deeply personal dynamic equilibrium. Again, the challenge is not "balance," it's balanc*ing*. It's creating the *capacity* to balance in the changing circumstances of life.

MYTH 3: FASTER IS BETTER

Some of us tend to see "balance" in terms of a baseball metaphor. The objective is to run around the diamond fast enough to touch each base each day. The expectation is, the faster we run, the higher our chance of succeeding; and the more bases we actually touch, the more balanced we'll feel.

But the reality for most of us is that the faster we run, the more exhausted—and less satisfied—we feel. Somehow, additional bases keep popping up. And as we run faster and try harder to touch more of them, we still deal with a vague discomfort that we're running in circles and still leaving vitally important things undone.

Suppose, for example, you know you need to exercise. So you tell yourself: "I'll go to the gym for an hour after dinner tonight to work out."

But you also realize that you need to spend time with your daughter. So you tell yourself, "Okay, I'll take my daughter with me to the gym while I work out."

But you also realize you need to catch up on some important new information in your professional field. So you think, "I'll listen to that new book on tape while I take my daughter to the gym to work out."

But you also realize you need to contribute to your community. So you add: "I'll stop by the soup kitchen and help out for an hour before I listen to that new book on tape while I take my daughter to the gym for an hour after dinner to work out."

On and on it goes, and we somehow think if we can just run fast enough and jam enough in, life will be better.

Right?

Not necessarily.

Imagine that you're traveling down a road. The weather's great, your car's working fine, you're getting 30 miles per gallon and feeling good. Suddenly, you come across a new freeway that wasn't on your map. Instead of going 40 mph, you find you can now go 65. You're elated.

But what if—in the midst of your highly efficient trip—you suddenly discover that you've been traveling south down the California coast, while your destination is New York City, over 3000 miles to the east?

Unless you're headed in the right direction, increasing your speed will only get you to the wrong place faster. In addition, you'll miss many of the rich, satisfying moments of living along the way.

Consider your own life experience. Are you getting more done now than you did a year ago? Five years ago? Ten? You probably are. But how much more balanced do you feel as a result?

Speed isn't everything. In fact, it's worse than nothing if it moves you in the wrong direction faster and cheats you out of some of the best moments of the journey.

MYTH 4: WORK AND FAMILY ARE NATURAL ENEMIES

When we're feeling pulled between work and home, it's hard not to view them as enemies in competition for our limited available time. It appears that we can only satisfy one at the expense of the other.

But in fact, this is a distorted 20th-century—and primarily Western—view. As we consider work/home balance, there's a much bigger picture of "work" and "home" we need to see.

Professor Kathleen Bahr and Cheri Loveless have provided insightful contributions in this area.[6] As they point out, until the 20th century "work" was "family work." Rather than pulling families apart, work was something that, by its very nature, bonded families together. Children worked beside—and talked to and listened to and learned from—their parents as they labored at the workbench and in the fields to accomplish the life-sustaining tasks that drew them close.

But as the 20th century unfolded, dramatic change began taking place. Historian John Demos observes:

The wrenching apart of work and home life is one of the great themes in social history. And for father, in particular, the consequences can hardly be overestimated . . . Of course, fathers had always been involved in the provision of goods and services to their families; but before the nineteenth century such activity was embedded in a larger matrix of domestic sharing. With modernization, it became "differentiated" as the chief, if not the exclusive, province of adult men. Now, for the first time, the central activity of fatherhood was sited outside one's immediate household. Now, being fully a father meant being separated from one's children for a considerable part of every working day.[7]

"As the century wore on," Bahr and Loveless observe, "fathers were home less and less with their children until, during the 1950s, father became a guest in his own home—someone who was catered to when present and had little to do with the day-to-day family work."[8]

With industrialization, the role of women also changed. "Labor saving" devices made work more efficient, noisy, and isolated. Tasks that used to provide opportunities for rich interaction, deep discussion, and shared contribution became basically isolated and boring.

With husbands at work and older children in school, care of the house and young children now fell almost exclusively to mothers, actually lengthening their workday.

... Tasks once performed to nurture and care for each other in response to life itself were reduced to "housework" and . . . the homemaking arts dwindled into dull, efficient routine . . .

Much of a mother's work began to be done in isolation. Work that was once enjoyable because it was social became lonely, boring, and monotonous. More seriously, the labor of caring for a family increasingly lost value in the sight of society. Our culture began to determine worth by "exchange value," or the dollar value something would bring in the marketplace. Since work in the home had only "use value," it remained outside the market economy and its worth became invisible. No wonder women eventually followed men into the workplace to labor for money, weakening the one remaining connection of any depth between parents and their children.[9]

Industrialization also changed the nature of family life for children.

Prior to modernization, children shared much of the hard work, laboring alongside their fathers and mothers in the house and on the farm or in a family business. This work was considered good for them—part of their education for adulthood. Children were expected to learn all things necessary for a good life by precept

and example, and it was assumed that the lives of the adults sur-
rounding them would be worthy of imitation.[10]

But industrialization drew children out of the home and into
parentally unsupervised and abusive labor. Laws designed to protect
children and prevent such abuse in effect ended child labor.

Eventually, the relationship of children and work inside the fami-
ly completely reversed itself: children went from economic asset to
pampered consumer. What it meant to be a loving parent was even
revised. Loving parents were once those who taught their children
to contribute their labor and their income to the support of the
whole family; now loving parents were those who gave their chil-
dren advantages in life and enhanced their self-esteem . . .
  Over the course of the century, parents internalized this mes-
sage until, in 1970, Kenneth Kenniston could state in the report of
the Carnegie Council on Children that "[Today] children rarely
work at all." More recent time-use studies show children do some
work around the home, such as cleaning their bedrooms, fixing
their own snacks (though not usually cleaning up the mess), and
shopping, including recreational shopping. Meanwhile, when
children do earn wages outside of the home, they usually keep
the money as their own and primarily use it for recreational
"needs."[11]

We live in an isolated time in history, one in which men, women,
and children try to interact from the distant ends of the universe
where they have been flung as a result of the "big bang" of social
"advancement." Yet, we yearn for family togetherness and we try to
achieve it apart from the "enemy" of work.

We "bond" with our children by getting the housework out of the
way so the family can participate in structured "play." We improve
our marriages by getting away from the house and kids, from
responsibility altogether, to communicate uninterrupted as if

work, love, and living were not inseparably connected. We are so thoroughly convinced that the relationship itself, abstract and apart from life, is what matters that a relationship free from lasting obligations—to marriage, children, or family labor—is fast becoming the ideal.[12]

For most of the world throughout most of history, "work" and "family" have not been at odds with each other; they have been complementary parts of a whole life perspective that bonds families in love, contribution, and victory in the struggle to survive. Even though we live in a challenging, perspective-limiting time, we need to understand that *work is a principle* and *family is a principle*, and genuine life balance demands that we create a synergy—rather than a chasm—between the two.

THE IMPACT

Consider the four myths we've just explored:

- The ideal life is worry free.

- Balance means equalizing the scale.

- Faster is better.

- Work and family are natural enemies.

Clearly, paradigms such as these can have a significant influence on our ability to create life balance.

And these are only a few of many such paradigms. As we move on in the book, we'll take a look at other myths that deal specifically with work, family, time, and money. We'll explore how they skew our effectiveness in each of these arenas of life, and in life as a whole. We'll also identify some of the more "real" and "realistic" paradigms that lead to life balance success.

The point we want to make here is that it's vital to life balance to validate expectations in terms of what is both "real" and "realistic." This will ensure that the fundamental beliefs that give birth to our thinking, doing, and getting are a firm foundation in which we can have confidence and trust.

WHAT YOU CAN DO NOW

- Begin to take a hard look at your expectations. Get them out in the open so you can evaluate them. Are they based on any criteria that would indicate they are "real"? (On "wisdom literature," the lessons of history, your own experience, or the experiences of those you trust?) Do they take into honest consideration the realities of your own situation?

- As you read through this book and live through the experiences of each day, keep working constantly to examine and validate your expectations. Throughout the day, if you feel frustrated, stop and ask yourself why. What expectation do you have that's not being fulfilled? Is it real? Is it realistic? Look for specific areas of misalignment you can correct for greater effectiveness.

GOTTA DO 2: OPTIMIZE EFFORTS

Once you've created valid expectations, there may be hundreds—even thousands—of things you can do to improve in a particular area or move toward a goal. But unless your efforts are (1) aligned with valid expectations and (2) leveraged for maximum results, you will never get the greatest return on your investment.

REBECCA

In the late 1970s, when Roger first suggested buying a computer, I was against it. I don't particularly relate to technical "gadgets" and I was far from convinced that it would (or should) fit into our budget.

But then Roger showed me an amazing thing. He showed me how I could take words, sentences, even whole paragraphs, and change them, move them around, or even delete them—without having to retype the page. What a dramatic change from the type-

writer I was used to! I couldn't believe the freedom and increased efficiency that one feature would offer.

We bought the computer. We really had to pinch the budget to do it, but it turned out to be one of the best investments we ever made. It dramatically affected my ability to write. It also provided a far more efficient way to keep track of our finances. In addition, it enriched our lives (in the pre-Nintendo days) with hours of family fun and games.

We've come a long way since that first Atari computer some 25 years ago. I still don't particularly relate to the technical aspects of computers and communication systems. But I love the results! I can write, research, pay bills, organize my life, work on family genealogy, communicate with family and friends, and surf the Net! And I really can't even begin to calculate the increase in efficiency and effectiveness because of it.

ROGER

Different from Rebecca, I love gadgets. I read the magazines, scour the research, and try to keep up on the development of almost any technology that promises to genuinely increase effectiveness.

However, I've discovered that there is a significant price attached to the learning curve. I've spent hours laboring with new software, only to finally end up calling product support to have them tell me there's a "glitch" in the program, they're working on it, and they will be coming out with the next version in a few weeks. I've finally determined in most cases to wait until version 2.0 comes out to even invest time and money. That way, I may not be on the very cutting edge, but with the rate of technological change, I'm not far from it. And I believe the significant savings—especially in time—is worth the wait.

I've also discovered that, even with our lifelong focus on time management, it's easy to get sucked into the "black hole" of cyberspace. It's far too easy to click from one site to another on the Internet, pursuing paths that are interesting, but may only be a four or a five on a top-10 priority list. The "Web," it appears, was well named.

As we indicated at the beginning of this chapter, we live in a time when we're literally inundated by good things we can do to improve our lives. Global awareness and dramatic and rapid changes in technology significantly increase our options for increasing effectiveness. But they also increase the complexity of our lives and can create "black holes" in which time, money, and many good things in life—including relationships—can disappear.

So out of all the possibilities, how do we determine the most effective things we can do with our money and our time?

Gotta Do 2—optimize efforts—deals with deciding on and planning to accomplish the most aligned, high-leverage activities that grow out of valid expectations.

ALIGNMENT

Suppose you've validated an expectation in the area of money. For example, you've determined that having financial security is important. It's "real." It's based on the principles of self-reliance and sustaining a life that creates satisfaction, happiness, and peace.

But you've also determined that, "realistically," you're a long way from where you want to be. You have an expensive house, two cars, and a boat. You have four credit cards with a combined balance of $16,027, and a $15,688 home equity loan—all of which you're making minimum monthly payments on. You have two children in grade school and one in junior high. You have no money set aside for their education, and the only retirement assets you have are in a mutual fund account that recently lost half its value.

Now today is Friday, and you and your spouse have the weekend off. So how are you going to spend your time and/or money?

1. Go on an "overnighter" at an expensive resort to get away from it all.

2. Buy a new big screen TV so you can enjoy the Saturday afternoon football game.

3. Go to the zoo with your children.

4. Attend a financial planning seminar some friends told you was really good.

5. Take some time to discuss ways you can get out of consumer debt.

Obviously, some options are aligned with your principle-based expectation of achieving financial security . . . and some are not. You may have important reasons for choosing to do things that are *not* directly aligned with this specific expectation—for example, maybe you have another expectation around "family" and it's more timely to spend the weekend building those relationships (though, as we'll explain in the chapter on money, building financial strength is a *fantastic* way to build relationships with your spouse and children).

But if you really want to get the benefits of financial security in your life, sooner or later you've "gotta do" the things that are aligned with that expectation. (And, no, that doesn't mean win the lottery or inherit a fortune. As we'll explore in greater depth later, those "windfalls" often only exacerbate financial problems. Research shows that the vast majority of people we would probably consider "financially secure"—who have a net worth of over $1 million—did not win the lottery or a game show prize or inherit someone else's money; they are simply ordinary people who have learned and lived the "real" principles of creating and sustaining wealth.[13])

So the first thing to do to optimize your effort is to make sure it's aligned with what is both real and realistic. In the above example, you might attend that financial seminar your friends recommended. Often, such seminars are accompanied by a free dinner, which would make it a fun date for you and your spouse. Or you might take your kids to the zoo in the afternoon and then let them watch a video at home while you and your spouse spend some time talking about ways you could get out of consumer debt. Either of these things would be good things to do.

What probably would *not* be helpful is spending money on an expensive resort or big screen TV. In your situation, those choices would not be aligned with valid expectations about financial well-being.

LEVERAGE

The second thing to do to optimize your efforts is to make sure the effort is leveraged—that you're getting the most results for the effort you put in. And that involves both *what* you do and *how* you do it.

Consider the *what*.

Going back to our example, if that financial seminar is a onetime event being taught by a highly reputable financial counselor who is only in your city that day, you might prioritize the seminar. On the other hand, if there are other time options and you and your spouse feel you need to create shared vision around your goal of being debt-free, you might prioritize time together instead. Or you could do one of a number of other aligned activities—balance your checkbook, sign up for online banking, review retirement plan options, check into the probable cost of college for your kids, or read a few chapters in a book on the principles of sound financial management.

There are usually a number of activities that are aligned with valid expectations. The key is to prioritize the one or two aligned activities you feel will bring the greatest return in your situation.

Then consider the *how*.

Let's say you prioritize time with your spouse discussing options for getting out of consumer debt. You sit down together, and after reviewing the facts, determine that if you charge nothing else and simply continue to make your current minimum payments on your credit card and home equity debt, it's going to take you 13 years and one month to get out of debt, and you'll end up having to pay $14,380.91 in interest, for a total payoff of $46,075.91.

DEBT	AMOUNT	INTEREST RATE	PAYMENT
Credit Card 1	$6,703	18.0%	$175
Credit Card 2	$1,833	15.99%	$50
Credit Card 3	$4,822	18.00%	$160
Credit Card 4	$2,669	21.00%	$50
Total credit card debt	**$16,027**		
Home Equity Loan	$15,668	6.50%	$250

	Principal Paid	Interest Paid	Total Payments	Time In Debt
Current Course	$31,695.00	$14,380.91	$46,075.91	13 yrs 1 month

As you consider alternatives, you conclude that the best option would be to sell your boat and apply the money toward your debts. Since you made a healthy down payment on it, you think you'll be able to find someone to take over the payments. That will give you $375 more a month to put toward your debt.

One way you could implement that decision would be to divide the $375 each month into five equal payments of $75 each, which you could then apply toward the four credit cards and home equity loan. With that one simple decision, you could save $7998.52 in interest and reduce the time it would take you to get out of debt by eight years and four months!

	Principal Paid	Interest Paid	Total Payments	Time In Debt
Current Course				
+ $75 to each debt	$31,695.00	$6382.39	$38,077.39	4 years 9 months

That would be fantastic! It would be a great step toward reaching your expectation of financial security.

But is that the highest leverage way to do it?

What if, instead of dividing the $375 equally between your five debts, you followed the more high leverage debt elimination strategy suggested by our friends at themoneyplanner.com[14] and applied the entire $375 to the debt with the highest interest rate until that was paid off . . . and then added the payment you'd been making on that debt to the $375 and applied both to the second highest interest debt until it was paid off . . . and then added the payment you'd been making on that debt to the other two figures and attacked the third highest interest debt . . . and so on until all your debts were paid?

That one adjustment to your approach would enable you to save an additional $1,148.06 in interest and be out of debt an additional one year and 10 months sooner!

	Principal Paid	Interest Paid	Total Payments	Time In Debt
Current Course				
+ $375 roll down	$31,695.00	$5234.33	$36,929.33	2 years, 11 months

Just compare the difference!

	Dollar Savings	Time Savings
Adding $75 to each payment	$7998.52	8 years, 4 months
$375 roll down	$9146.58	10 years, 2 months

In today's fast-paced world, it's not only what you do, but also how you do it that makes the difference. The smarter you work, the more traction you'll create to move ahead.

As we move into the following chapters, we'll share with you more aligned, high leverage ways you can increase your effectiveness in each of the four major areas—work, family, time, and money—and also generate a positive, balancing synergy between the four.

WHAT YOU CAN DO NOW

* Begin to think about what you do in terms of *alignment* and *leverage*. Make sure you're not wasting time or money on activities that don't grow out of what matters most to you, or activities that don't maximize the time and money you invest.

* Start a "perhaps" list. As you continue to read this book and as you live through the experiences of each day, when you come across an idea you like and might want to implement, write it down. You might find it helpful to organize your list by "role": individual, spouse, parent, manager, PTA president, etc. This will enable you to capture good ideas without becoming distracted or overwhelmed by them. It will also provide a rich resource to help you sort through alignment and to leverage priorities when it's time to plan.

GOTTA DO 3: DEVELOP "NAVIGATIONAL INTELLIGENCE"

Your expectations may be real and realistic; your effort may be aligned and leveraged. But you still need to deal effectively with the challenges and opportunities of living each day. So how do you tell if the unanticipated is opportunity or opposition? How do you deal with the tension between the need to focus and the need to be open to the unexpected? The key is to develop your gift of discernment—the gift that empowers you to consistently recognize and respond to what matters most.

Most of us tend to think life would be a lot easier if we could simply plan and execute the plan—no interruptions, no changes, no surprises; just do exactly what we set out to do.

There's just one problem: Life is unpredictable. There's no way we can know in advance everything that's going to happen. We can do our best to anticipate, but we really don't know for sure what challenges, problems, or opportunities any day or any moment will bring.

That's why success in life balance is more than simply planning and executing—it's also developing the wisdom and judgment to make good choices in "decision moments." It's learning to navigate effectively through the myriad challenges we face each day.

"Navigational intelligence" is the ability to make good judgments in these decision moments. It's the ability to plot a good course, ride the waves, weather the storms, respond to the currents, and effectively course-correct. It involves the ability to know and do what matters most in life as a whole and also to know what matters most *now*—when you're working on a project and your daughter calls with a problem she wants to discuss, when you're sitting down to work on your taxes and you suddenly feel like going to a movie instead, when you're in the middle of your annual garage cleaning and your neighbor's car breaks down in the driveway, when you finish your low-fat lunch and you smell the aroma of fresh-baked chocolate cake.

This is where we face the real, gut-level, rubber-meets-the-road challenges of wisdom and life balance. And this is where we face one of the most difficult life balance dichotomies: the tension between focus and awareness.

If we totally immerse ourselves in a project, we're afraid we'll lose awareness of the people and opportunities around us. On the other hand, if we try to be aware, we can't give projects the intense focus they require for successful completion. As a result, we often live suspended in a mediocre middle world, only moderately aware, essentially unfocused, feeling victimized by the things coming at us and guilty about what's not getting done.

The solution to this dilemma—and to the problem of making good decisions in all moments of choice—lies in discovering, calibrating, and regularly using a wonderful gift we have called the *gift of discernment*. Properly developed, this gift empowers us to constantly scan for, recognize, and respond to what is most important— even when we're focused on something else.

REBECCA

I work at home—and so does Roger, much of the time. We have home offices across the hall from each other. We also have two children living at home, one in a nearby university, and four married children and 15 grandchildren, all living within 10 minutes of our house, and my mother living next door. Three of our children have significant health problems and sometimes require additional attention or help.

One of my biggest challenges is balancing the need for intense focus needed for writing with the flexibility of "being there" for the people I love.

I learned long ago that there are "teaching moments" with children that never come again. There are grandchildren whose births and special birthdays only come once. There are singular times when helping my mom or responding to a question from my college age daughter, helping my husband with a project or being available to tend grandchildren, really makes a difference.

I don't want to miss those opportunities. I don't want to shut the door and shut out the important people in my life. At the same time, there's no way I can write without times of intense focus.

So I try to plan based on the importance of the projects I'm working on and the needs of the people I love. I schedule regular writing times. I also plan special birthday "sneak-outs" with the grandchildren, regular dinners, family nights and other activities with the children at home, and a date with my husband once a week. I try to call my mother or see her every day.

But in the process of carrying out my plans, I find that nearly all the time—even when I'm engaged in high focus work—I have available a sort of subconscious "background scanning" capacity that can alert me to higher priority opportunities and needs that may arise. This capacity often allows me to quickly shift focus when Roger or one of the children comes into my office, or prompts me to prioritize a day differently than I had planned.

Learning to recognize this "auto scan" capacity and quickly shift gears is something that's been hard for me to do. By nature, I'm singularly focused. (I'm one of those people who finds it challenging to even cook and talk to someone at the same time!)

But it's not been nearly as hard as struggling with the discomfort that I may be missing important things, which I may later regret.

As long as my overall life values are in place and my scanning sensors are on, I find that responding effectively in the moment is generally much easier to do.

This "background scanning" is one of the ways the gift of discernment works in our lives. It doesn't take much bandwidth when it's on automatic. The key is to learn to recognize it and respond to it . . . and to "calibrate"—to adjust, regulate, or attune—it for maximum results.

ROGER

A few years ago I took our youngest son to Alaska. We went out on a fishing boat, and as we got farther out to sea, the shoreline became less visible and finally disappeared from view.

The captain of the boat showed us how to fish for the 50-pound halibut lurking below. As we fished, we could hear various beeps and other noises coming from the radar, sonar, and GPS (global positioning system) equipment on the boat.

The captain appeared to essentially ignore the sounds. But at one point a beep sounded that was different from the others. To this sound, the captain responded instantly. He immediately went in the cabin to check it out.

A few minutes later he was back. He informed us that his equipment indicated that there was a small weather disturbance moving into the area. After checking all the facts, however, he had concluded that it wasn't bad enough to return to shore. So we continued fishing. After a while, the winds came, but they passed without cause for concern.

The response of the captain to that particular sound illustrates the ideal response to impressions that come to us through our gift of discernment. There are many noises around us all the time, but our ability to hear and respond to the particular sound of our own inner "radar" is what empowers us to be aware of and act upon what matters most.

So how do we calibrate this inner radar? By doing three things:

* Valuing principles
* Evaluating experience
* Inviting inspiration

VALUING PRINCIPLES

We've already talked about the importance of validating our expectations in terms of the "real" principles that govern in all of life. As we gain confidence in the existence of these timeless principles and come to personally value, seek, and embrace them, we calibrate our discernment capacity. We adjust the settings so our automatic default mode reflects the natural laws and priorities that bring the greatest life balance results. In this way, we are constantly and naturally "scanning" for priorities aligned with principles that create positive results.

One powerful way to calibrate is by creating a *personal mission statement*, a process we've taught for years and written about in *First Things First*. Such a statement will create a basic framework against which the value of goals and unexpected opportunities can be quickly and naturally measured.[15]

Another way is to create a constant input of "wisdom literature"—that portion of world literature that embodies principles dealing specifically with the art of living. This is another process we've taught and written about, and we'll give this concept some additional attention and development in the chapter on wisdom.

When we clearly identify and frequently review principles and values, they become the foundation of our discernment and a standard against which the value of any activity is automatically measured.

EVALUATING EXPERIENCE

A good friend recently related her experience some years ago as a first year public school teacher. Having just received her degree, she was anxious to do well and was concerned about her lack of experience. As she talked with her father—a school principal—she expressed the sense of awe she felt about a teacher in his school who had taught for 35 years.

"How wonderful it must be to have 35 years of experience!" she exclaimed.

Her father thought for a moment, then replied, "There's a difference between 35 years of experience . . . and one year of experience 35 times!"

Sometimes it seems we go through life making the same dumb mistakes, getting the same negative consequences, over and over. And we never "learn." If you've seen the movie *Groundhog Day*, you've probably laughed at the character played by Bill Murray who—through some quirk of fate—actually did live the same day over and over until he finally realized the consequences of his choices and learned to make better ones. In repeated and often comical efforts to live through the day, he gradually changes from a self-centered, arrogant, offensive, "what's in it for me?" schlock to an honest, humble, genuinely nice guy who spends his time reading good literature, developing his talents, and helping others. In making the change, he's finally able to develop enough character to create a quality relationship with a wonderful woman who would never have considered him otherwise.

Sometimes it's easy to laugh when we watch a funny movie and see someone making the same stupid mistakes over and over again. But the reality in our own lives is not so funny. In fact, it's inefficient, ineffective—and often painful.

So why do we do it? Experience is supposed to be the great teacher. Why don't we learn?

The answer is that most of us don't take the time to evaluate and course-correct. We live with the invalid expectation that "success" somehow does not involve making mistakes, and so we see our mistakes as failures, and they make us feel disillusioned and weary. As a result, we fail to tap into the power of our mistakes as high leverage feedback and course-correction tools.

In his book, *Peak Performers*, achievement expert Charles Garfield refers to a study conducted by Warren Bennis of ninety leaders in "business, politics, sports, and the arts, including sixty board chairmen and CEOs of major corporations." Garfield observes:

With their attention on achieving their mission, the word failure *seldom enters a conversation unless someone else brings it in. The scores of synonyms for it—glitch, bug, hitch, miss, bungle, false start, to name just a few—convey their view that what someone else might call a failure is something from which they intend to learn. As one of them said, "A mistake is simply another way of doing things."*[16]

As anyone who's every tried to navigate a boat or a plane can tell you, arriving at a particular destination is a function of making constant course corrections. You have to allow for the impact of the currents, the weather, and other elements, and you have to adjust for them.

It's only when we don't *expect* to course-correct that we run into trouble. Then we're afraid of feedback—of the very information that can best empower us to get on track and reach our goal.

One excellent way to evaluate experience is to keep a personal learning journal. We'll look at this and more high leverage ideas in the chapter on wisdom.

INVITING INSPIRATION

Even beyond what we can learn about principles and from experience is a quiet but powerful insight that gives specific personal direction and highlights what we need to work on or respond to at any given time. But we only receive the full benefit of this insight when we open ourselves to it.

If you've ever been on a personal retreat, gone through the process of writing a personal mission statement, or taken a quiet moment to reflect before setting a goal, you've probably felt this kind of inspiration. If you've learned to pay attention to it on a regular basis, you probably found yourself doing things that bring a great deal of satisfaction in your life.

In the words of the poet John Greenleaf Whittier:

He is wisest, who only gives,
True to himself, the best he can:
Who drifting on the winds of praise,
The inward monitor obeys.
And with the boldness that confuses fear
Takes in the crowded sail, and lets his conscience steer.[17]

We have one friend who has a firm grasp on what's important in life. He plans and executes and accomplishes a great deal. But a real key to his inner peace and life satisfaction is symbolized by the small notebook he keeps with him at all times. He's constantly on the alert for inspiration. When he receives an impression, he immediately writes it down and he holds himself accountable to follow through with whatever it was he felt impressed to do. As one by one these things are carried out, little by little this man adds to his store of personal strength and confidence in his ability to recognize and respond to the whisperings of his conscience . . . and to his sense of deep, personal fulfillment.

As we go through the chapters on work, family, time, and money, we will identify principles in each of these four areas with the goal of helping you build your discernment capacity. We'll also focus—particularly in the chapter on wisdom—on evaluating experience, course-correcting, and inviting inspiration.

WHAT YOU CAN DO NOW

* Begin paying attention to your discernment capacity. Nurture it with meditation and wisdom literature; exercise it and strengthen it by using it. Notice that the more you pay attention to it, the more active it becomes.

IF YOU DON'T DO THE GOTTA DO'S

The three Gotta Do's we've discussed in this chapter validate expectations, optimize efforts, and develop your navigational intelligence —are vital life-balancing tools. You can tell they're Gotta Do's by asking yourself what happens when you don't do them:

* What happens when you don't validate your expectations—when you operate out of paradigms that are incomplete, inaccurate or distorted?

* What happens when you work hard, but what you're doing is not aligned with valid expectations or leveraged for optimum results?

* What happens when you lack navigational intelligence, when you don't have the discernment to determine what matters most in moments of choice?

Can you see the impact on your ability to create balance and momentum in your life?

Validate.

Optimize.

Navigate.

Let's now use these Gotta Do's as a framework to look specifically at work, family, time, and money. The objective of these next four chapters will be to explore the ways we think about these arenas of life, to align our expectations with what is both "real" and "realistic," and to identify high leverage optimizers that will increase effectiveness in each arena and enhance the synergy between the four.

Then, in the chapter on wisdom, we'll look even deeper into creating synergy and positive momentum in our lives, and into increasing our navigational intelligence and making good choices every day.

3

WORK MATTERS

Work is love made visible.
—Kahlil Gibran

Have you ever known people who really hate their job? And do you recall what they're like to be around—grouchy, testy, frustrated, complaining, depressed? Being with them—at work or at home—is generally not pleasant.

ROGER

As I was conducting one particular seminar and we began talking about work, I noticed discouraged looks on the faces of several employees from the same organization. I could tell there were issues we needed to address.

One woman was particularly negative. She seemed to be seething, boiling inside. She spat out her bitter words with venom and issued a defiant challenge: "So what if you work at a place where the harder you try, the worse it gets?" Her words and her body language communicated to everyone that she was convinced there was no answer to the problem.

Over the next couple of hours, as we talked about work prob-
lems and solutions, I saw the discouraged looks gradually change
to hope and commitment as people began to see how they could
improve their situation and make a difference—except for this
woman. For some reason, she seemed unreachable.

During the lunch break, she came up to me. "I've been in this
organization 25 years," she said bitterly, "and this other woman
who's been here only a few years just got promoted five levels.
Well, you know what she's been doing!" She was angry and frus-
trated and seemed to want to keep on dumping.

As I listened to her, I found myself thinking two things. First—
what a tragedy! I felt terribly sad that this woman perceived her
situation to be so difficult, and that her bitterness blinded her to
the possibility that things could be better.

And second—I am so glad *I'm not married to this woman! I*
knew what she must have talked about at home, what she talked
about on the weekends, and what she was going to talk about
when she retired. If something didn't change, she'd become one of
those unhappy, bitter people who spend their retirement years
complaining about how miserable their work years were, how
people took advantage of them, and how they were trapped in
their jobs but had to stay to collect retirement benefits.

This woman was obviously "hate your work" centered.

Now contrast this woman's response to her "work" with the sen-
timent expressed in the Kahlil Gibran quote that began this chapter:
"Work is love made visible."

How can it be that to some people "work" communicates a sense
of drudgery, a grindstone, a necessary evil, a tearing away from family and quality personal time, a highly charged and unfair political,
sexist environment, a monotonous toil—while to others it represents
career, fame, recognition, fortune, status symbols, and identity—and
to still others it represents a life's mission, a great contribution, a
noble endeavor, or a beautiful gift of love crafted with excellence,
personalized talent, and individual care?

Clearly, there's a difference in the way people *see* their work. And that difference in seeing leads to a difference in *doing* . . . and, ultimately to the results they're *getting* in their lives. It's the "see-do-get" cycle we discussed in Chapter 2.

When you hate your work, nobody wins—not you, your boss, your organization, your coworkers, customers, suppliers . . . not even your family. But when you truly love your work, everyone wins. In fact, being excellent, joyful, and inclusive in your life's work can be one of your greatest contributions to your family.

In this chapter, we'll ask you to explore:

- How you see work

- How you see *your* work

- How you see yourself as a worker

Then we'll look at aligned, high leverage ways you can optimize your ability to contribute on the job and navigate competently through issues of work and life balance.

At the end of this chapter, we'll also suggest some ways to transform work into a bonding rather than a divisive family experience. Work doesn't have to cause frustration and conflict; it can be a great source of family bonding—particularly when you focus on *why* and *how* you work. The goal is for you and your family to be able to say with joy and satisfaction: "*Our* work is *our* love made visible."

HOW DO YOU SEE WORK?

Work is one of the most confusing words in the English language. We talk about "having to go to work." We want to "get off work." Why? So we can go enjoy a good "workout." A professional photographer considers taking pictures "work" and gardening a hobby, while a professional landscaper considers gardening "work" and taking pictures a hobby.

Many of us work very hard at games and sports and call it "play." Some expend tremendous effort and energy training to run in a marathon. Teenagers who cannot be convinced to get a job or clean their room will submit to incredible pain and struggle at a football camp to prepare themselves to play the game they love. Somehow, it seems, these things are not really "work" at all.

What's the defining line? The minute you get paid for "work," does it suddenly lose its appeal . . . or does it immediately take on meaning or importance? When the amateur golfer goes professional, does he lose the joy of the game? Is work at home "work"? Is it somehow less noble, less fulfilling, more demeaning than other work? Is the only "work" that counts the work that's recognized by others in terms of financial reward?

In physics, work is described as "an expenditure of energy." By definition, then, anything you do that requires energy is work.

REBECCA

Before I became involved in writing professionally, people would sometimes ask me, "Do you work?" I had to laugh. "Are you kidding?" I'd say. "I have seven children. Of course I work!"

Work is what you do. Whether you're paid for it or not, whether it's in the home or out, work can be noble and fulfilling. It can contribute to the health, welfare, and encouragement of others. It can transform people and situations. It can uplift and inspire.

As many have affirmed over the years, work is a timeless and universal principle of quality of life.

> *It is the working man who is the happy man. It is the idle man who is the miserable man.*
> —Benjamin Franklin

> *The world is moved not only by the mighty shoves of the heroes, but also by the aggregate of the tiny pushes of each honest worker.*
> —Helen Keller

And your own work—your life's work (including your work in the family)—is a profound and meaningful expression of your self.

HOW DO YOU SEE YOUR WORK?

So how do you see *your* work? Whether it's outside the home or in the home—as a homemaker or "telecommuter" or both—do you feel a sense of joy and contribution in it? Do you look forward to it, feel grateful for it, take pleasure in doing it well? Is it personal development for you? Or is it escape . . . or monotony . . . or drudgery? Can you hardly wait until the day is over so you can "crash," move on to recreation, or do something else?

In addition to *what* we do, the joy and satisfaction we derive from work is a function of *why* and *how* we do it. Conventional thinking seems to suggest that the *what* is the most important factor. But we suggest that at least as important as the *what* are the *why* and the *how*.

An old story from Italy tells of a priest who comes up to three stonecutters working in the hot afternoon sun. The priest asks the first, "My son, what are you doing?"

The man replies, "I am cutting stone."

The priest then asks the second man, "What are you doing?"

The stonecutter replies, "I'm making 100 lira a day."

Finally, he asks the third stonecutter the same question.

This worker replies, "I am building a beautiful cathedral."

What's the difference? It's the *context*. It's the reason for working.

It's fairly easy to see how you can love your work if you love the thing you do—particularly if you're not stressed out about family or other issues. But the truth is that *all* of these reasons can bring fulfillment and joy. It's fine to cut stone if you love to cut stone. It's also wonderful to cut stone if that's the best way you can provide for those you love. And it's wonderful to cut stone if you really love the idea of building a cathedral—even if stonecutting is not your favorite thing to do. You may not love the task itself, but the context of love is there.

REBECCA
Though I love a clean house, I haven't always loved scrubbing floors or cleaning toilets. Though I've loved to contribute through writing, I haven't always loved the deadlines, the intense pace, the struggle to find the right words, the things I've left undone as I've been writing.

But in both cases, the context has always been there. I love my family. I love helping people. I love the incredible material I've been privileged to work with. And that love has literally swallowed up the challenges, the inconveniences, the setbacks.

For me, the context of my work—my love for people and principles—has been a deeper "Yes!" that's made it easier to say "No" to other things.

So what is your reason for working? And how does it affect the way you see and feel about your work?

For most people, the primary reason to work is a matter of economics: "I owe. I owe. It's off to work I go." Or "I *have* to work . . . " Or "I need to provide for my family . . . "Or "We just can't make it without two incomes."

For many, this economic factor is a huge consideration, and it has an enormous impact on the way they see their work. Much of the pain around the issue of balance, in fact, is driven by economic fear—especially in a time when many businesses are dramatically downsizing or going belly up. There's a nagging worry: "I can't lose my job. If I did, we'd be lucky to pay our bills for two months." As a result, people feel trapped in their jobs, compelled to work long hours and afraid to do anything that might make waves.

Too, in recent years, there's been great social value placed on working for a sense of personal fulfillment and self-worth, career development, recognition, and the "stuff" money can buy. This focus has also had a huge impact on the way we feel about our work. When the primary reason we work is economic—but the social emphasis is on working for individual recognition, personal aggrandizement, or material reward—it's easy to think that noncareer work is somehow demeaning, that working to provide for the economic welfare of the family is less noble and less satisfying than working for personal satisfaction, recognition, money, and fame. Inadvertently, the task has become enthroned at the expense of the value of work itself.

Certainly, it's wonderful if you do something you naturally love to do. And there are many things you can do to help create this kind of alignment. But keep in mind: Research indicates that most people entering today's work force can expect to go through a number of job changes during their lifetimes, some of which are so significant they could actually be considered career changes.[1] Research also shows that most people who have accumulated significant wealth and also feel a significant degree of balance in their lives do not have the "glamorous" jobs. They are "welding contractors, auctioneers, rice farmers, owners of mobile-home parks, pest controllers, coin and stamp dealers, and paving contractors" who have simply learned to live high investment, low consumption lifestyles.[2]

The point is, you don't have to have the most exciting, thrilling, high profile job in order to be successful or to love your work. That very expectation can cause you to waste years feeling dissatisfied and unfulfilled. And that waste is a loss for everyone—for you and your family, as well as the company you work for.

The reality is that you can find deep joy and satisfaction in knowing that your work is your love for your family made visible. And, as we'll see in Chapter 6, "Money Matters," there are ways you can manage your money so you're not continually driven by economic fear.

ROGER

Recently, I did a seminar for a well-known company with a reputation of hiring smart, successful people. During the discussion, two of the participants shared an experience they'd had the evening before.

They said that during the dinner hour, they decided to jump in their Mercedes and take a run by the ocean before the evening meetings. They parked near the beach, and as they were sitting there, talking and enjoying the cool ocean breeze, they noticed a man getting some things out of an older car. As they watched, this man began to canvas the area and pick up old bottles, paper plates, and other garbage people had left on the sand. Because of his dress, they could tell that this was his job—perhaps even a second job.

These men commented to each other: "Look at that poor guy. What a waste! Cleaning up the beach is all he can do." Their unspoken attitude was, "Look at us. We're so educated, so smart. We make all this money and we've got this beautiful car. We're so much better than he is."

After a few minutes, a young girl came up to the man and begin helping him. She'd been sitting on a blanket with several others—evidently her family—a short distance away. As the three men watched, it became apparent that the family sitting on the blanket was this man's family. One by one they finished their picnic dinner and came over to help him.

Before long the cleanup was complete and everything was put away. Then the man and his family began to play together, to roll in the sand, to laugh and chase each other on the beach. Obviously, they were having a wonderful time.

The initial attitude of the men who were watching slowly changed from disdain to poignant envy. They realized that while they had been sitting there basking in their own accomplishments and preparing to go to more evening meetings, here was someone who had somehow integrated part of his work life with his family, and, in many ways, seemed to be happier than they were.

Working to provide for those you love is very likely the highest, noblest, most fulfilling motive you will ever have. It's one of the most important ways you invest in your family. As one study suggests, breadwinning can be "active, responsible, emotionally invested, demanding, expressive, and measuring real devotion."[3] And if it's done with excellence, it can provide a marvelous legacy of character for your children as well as economic well-being.

As we've said before, at the core, it's not "work" and "family" that are at odds. What is at odds with both work and family is the cultural notion of *my career* and the focus on all the *stuff* that accompanies "success" in a materialistic world. And it's a heart set on those things—rather than on the principles of work and family—that often masquerades as "imbalance."

ROGER
In personal interviews, some people have told me that the more they try to create balance between work and family, the worse the situation gets. For a while, this didn't seem to make sense.

But the more I listened, the more I came to realize that these people hadn't really come to grips with the long-term preeminence of family. In effect, they were putting family—which is inherently a deep, permanent, lasting emotional commitment—on the same level as a job—which, even at its best, is inherently temporary, unstable, and subject to change.

As a result, family members were feeling insecure. Spouses felt like no more than live-in roommates. Relationships were suffering. Efforts to appease family members came across as token and insincere.

The reality is that temporary emotional relationships will never produce permanent love. And as long as people genuinely struggle with which is more important—family or career—relationships come across as temporary.

If you feel the need to consistently apologize to your family about your work, you might want to ask yourself: "Am I really doing *our* work—work that's a vital, contributing part of a robust physical, mental, social, and spiritual family economy—or am I doing *my* work—focusing on *my* career, *my* personal fulfillment, *my* independent achievement?" If it's *my* work, you may want to consider the impact it's having in your effort to create balance. If it's *our* work, make sure your family knows.

At the core, *my career*/home balance and *stuff*/home balance—as distinct from *work*/home balance—are not scheduling issues; they're issues of the heart. And until you're resolved on a heart-set level, no amount of effort to create balance is going to fully succeed.

THE DUAL INCOME CHALLENGE

Another factor affecting the way we feel about our jobs is the issue of both parents working when there are children at home. In many ways, this has become the icon of the work/family balance struggle.

For many young parents, it's almost an unexamined expectation: "Of course we'll both work. Everybody does." For others it's a highly sensitive issue, touching on everything from disturbing social statistics, "latch-key children," and cell phone parenting, to social contribution, religious beliefs, and women's rights. Though women have been in the limelight because of their increasing involvement in work outside the home, this subject has also created a growing concern for many men who increasingly worry about the welfare of their children, especially now that mothers, as well as fathers, are gone from home.[4]

Many parents want to be with their preschool children as they take their first steps and say their first words. Some don't want school-age children to come home to an empty house. These parents are aware of the social statistics that indicate a significant increase in drug and alcohol abuse, teen pregnancy and suicide, and other severe problems apparently exacerbated by the absence of parents in the home.

But they also feel compelled to work outside the home in order to provide for their children's economic needs—and house payments, car payments, medical bills, education expenses, diapers, braces, and piano lessons all add up. As a result, parents feel torn and imbalanced. They tend to see work as a "necessary evil." While it enables them to provide for their children, it also devours irreplaceable quality family time.

If the two-working parent issue is creating stress for you, you may be interested in "second shift" research that has turned up some interesting facts.

In married households, the traditional one-breadwinner family of the past has dwindled now to only 21 percent.[5] Along with several major articles, two books—*Two Incomes and Still Broke* by Linda Kelley, and *Shattering the Two Income Myth* by Andy Dappen—suggest that in most cases, financial reasons alone do not justify the second income. In simple terms, the second income usually needs to reach $30,000 before even one dollar is contributed to spendable income in the family. And after that, for every three dollars earned, only one dollar is actually spendable income.[6]

Here are some of the reasons:

- The second income puts you into a higher tax bracket.

- You have to pay for extra goods and services—things you wouldn't have to buy if you didn't have the job, such as:

  ○ work-related clothes and tools

  ○ child care (for families with children)

- ○ additional transportation
- ○ meals out
- ○ home services (house cleaning, lawn care, home repair, shopping help)
- ○ convenience shopping items (microwave dinners, packaged "quick fix" and deli foods)
- ○ guilt gifts ("Mom and Dad will both be gone, so we bought you this new video game")
- You engage in higher (gross income) spending, even though the disposable income doesn't go up that much ("Look—you're making $50,000; I'm making $45,000. Together, we're making $95,000! We can afford this!")

In many instances, the only thing the second income really "adds" to the family is the tremendous stress of trying to handle home and family needs with both parents gone from home. The real tragedy comes when a parent who doesn't want to work ends up working, and—bottom line—there's no economic gain.

Obviously, every circumstance is different. But knowing the facts and options with regard to a second income can help you make the decision that's right for you. The important thing is to make sure you're connected with your inner compass so that you don't just play out some unexamined social script, but instead you're clear about *what* is important to *you* and *why* you work. It's also vitally important to ensure that you and your spouse see eye-to-eye on work priority decisions.

REBECCA

When Roger and I began dating, there was tremendous social pressure for women to focus on career. I loved learning and was grateful to have received a full academic scholarship to a wonderful university. I had started on a path that included plans for both undergraduate and graduate degrees, and marriage was not even on my mind. But it didn't take many dates with Roger for me to start thinking that I might want to consider changing the plan.

The following summer, we were married. I continued for another year at the university. But when we had our first child, I came to a major fork in the road. Though I took a few more classes off and on, I discovered that deep inside me was a compelling and growing conviction that the greatest life contribution I could make was to really focus on loving and nurturing this child and others we wanted to have. I didn't fully understand it. Almost everything around me seemed to contradict it. But I felt it. And somehow I knew that listening to that inner voice was the one thing that would bring the greatest fulfillment and joy. So I made the decision to invest what time, talent, and energy I had primarily in our family.

Over the years, carrying out that decision has not always been easy. There have been times when messy diapers, skinned knees, runny noses, and teenage identity crises seemed overwhelming. There have been times when I have felt mentally understimulated, physically overchallenged, and occasionally unappreciated. There have been times when we had to scrimp and save and do without some of the things two incomes could have provided.

But there have also been times when I felt real joy in discovering creative ways to engage talent and capacity in family leadership and home management. And there have been times when I knew that just being there—listening and loving—really made a difference.

Now, as I look down the table at our family gatherings—as I feel the love and see the choices our children have made in their lives—I realize there's absolutely nothing else like it. I'm so glad that the quiet voice inside was somehow stronger than the louder voices outside. And I'm grateful that Roger willingly supported my decision to be at home.

I am also glad that the past 15 years have brought the opportunity to work with Roger and with Stephen Covey. I feel a great sense of fulfillment in being able to contribute through writing. But I am intensely grateful that the opportunity to write came the way it did . . . and not in the way or the order I would have supposed. I will never regret spending that once-in-a-lifetime season

*with my children. Living and learning with them has given me
something to write about.*

One of the advantages of today's work world is the significant
increase in options. Though still tough, it's easier now than it's ever
been to take breaks and then come back into the work force.
Companies are moving toward more family-friendly policies such as
job sharing and part-time work. Technology makes it possible for
many parents to work from their homes.

Also, as we'll discuss in Chapter 6, "Money Matters," the conflict
can be enormously lessened if you buck the trend and learn to live a
high-investment, low-consumption lifestyle.

THE SINGLE-PARENT CHALLENGE

If you're the head of a single-parent family, you probably don't have
the luxury of considering whether or not to work. Gainful employment is most likely an economic necessity. Again, there's the temptation to see work as a "necessary evil."

But some single parents tell us it's possible to turn the fact that
you work for your family into a source of family bonding—especially if you regularly communicate to your children that you love them,
you love being with them, and providing for their needs is one of the
few things you would consider important enough to justify spending
time away from them.

Again, we'll examine ways to manage your resources to econo-
mize and improve your financial position so you don't have to spend
extraordinary hours away from home (see Chapter 6). In addition,
you might want to investigate other options, such as job sharing or
creating an in-home business, which is one of the fastest growing seg-
ments in today's market.

But when you do have to be away, through your example you
can teach your children the nobility of work and sacrifice for those
you love. You can teach them to be cheerful in the midst of challenge. Through your work, their own chores at home and outside
jobs as they get older, they can learn the importance of all family
members working for the good of the family. You may even be able
to involve them in your work so they understand what you do and

perhaps even help you do it. In any case, it's far more psychologically and emotionally healthy to cultivate a sense of gratitude for each other's contribution than to fall into the trap of reinforcing each other in feelings of powerlessness, injustice, or martyrdom.

At the end of this chapter, we'll share some practical ways that parents—single or otherwise—can build bridges between work and home, and also help children to learn to love their work.

OTHER REASONS FOR WORKING OUTSIDE THE HOME

Of course, there are reasons for working outside the home besides economics. Some are fairly obvious, such as making a contribution, building meaningful and productive associations, finding an outlet for a particular talent, relieving human suffering, or bettering the world. Working for these reasons can bring you great joy, help you create a rich, balanced life, nurture the principle of work in your family, and even bond the family through shared work effort . . . *provided your priorities are clear and you ensure that you devote sufficient time and energy to those things that matter most to you.* Again, the key is to connect to and align with your own inner guidance system.

Other reasons for working may be less obvious. Some, in fact, are subtle and often unrecognized. But they are also vitally important to understand. As sociologist Arlie Hochschild points out in *The Time Bind*, many people simply find it more satisfying to be at work than at home. At home they face "unresolved quarrels and unwashed laundry"; at work they find compensation, recognition, promotion, "reliable orderliness, harmony, and managed cheer."[7] Often, without realizing it, both men and women are seduced into spending unnecessary hours at work simply because it seems more satisfying in the short run.

Seeing "happiness" in terms of immediate personal comfort rather than long-term family relationships and quality of life, some people may seem to love their work in the short run—or at least the escape their work provides. But this is not the kind of principle-based love of work that brings deep inner satisfaction and real life balance. And if we expect it to, we're going to be disappointed.

Again, we're back to validating expectations. The question is: Are we doing the things that will create the long-term results we really want?

SHOULD YOU WORK OUTSIDE THE HOME?

So should you work outside the home? And if so, how much? And when?

Of course, basic economic needs must be met. But to have a loving, successful family also requires that basic mental, social, and spiritual needs are met. And those needs are often greater in certain seasons—when children are very young or parents are very old, or there's some other challenging situation at home.

Ultimately, there's not one "right" answer for everyone—or for anyone in every season of life. People are different. Situations are different. Seasons are different. That's why we affirm once more that real "balance" is "balancing." It's the process of making good choices on a regular basis. It's making sure that you're *seeing* your life and your choices in terms of your own navigational intelligence rather than through popular social paradigms, and that you're *doing* based on timeless principles and what really matters most.

Whatever your situation, creating and deeply pondering over a personal mission statement is a powerful way to keep connected. A mission statement is the standard against which you can weigh alternatives and options. It helps you clarify—and remember—*why* you work and why you do whatever you do in every season of your life.

HOW DO YOU SEE YOURSELF AS A WORKER?

It doesn't take much life experience to realize that there's an enormous disparity in the way people work. You can walk into almost any department store and find salespeople who greet you with a smile and go out of their way to help you find just what you need ... and others who sit behind the counter talking to each other and act as if your questions are an intrusion on their conversation. You find builders, subcontractors, suppliers, and craftsmen who take time to do a job well, pay attention to detail, and take pride in their work ... and others who rush through a job, cut corners, and focus more on increasing their profit than on turning out excellent work.

As well as how these people *see* work and how they see *their* work, the quality of their work grows out of how they see *themselves as workers*—and, as a result, how they work.

In a social environment that gives many mixed messages about work, where do great workers get their paradigms of great workers?

Some have been raised in families or cultures that value a strong work ethic. Asian immigrants to the United States, for example, have earned a reputation in the workplace for their solid work ethic.[8]

Others work in strong, value-centered organizations that teach employees to see themselves as excellent workers. It's a pleasure to go into those environments. If they're part of a national or international chain, you feel comfortable that wherever you go, you'll receive the same high quality service. Hopefully, wherever these employees go in the future, they take with them the vision they acquire through training on the job.

Some have learned to be great through observation and experience. They've seen qualities that have led to the recognition and promotion of others and have chosen to integrate those qualities in their own lives.

Others seem to have an innate disposition to work. Regardless of their upbringing or environment, they seem to recognize the satisfaction and fulfillment that come from working hard to accomplish a meaningful purpose or goal.

Whether or not you have the advantage of family or cultural influence, corporate training, experience, or innate personality, you can choose to become a great worker. You can choose to be excellent in whatever you do.

And why not? If you're going to work, you might as well work wonderfully. Mediocre employees are poor leaders, poor team players. They get passed up for pay raises and promotions. They're generally frustrated and bored. They find little or no satisfaction in their work.

So why not commit to excellence? You'll contribute more. You'll feel better. You'll make more money. You'll generate more credibility and have greater opportunities. Whether your work is in the family or out of the home, the more you learn to see it in terms of excellence, the greater fulfillment you will find in it.

OPTIMIZERS AT WORK

Virtual mountains of material have been written and taught on improving performance in the workplace. It's been Roger's privilege to work in this field for several decades and to have been close to the development of many outstanding ideas. At the end of this book we have included a bibliography of what we feel is some of the most significant material in this area.

At this point, though, we'd like to share seven of the most aligned, high leverage optimizers in the area of work. In highlighting these seven, we do not mean to imply that effectiveness in time and money management are not among the highest leverage optimizers in the area of work. They are. Consider the following:

- **Time.** According to a recent article in the *Harvard Business Review*, fully 90 percent of managers squander their time in all sorts of ineffective activities.[9] Also, a recent FranklinCovey/Harris Interactive survey[10] shows that employees in the United States spend:

  o Only 49 percent of their time on activities directly linked to their organization's key priorities

  o 32 percent of their time on activities that demand immediate attention, but have little relevance to their organization's most important goals

  o 19 percent of their time on petty politics and bureaucracy

- **Money.** An employee's ability to manage money affects not only the dimensions of his or her job that relate to the company budget, but also other factors related to work. Research shows:

  o Two-thirds of employees say they have trouble paying their bills on time and "worry about money."

  o On average, 15 percent of employees in the United States are so stressed by their poor financial behaviors that their job productivity is negatively impacted. (This figure is 20 percent in the military, and, in some work places, it's as high as 40 to 50 percent.)[11]

These areas are so critical, both at work and at home, that we have included an entire chapter in this book on each.

But in addition we suggest the following seven optimizers as effective ways to enhance your performance on the job. They are not new, but are time-proven to bring significant results. The reason we've chosen these seven is because they are not only based on timeless and universal principles but are also particularly relevant in dealing with the challenges in today's world.

OPTIMIZER 1: BE PROACTIVE

When you're unhappy or frustrated or things are not going well, it can be tempting to say, "It's the economy (or the board, or the stupid policies, or the change in the marketplace, or what's happening in technology, or my dumb boss)!" People can always come up with reasons to blame as to why the job's not getting done.

But if you're going to be effective on the job, you'll see things differently. Effective workers acknowledge their "response-ability" to take what action they can to create change. They focus their efforts on the things they can do something about.

In his *7 Habits of Highly Effective People*, Stephen Covey lists proactivity as Habit 1.[12] Proactivity is accepting responsibility (or "response-ability") for your own work and for your own thoughts, feelings, actions, and life. It's acting based on principles and values instead of *reacting* based on emotion or circumstance. It's focusing your time and energy on those things you can influence and letting go of those things you can't. Proactivity is foundational to both personal and professional success and to every other habit of effectiveness.

Proactive people are a great asset to any organization. They generate ideas and action that make a difference. They take the initiative. They seize opportunities and make things happen.

ROGER

Some years ago I was put in charge of developing a training program for a large organization. When I arrived, I inherited an administrative assistant who had been there for a while. In the midst of my challenges, I hurriedly checked her off on my list—"competent assistant"—and quickly moved on to more important things.

In the following weeks, though, I came to realize that she was one of my "most important" resources. This woman did everything I expected an administrative assistant to do very well. But she gradually began to do more. After a few sessions of dictation, she brought the letters in for me one day, opened and sorted, and she said, "If there are any of these letters you'd like answered in a way similar to the ones we did yesterday, I'd be happy to draft them for you to save you time. You could look them over and see what you think." I was feeling a time crunch, so I thought, why not? The drafts she gave me were well-written and sensitive—better than I could have done myself. Soon, she was doing 95 percent of the letters without my dictation.

Because I was impressed with her writing, I asked if she'd like to be involved in creating a training manual. She agreed, so I gave her a particular section and asked her to jot down a few ideas. She not only put down her ideas; she produced an excellent draft of the proposed material. Eventually, she ended up as a trainer and assistant manager in the department. Finally, I discovered that she had a master's degree in communication and had accepted the administrative assistant position at the time because that was what was available. She was one of the major reasons why that training program was so successful.

I've always appreciated human potential, but this woman raised my vision of how effective someone could be in proactively fulfilling a work role. Since that experience, my view of administrative assistants has forever been changed, and it's affected the way I've interacted with every assistant since. Some of my greatest work associates have been people who started out as administrative assistants and increased their capacities and moved on, or became incredible assistants because that's what they wanted to be.

Proactivity is at the root of personal job satisfaction, organizational and societal success.

REBECCA

Several years ago, as we were working on a "wisdom literature" project, we ran across an amazing example of proactivity in the workplace and in society as a whole. We were in Australia and had the opportunity to interview some of the Aboriginal tribal leaders in several cities along the coast and also in the heart of the outback in a village called Yuendumu.

In sharing their ideas with us, these tribal leaders told of what they called the "cultural genocide" of their people—how early Caucasian arrivals sought to "civilize" and "educate" Aboriginal children by taking them away from their land and families—the two things that were deeply connected to their sense of identity—and relocating them in white foster homes so that they could be raised in the cities. The resulting social problems among the displaced Aboriginals—alcoholism, domestic abuse, etc.—were immense.

However, these leaders told us about the great proactivity of the women of their tribes. These women had recognized what was happening and took it upon themselves to initiate efforts to create a sense of identity and purpose among their people in their new and difficult situation. They worked hard to set up businesses or "co-ops." They got them running successfully. Then they approached the Aboriginal men and asked them to run them. They also asked them to return to their positions as spiritual leaders of the tribes.

The sense of respect with which the tribal elders spoke of the women was very impactful. Though this kind of leadership was not their natural role in the society, it was easy to see that these women had risen to the need and taken significant steps to restore a sense of dignity and purpose so vital to the well-being of their people.

Proactivity is learning to *see* yourself as "response-able" and *do* response-able things.

How do you develop it? Take initiative. Always think, "What can *I* do?" Learn to listen to your own language. If you ever find yourself blaming or accusing someone or something else for your discontent—in word or in thought—STOP! Always focus your thought and energy on what *you* can do to make a difference.

ROGER

In seminars, I often teach the principle of proactivity by dividing participants into teams of two. I then ask them to think about a problem or challenge they have at work, and to take turns describing these problems to their partners, doing everything they can to convince them that there is no way this problem is their fault and there is really nothing they can do about it.

After what is often very animated sharing, I ask people how they feel. The immediate responses are most often, "I feel justified!" or, "I feel so unburdened and relieved!"

But as we continue to interact, more and more I hear, "Yes, but I don't really feel satisfied," and, "This feels familiar—too familiar. I'm afraid I'm too good at this."

I then ask them to take this same problem and accept "response-ability." I ask them to use only proactive language:

"I can . . . "

"I think . . . "

"I feel . . . "

"My next step is . . . "

I ask them to do everything they can to convince their partner that they can make a big difference.

Again they interact. This time, when I ask them how they feel, their responses are significantly different:

"I feel much more energized!"

"I feel empowered."

"I feel hopeful."

They begin to realize that the only people who were making them victims were themselves.

Consider the dramatic contrast between these two approaches. Most of the time, whether we *see* something as a problem or an opportunity is what *makes* it a problem or an opportunity.

OPTIMIZER 2: FOCUS ON JOB ONE

The problem many people have in making the commitment to excellence is the tendency to translate that commitment as, "I now have to do everything everybody wants me to do perfectly."

That's impossible. It's also strategically unsound.

Whatever your job, you will probably never be able to do everything that could be done . . . or everything you would like to do . . . or everything other people would hope that you would do. The key is to proactively determine what we call your "Job One" and to do that job very well. To do that *one thing* with excellence is far more important than doing *everything* with mediocrity.

One significant challenge to focusing on "Job One" is the focus/awareness dichotomy we described in Chapter 2—the tension between the need to concentrate and the need to be aware of and respond to other things that are going on. Nowhere is this dichotomy more evident that in the highly charged political environment of many organizations. While employees struggle with the need to focus on high priority projects, they also feel compelled to respond to the power plays, rumors, innuendos, and second guessing that goes on in the organization. As a result, a huge percentage of time and effort is wasted. The loss is not only the company's; it's also a loss to all the employees who go home feeling unproductive and dissatisfied. So what's the solution?

Take the steps necessary to focus on Job One.

First, understand your organization. Whether your business is supplying bread to supermarkets, designing or constructing buildings, renewing drivers' licenses, servicing automobiles, or selling computers, ask some key questions:

- Why are we in business?
- What goods or services do we provide?
- Who are our customers?
- What value do we contribute to our customers' lives?
- How do our customers pay for the value we provide?
- What results are we trying to achieve?

Seek to understand your organization from the point of view of your boss, your peers, your customers, and your competition. If your company has an organizational mission statement, review it carefully. Inquire. Observe. Do all you can to understand the organization you work for.

Second, understand your role in the organization. As business consultant Peter Drucker put it: "The effective executive focuses on contribution. He looks up from his work and outward toward goals. He asks: 'What can I contribute that will significantly affect the performance and the results of the institution I serve?'"[13] Define your contribution, not in terms of activity, but in terms of results. Create a "work" mission statement if you'd like. Make sure the contribution you define is aligned with the organization as a whole and leveraged for maximum positive impact.

Third, make sure your vision of your role is aligned with your boss's vision and that of your peers—that there is agreement on what your Job One is. Ideally, this alignment would grow out of a goal alignment or performance planning meeting initiated by your boss. But if it doesn't, be proactive. Make sure that you and your boss are on the same page.

ROGER

One day a fellow consultant got a call from the CEO of a company he was working with. The CEO said, "George, I need your help. It looks like we're going to have to let 'Fred' go. I hate to see this happen, but the results aren't there. Could you visit with him to see if there's any chance we can save him?"

George said, "Sure, I'd be happy to visit with him."

In talking with Fred, George said, "Would you mind telling me what this CEO holds you accountable for?"

"Not at all," Fred replied. He rattled off a list of responsibilities, and George wrote them all down. Then he showed the list to Fred.

"Is this right?" he asked.

"That's right!" Fred confirmed. And he indicated that in his mind, he was fulfilling those responsibilities well.

Later, George was talking with the CEO. He said, "Would you mind telling me what you hold Fred accountable for?"

"I'd be happy to," was the reply. And he rattled off the list. George wrote it all down.

When George put the two lists side by side, there were significant differences. He went back to Fred and said, "Would you be interested in the list the CEO came up with when he was asked the same question?"

"Sure!" Fred replied. He went over the list with increasing astonishment. "Oh, man!" he exclaimed, "This is really amazing!"

A few months later George got another call from the CEO. "I can't believe the change in Fred!" he exclaimed. "There's been a total turnaround. You've got to come and do this to the whole department. What did you do to the guy?"

George replied, "I gave him your list!"

Effective employees know that it's critical that their list and their boss's list match, even when their boss doesn't. In the situation we shared above, what actually happened when George said, "I gave him your list," was that the CEO paused a long minute and then replied, "I knew it! He cheated!"

Astonishing as it may seem, the sad truth is that in some people's minds, good employees are just supposed to *know*. And if they have to talk about it, they're either not qualified for the job or they're wimps.

But excellent employees don't settle for not knowing the key activities they're responsible for. If they're in a situation with a boss who doesn't understand, they proactively make it happen. They approach their boss and say something like: "I've listed my strategic tasks for the next month, and I just left a copy on your desk. If you see anything differently, would you let me know?" Or, "I'm planning my priorities for the coming year and I want to make sure I have everything in the right order. Would you mind looking over this list and seeing if I've left anything out?"

If you haven't taken steps to make sure your lists match, they probably won't. And no one else is going to make it happen. So be proactive. Take the "response-ability" to make sure there's alignment between what you do and the key strategic objectives of the organization, and that you and your boss—and also your peers—are on the same page.

Then stay focused on Job One. To paraphrase Peter Drucker: "Starve problems; feed opportunities."[14] Let the politicking within the organization die from lack of nourishment. Trust your inner navigational intelligence to let you know if there's something that needs your attention. Other than that, stay focused on what matters most.

ROGER

I'm currently working with a small company of world-class software developers. The trust level in the organization is so high that there is absolutely no politicking. The developers focus exclusively on their work, and the amount of creativity and development that comes out of that group as a result is amazing. We've had large organizational clients literally shake their heads in amazement at the quantity and quality of the work these people have been able to turn out.

Doing your Job One well will make an enormous difference in the effectiveness of your organization. It will also give you a greater sense of personal job satisfaction. In addition, it will generally buy some forgiveness as you work to develop other capacities.

If your job is sales, for example, and your performance is just mediocre, the level of tolerance may be very low if you have difficulty learning to turn in accurate and timely expense and sales reports. On the other hand, if you perform superbly, significantly exceeding expectations, it's almost a given that the tolerance for your learning curve on the reports will dramatically improve. You'll probably never get a bonus or a raise from turning in good reports, but by doing the critical things that benefit everyone on the team well, you'll probably secure the support you need to produce the results required for compensation and promotion.

OPTIMIZER 3: THINK "TEAMS"

With the intense focus on career and competition, it's easy to view work through a paradigm of independent achievement—to think of *my* career, *my* accomplishment, *my* success.

But when we think about it, it's obvious that "success" is very much an interdependent effort. We all stand on the shoulders of those who've gone before us. We all rely on the talents and skills of those around us. Even "independent" contractors contribute to interdependent projects, and they generally have support systems— from administrative assistants to suppliers—who help them make their contributions.

The truth is, we're better together than we are alone. And excellence demands the ability to maximize the effectiveness of our interdependence.

REBECCA

A couple of years ago I was asked to accept an assignment in a women's service organization to which I belong. The task was to plan and carry out a monthly activity for the hundred or so women in the organization that would enrich their personal and family lives and provide opportunities for them to learn new skills and give service to others.

I was happy to fulfill the assignment, but I realized that the contribution would be much greater if others were involved. A good part of the purpose of the assignment would best be fulfilled as these women really got to know each other, contributed to the planning and execution of the activities, and shared their talents and skills with the others.

My first decision was to engage the help of two of the women as assistants. Together, we determined to rotate the primary responsibility for the activities so we would each be in charge one month out of three and have supportive roles the other two months. This immediately gave each of us a sense of focus, freedom and creativity in planning, and a dependable network of support.

We then examined the functions involved in our roles and determined to create a committee of specialists to handle regularly needed tasks such as food assignments and PR. We ended up with eight women on the committee who all contributed time and talent to make the monthly meetings a success. We then made an effort to learn as much as we could about the talents and interests of each woman in the organization and to structure our activities around the sharing of those talents and interests.

It has been thrilling to see how the committee has developed and to see the tremendous contribution each committee member and each member of the organization makes to the success of the whole. By working together, we've been able to do some good things—without creating excessive demands on any one person's time and resources.

One month, for example, during our two-hour activity, we were able to put together 50 kits for children fleeing from domestic violence. We made blankets and gathered contributions of stuffed animals, coloring books and crayons, and personal hygiene items for children who often run from home with nothing more than the clothes on their backs. Another month, we were able to assemble 200 hygiene, new baby, sewing and education kits to be sent to Third World countries.

By working effectively together, we've been able to maximize the time and resources we each have to give and to accomplish something that none of us could have done on our own.

Whether or not you're in a leadership role, thinking in terms of teams enables you to work with others to maximize strengths and compensate for weaknesses in accomplishing shared goals. It encourages you to appreciate the talents and skills of others and to celebrate shared success.

OPTIMIZER 4: CREATE PARTNERSHIP AGREEMENTS

One of the most destructive myths in our society is the often unspoken and unrecognized myth that you can have a balanced life or be a great highly productive employee, but not both. The facts are that most workers are very busy, but according to the FranklinCovey/ Harris Interactive Survey of U.S. workers (available free at www.franklincovey.com/lifematters):

- Only 44 percent clearly understand their organization's most important goals.

- Only 19 percent have clearly defined work goals.

- Only 9 percent believe their work has a strong link to their organization's top priorities.

- Only 19 percent feel a strong level of commitment to their organization's top priorities.

Can you imagine the impact of this lack of communication and alignment—not only on the organization, but also on the employee's sense of purpose and job satisfaction? Can you see how paradigms that don't recognize the reality of this situation translate into pressure to work longer hours in order to get things done?

The truth is, it's not a matter of working longer; it's a matter of working more effectively. And that's something that's in your proactive control.

Whether you're working with a boss or a peer, your ability to align and focus makes an enormous difference in your job satisfaction, in your value to the organization, and in your ability to create life balance. As we said earlier, proactive employees make sure their list and their boss's list match. They also make sure there's shared vision with other members of the organizational team.

One way to create shared vision, vertically or horizontally, is to create partnership agreements. These agreements can be formal or informal, written or verbal. They can be as simple as a five minute conversation. The goal is to make sure there's shared vision and—alignment regarding:

- *What* you're trying to achieve

- *Why* you're trying to achieve it

- *How* you plan to achieve it, and how you'll know it when you do

By creating well-functioning partnership agreements, you make it possible to focus time and energy into top organizational priorities—instead of wasting them on nonaligned activity and internal politicking. You open the door to effective synergy and joy in shared accomplishment. You develop a reputation of being a dependable employee and a "team player." You significantly increase your value to the organization.

Keep in mind: you don't have to be the "boss" to initiate the partnership agreement process. You can proactively seek to create shared understanding wherever you are in the organization. Just make sure that the agreements you work to create are always in the true spirit of "win-win."

The key to the success of partnership agreements is to always honor them—or to modify them together, should the need arise. The only surprise your partners should ever encounter is when you exceed expectations.

OPTIMIZER 5: BUILD ON YOUR STRENGTHS

ROGER

Some years ago, I worked with the personnel department of a large corporation. Don, a recruiting and placement consultant on my staff, did his work with about average performance.

One day, I had the occasion to ask Don if he would do one of the tasks I delegated to staff members on a rotating basis. It was a project that required statistical analysis of a number of factors in the department. Though he had never done this task before, he agreed to do it.

When Don turned in the assignment, I was taken by surprise. The report had a quality of excellence and added value that I'd never seen him display in fulfilling his normal job. I immediately went to find him.

"Don!" I exclaimed. "This is phenomenal! You've done an excellent job on this report!"

He gave me a little smile. "I enjoyed doing it," he replied. "I've always been good with numbers."

Now he had me puzzled. "Why in the world are you in recruiting and employment?" I asked. "You seem to be doing all right, but you obviously have a great talent in the area of analysis. Why did you choose this particular job?"

Don looked sheepish. "That's just it," he replied. "I know I'm strong in analysis. But I never have been good with people. I felt I needed to improve in that area of my life."

I shared with Don an important concept of effectiveness I have seen validated time and time again. By focusing on our strengths, we not only increase our productivity and personal happiness, but we also use our unique talents to make significant contributions that would otherwise not be made. Of course we need to improve in areas of weakness. But to become overly focused on weakness keeps us from connecting to our inner strength and areas of greatest contribution.

A short time later, when an opening for an analytical job came up in another department, with Don's approval I recommended him for the job. He enjoyed the assignment and performed with excellence. Within a year he was managing the section. Interestingly, as his confidence in his new job grew, he became more relaxed about interacting with people, and, for the most part, his weakness took care of itself.

As we've said before, it's not necessary to have the "perfect fit" job in order to love your work. But when you can align your work with your talent without sacrificing your most important priorities, why not? Working in your area of greatest strength enables you to maximize your contribution and increase job satisfaction.

OPTIMIZER 6: CONTINUALLY IMPROVE

The only time you can coast in life is when you're going downhill. So if you want to be an excellent worker, you need to be involved in continuous improvement. And there are at least two effective ways to do that.

The first is to seek feedback.

Most of us don't really like feedback. We like to do what we want to do, and we assume that if anyone disagrees or gives us flack, it's his or her problem. But effective employees recognize that we all have blind spots—problems and weaknesses in ourselves we just can't see. By asking for feedback, really listening to it, weighing it thoughtfully in light of our own heart-set, and implementing what our inner wisdom tells us to do, we can become much more effective . . . and build relationships in the process.

REBECCA

As a writer, I remember the fear and trepidation I felt when I received one of my first magazine articles back from the editor. In my mind was the vivid image expressed by Jo in Louisa May Alcott's Little Women *when she saw the editor's marks on her work and felt "as a tender parent might on being asked to cut off her baby's legs in order that it might fit into a new cradle."[15]*

But as I opened the envelope and cautiously began to go over what he had done to my "baby," I found myself slowly becoming more impressed. This wonderful editor had not diminished the content or altered the style, but his well-placed suggestions genuinely improved the capacity of my words to communicate authentically and effectively.

Over the years, I have learned to respect a good editor. I have also learned the value of having many eyes review my work. After spending hundreds of hours on a project, I find there are small errors I can read over 20 times without spotting. And as others express different ideas and perspectives on content or style, I find an increased ability to look at my work more objectively and to change it to better communicate with a wider range of people.

Often, I listen and implement. Sometimes, I listen and decide not to implement. But I have learned to always listen. And in the process, I have become very, very grateful to those who are willing to give feedback.

When people sincerely respect and pay attention to others, it often enhances their own work, but it almost always enhances their ability to interact effectively and to solve problems on the job.

One simple but effective way to seek feedback is to select a sample of people—bosses, peers, customers, reports—and send an anonymous questionnaire. Attach a memo along these lines: "I'm trying to find ways I can improve. Would you please take a few minutes and give me some honest feedback?" Ask someone else to type up the results so that complete anonymity will be preserved.

You might ask questions such as these.

- From your perspective, what do I do that is most useful?
- What are my greatest areas for improvement?
- What one thing do you think I should continue doing?
- What one thing do you think I should stop doing?
- What one thing do you think I should start doing?

If you send out that questionnaire once or twice a year, you'll get some great information. You can read it, think about it, and look for ways to implement it.

Of course, you don't want to become feedback centered—like the politician who was asked his position on a particular issue and replied, "I don't know. I haven't read the polls yet!" You may want to have your own mission statement firmly in place first so you can measure feedback against it.

Your objectives in getting feedback are to see how others perceive what you're doing, to evaluate how what they see relates to your own center of principles and values, and to become aware of any blind spots you may have.

It's generally a good idea to send a thank-you note to those who respond: "Thank you so much for taking the time to contribute to the feedback I have recently received. As a result of this feedback, here are some things I'm going to work on." This kind of specific thank-you increases the likelihood that people will respond to questionnaires from you in the future. It affirms their investment of time and effort and lets them know you're paying attention to what they say. It also communicates to others that you're a person who is sincerely willing and trying to improve.

Now you may say, "Wait a minute! I'm not so sure I want to do this. I might hear something I don't want to hear." Our answer to that is: "That's the best stuff *to* hear . . . and better now than later!" If there is something negative, it's much better to hear about it now— when you can do something about it—than in an exit interview several months down the road. What's more, if you don't hear about it now, you might never hear about it. Perhaps nobody will ever tell you the real problem, and you'll go on to job after job feeling haunted . . . unappreciated . . . wondering . . . never knowing . . . and not having enough information to see the problem and to change.

ROGER

Years ago I was working for a large corporation. When review time came around, I did not receive the evaluation I'd expected. From my perspective, I'd done everything I was supposed to do and I'd done it well. But the evaluation I received was only average.

When I expressed my concern to my boss, he told me there were other factors involved. Evidently, a few of my peers thought I was more interested in climbing the corporate ladder than in being a good team player, and that perception was getting in the way of my ability to contribute.

I was devastated. I had no idea. While I'd struggled with some ladder-climbing issues in the past, I had worked hard to resolve them and was satisfied in my own mind and heart that my motives were on track. I felt terrible to think that anything I'd done had kept me from earning the trust and credibility I needed to be effective in my job, and that our work may have suffered as a result.

As much as the feedback hurt at the time, I now appreciate the courage it took for that supervisor to give it. And I realize that if I had proactively sought feedback much earlier, there were things I could have done to deal with the problem so it would never have come to the point it did.

I will never forgot the lesson I learned on that job: Get feed back! Sometimes it's hard. Sometimes it hurts. But you're much better off knowing and doing something about it than living with the consequences of not knowing.

If you're ever feeling unappreciated on the job, it may be a red flag that the time to get feedback is *now*. And if the feedback hurts, here's one way to deal with it:

First, be grateful for the pain. You're normal. You're alive. Say to yourself, "All right! Now it's confirmed—I'm a normal person!"

Next, take the feedback, put it away for the night, and go do something that puts it in perspective. For example, go see a disaster movie—complete with wide screen and Dolby digital sound.

The bigger and more dramatic the disaster, the better. After you've spent two hours watching earthquakes, raging rivers, asteroids, or monsters wipe out half the earth, you'll be able to look at the feedback with much better perspective. With half the world's population being destroyed, the fact that one person wasn't happy about something you did on the job doesn't seem so critical. So go home and have a good night's sleep. By the next day things won't seem so bad.

Finally, look at your feedback *in context*. Remember that as important as what feedback tells you about yourself is what it tells you about others—about how they feel and what's important to them. So balance their feedback in light of your own mission and goals. And also use it to gain insight into how you can improve your relationships with those who've taken the time to share.

A second way to apply the principle of continuous improvement is to invest in professional development. As we indicated earlier, research shows that people entering today's work force can expect to go through six to eight job changes during their lifetimes. And technology is changing at such an incredible rate that if you don't keep up, you'll be quickly left behind.

So who is going to prepare you for the next opportunity, the next change? Who is going to update you on new technology? If you're waiting for someone else to do it, you may be in for a long wait. Fortunately, some companies provide resources and there are other opportunities available. But now—more than ever before—the individual is the one who has to take the responsibility to learn, grow, and prepare.

So make it a way of life to always be learning. Read books. Listen to tapes. Take classes. Peruse trade journals—in your own field and in related fields as well. If you're in construction, keep up on real estate. If you're in the restaurant business, keep up on advertising, tourism, and travel. Keep abreast of emerging technologies, issues, and trends. Expand your horizons. Be prepared so that if your job opportunity changes, you won't be left in the dust.

In Chapter 5, "Time Matters," we'll discuss how you can manage your time to effectively invest in professional development and keep up on personal effectiveness technology.

OPTIMIZER 7: JUST . . . WORK!

As we observed earlier, some people simply know how to work. Perhaps they were raised on a farm or in a family culture that valued hard work. Or perhaps they learned from experience or observation what it takes to get results, and they developed the capacity to do it.

However they may have learned it, when they come on the job, you notice it: "Boy, that guy is a real worker!" Or, "She really knows how to get the job done!" On the other hand, you also notice those who generate a lot of movement and noise but basically don't get much done.

People who have learned to work are a great asset to any organization. They've developed a skill that produces results, and they can transfer this skill to any job they have.

REBECCA

My father definitely knew how to work. He was raised on a farm. He spent many hours milking cows, picking cotton, and bailing hay. By the time he was eight, he was earning his own money for clothes and other personal necessities.

Following a bout with Malta fever as an adult, Dad was forced to change to a job that didn't involve animals. So Mom, Dad, and I (I was three at the time) moved into the city, where he worked at a service station for a number of years.

Dad was a great service station worker. Whatever amount of time it took most mechanics to do a brake job, my dad pushed his skill until he could do it in less than half the time. In the evenings and on his one day off a week, he worked for 18 months to build the house he and Mom lived in for 30 years.

At one point Dad decided he wanted to do something that would provide more income and allow him to be with his family on Sundays. So he worked and studied to pass stringent tests required to become a State Farm Insurance agent. I remember as a teenager helping him study for those exams.

Shortly after Dad was accepted as an agent, the company made a college degree a mandatory requirement for acceptance.

But Dad's lack of a degree didn't hold him back. During his 20-year career with State Farm, he broke every record in his region. With Mom helping as his office manager, he wrote several hundred "apps" a month in a time when one app a day was the standard for success. He won repeated awards for his success at the district, regional, and national level, eventually gaining recognition as one of the top 50 agents in the United States.

Following his retirement, Dad worked helping neighbors till their gardens and helping my mom create a family literacy center in our community. As long as he could work, he did work—even with significant health problems that would easily have slowed others down.

Dad was a man who knew how to work, and I believe his legacy of work will impact our family for generations.

In this day and time, it's easy to confuse "activity" with "work." People can be busy—even to the point of spending long hours on the job and coming home exhausted—without really "working." And the meager results bear little correlation to the amount of time and effort expended.

ROGER

I remember when we first moved onto our little minifarm. I was out digging irrigation ditches when a couple of older neighbors who had been lifelong farmers dropped by. After watching me for a minute, one of them remarked, "Well, at least he knows what to do with the business end of a shovel!"

They picked up a couple of shovels and proceeded to help. Even though they were considerably older, those two men were able to move a lot of dirt in a very short time. Through their lifetimes of work, they had obviously gained competence in using the principles of leverage, focus, pacing, effective use of energy and persistence.

This is a very simple example, but it impressed me with the truth that no matter what you do, you only really learn how to work by working.

You're much better off if you can learn to work *before* you move into the competitive workplace. But wherever you learn how to work, learn it. If you don't, you're much more likely to get caught in the "activity trap," where sheer busyness deludes you into thinking you're doing something important . . . when you're really not!

If you know how to work, you have the foundational skill that will enable you to be successful in any job situation.

NAVIGATIONAL INTELLIGENCE

There are two ways you can approach these seven "optimizers" we've just described. You can simply do them . . . and you will get results.

Or you can do them with awareness. You can do them in a way that will produce results *and* build your navigational intelligence in the process.

Remember from Chapter 2, you build your navigational capacity by:

- Valuing principles

- Evaluating experience

- Inviting inspiration

As you do these optimizers, you can discover and extract the principles involved. You can find at their root timeless principles such as *responsibility, focus, alignment, dependability,* and *contribution.* And as you learn to consciously recognize and value such principles, you build and strengthen your own framework for principle-based navigation.

As you evaluate your own experience in implementing these optimizers, you can improve your ability to discern when you're out of harmony with timeless principles. If you begin to feel victimized at work, for example, you can recognize that you're out of harmony with the principle of responsibility. If you find yourself being distracted from Job One, you can recognize that you're not in harmony with the principles of focus and alignment. You can learn to more quickly feel the deviation and immediately course-correct.

As you consider these optimizers, you can also invite inspiration to come up with effective ways to apply them and the principles involved in your unique situation. You can find personalized ways to become more proactive, for example, or to contribute in more meaningful ways.

Improving your navigational intelligence will help you make better decisions concerning your work—from major decisions concerning what you do and when you do it, to the seemingly small but vitally important decisions you make every day.

REBECCA

Several years ago I was invited to work on a project with Stephen Covey. He wanted to translate the life-changing material he had worked on and taught for 25 years into a book so it could reach many more people than those who had attended his seminars and speeches.

I was thrilled. I loved Stephen's powerful ideas and his unique way of capturing and expressing them. I had a strong feeling that The 7 Habits of Highly Effective People *would be a pivotal work that would impact many lives for good.*

But I also had reservations. For more than 20 years my chosen and primary focus had been on our own home and family. Though I'd taken some classes, participated in community affairs, and collaborated with Roger on a few articles and a short book on time management, we had managed our lives so that most of the time I could be where I felt strongly I wanted to be— at home, with mind and heart focused on raising our children.

We still had children at home, and I sensed that Stephen's project would require a great deal of time and effort and that this was something I wouldn't be able to "fit in" between all the things I was trying to do for our family. But after careful consideration, I also felt in my heart that it was something I really should do. So we hired someone to help out at home, and inspired by the material and by Stephen, I retreated to the basement and began the project with enthusiasm.

As the days went by, the struggle I had only anticipated became very real. More and more, I became aware of things I had always done for my family that I couldn't do now. I discovered that in addition to the big decision to work on the book, there were little decisions every day—the number of hours I worked, the way I interacted with family members during family time, how I handled interruptions, the priority I placed on various family activities—that flowed together to create the direction my life and our family life was taking. It was really difficult at first. But over time I discovered that the more I worked to develop and pay attention to my navigational intelligence, the better I became at responding to the highest priority need at the time.

When the final product was at last turned in, I snapped back like a rubber band, throwing myself into homemaking and mothering with a gusto that astonished even me. I was very happy to be back in my chosen career. But I was also tremendously grateful for the opportunity I'd had to contribute. I found that my months of working with the 7 Habits material had made me a better person. The content had worked its way more deeply into my personal life, into my family life. Despite the temporary season of imbalance it created in our lives, it seemed we were all better off because of the effort.

ROGER

On one occasion, the company I was working for was going through intense growth. Rebecca and I made the decision to go into a period of conscious imbalance for a while. Though it meant I would be away from the family an inordinate amount of time according to our standards, we agreed that I'd spend more time on the road. We felt it would make an important contribution to the business and would help us accomplish our shared long-term goals.

Things went well. We accomplished the company goals, and Rebecca and I teamed well to take up the slack at home. But when the agreed period of time was over, I found it was difficult to back off. There were many pressures to continue. The imbalanced lifestyle had become a way of life.

More and more, I found I was asking myself, "Am I allowing good things to take the place of best things?" As I thought through the situation and listened to my heart, I began to feel that I needed to take a stand and set some limits on the number of nights I would be gone each month.

Setting that limit wasn't easy. There were certainly pressures to do otherwise. But I'm convinced that, for me, that decision was right. It increased quality time with the family, gave me more freedom to contribute to church and community efforts, and allowed me to work on books we otherwise could never have written.

From the big work decisions to small ones, the quality of our decisions is directly related to the degree of navigational intelligence we have developed.

The two of us have tremendous respect for the power of navigational intelligence. The best decisions in our lives have come as we've developed and paid attention to it. Our worst mistakes have come when we've ignored it. We are convinced that the combination of timeless principles, examined experience, and inspiration simply can't be beat as a powerful tool for living in harmony with what matters most.

BUILDING THE WORK/FAMILY CONNECTION

As we said before, work and family are not natural enemies, In fact, one of the great things about work is that it can be a powerful tool in building family relationships and strength.

One of our sons recently shared the following experience:

When I was 10 years old I had the opportunity to fly down to Texas and spend two weeks with my grandparents. My grandfather was one of the top insurance agents in the nation, and he had plaques and awards all over the walls in their home. My grandmother was his office manager. She was an impressive woman—in fact, she'd been personnel manager at a major department store. They had about a dozen employees, and they ran a really tight ship.

They were the ones who gave me my first exposure to a really well-run office. They took me to work with them, where I would sit up on the filing cabinets while all these employees were writing up insurance applications and secretaries were answering phones and Granddad was talking to clients and Grandmom was supervising it all. I think that, more than anything else in my life, watching that well-oiled machine and the aggressive energy with which they pursued their goals instilled a sense of excellence in me in terms of performance and career.

The interesting thing was that they didn't just let me watch—they literally made me a part of the business. They took me in and exposed me to what it was like. They explained to me what they were doing and why. They treated me like a person—not like a little kid who was in the way. And I felt like I was 10 feet tall.

That experience was very formative for me. It made a profound difference in the way I've studied at school and in the way I've developed my work habits. I think there's a lot of wisdom that comes from however many decades grandparents have lived on the planet, and it's a shame that we don't pay much attention to that in this culture.

In today's world, you generally can't have your children working alongside you in the fields or making soap by the fire. But there are a number of things you can do to involve your family meaningfully, to build bridges between work and home, to help your children (or grandchildren) become contributing adults, and to increase the sense of wholeness in your own life.

To conclude this chapter, we'd like to share some ideas that can help you make that happen. As you read, keep in mind that we are *not* suggesting that you don't focus at work when you're at work. You need to do that. But if you have some of these bridges in place, it will make focusing at your work easier to do.

SHARE THE VISION

One of the most effective ways to nurture the principle of work and create work/home synergy is to share the vision. Whether your work is in the family or out of the home, let your family be involved in it. Let them know *what* you do and *why* you do it. Let them see *how* you do it. Let them know that to you, "*my* work" is a part of "*our* work." Let them know how what you do contributes to others and to them.

One way you can do this is by sharing related elements of your personal mission statement or your work mission statement, if you have one. Another way is to regularly share some of the positive benefits that come from the work you do, including how the products and services you provide are helping others. You could also make an effort to be open about family finances. Help your children understand the relationship between your work, your income, and meeting family needs.

It's wonderful when children can take a sense of pride in their parents' work. You may not have the most glamorous job on the planet, but whether you're a seamstress, a secretary, a rocket scientist, a sanitation engineer, or a homemaker, you can teach your children the value of principles such as excellence, interdependence, and contribution. And if for any reason you don't want your kids to know what you do, maybe you should question whether you should be doing it!

As your family understands more about your work and begins to feel a part of it, work ceases to be a mysterious and necessary evil that keeps you away from family events. It becomes a clearly defined avenue of contribution in which they see you investing time, energy, and creativity to enhance their well-being and the well-being of others. They will better understand the scheduling decisions you sometimes have to make. And it may even spark an interest—if not in the particular job itself, perhaps in some aspect of it, or even in the way that you do it—that might affect their future performance or job choice.

Sharing the vision can give children the context to see how their work—their schoolwork, their part in family work projects, or their daily chores at home—contributes to the welfare of the family as a whole. In addition, it provides many teaching moments in which children can learn that work—well done—is one of the fundamental principles and rich, satisfying experiences of life.

TEACH YOUR CHILDREN TO WORK

One of our biggest challenges in the work force today—as well as at school and in the home—is due to the fact that many children do not learn to work. Often, parents are not at home to assign, supervise, and follow through. In the limited time they have, they find it easier in the short run to do things themselves than to teach children to do them. For many teenagers, expectations around work are limited or nonexistent.

But they need to learn. Keep in mind that *work is a principle*. There is dignity in it. There is joy. The reality is that children are happier both now and as adults as they become competent and learn to contribute.

By far, the most high leverage way to deal with this problem/ opportunity is to set the example. Work hard. Work with excellence. Work with joy. Let your children see the manifestation of the principle of work in your own life. Your example can help them see work in ways that will empower them to love their own work and find joy in labor, peace in principle-based priorities, meaning in contribution rather than recognition, and satisfaction in subordinating excessive toys and glitter to financial security and quality family life.

In addition, you can give children work to do at home—even if it's inconvenient in the short run, even if it takes four times longer to teach them how to do it than to do it yourself. There are a number of excellent books on organizing home tasks to build character. (See Notes under "Family Matters.")

Another thing you can do is encourage excellence in schoolwork. Go to school with your children. Find out who their teachers are, where they sit, what they do. Let them know that when they do their schoolwork well, they benefit everyone: "I know this isn't your favorite class, but I can tell you're really trying. You're doing your homework. This is going to help you. It's going to help me. It's going to help the family. It's going to make a better world. Thanks for hanging in there." When appropriate, offer to help. Kids can have positive work experience doing what they do anyway; part of it is simply in the way we frame it.

Whatever work your children do, appreciate it. Celebrate it. Help them understand that their work is a great contribution to all.

TEACH YOUR CHILDREN TO LOVE WORK

ROGER

One summer when some of our children were quite young, I decided to teach them more about how to work. The principal vehicle for doing that was the family garden.

Early one evening, I took the children out, hoes in hand, and proceeded to teach them how to weed. As their hoes hit the dirt, bean, potato, and carrot shoots began to suffer the onslaught along with the weeds. I became increasingly agitated. "Hey, watch out for that plant!" "Wait! Be more careful!" "No, don't do it that way!" After half an hour, I was a nervous wreck and the children were totally discouraged.

Then Rebecca came outside. She watched what was happening for a moment, then picked up a hoe and started in. She took quite a while to do one row, but as she worked she constantly made little comments. "Oh, look at this row! Aren't we doing a nice job?" "Let's get all those nasty weeds away from the little plants so they can get all the nourishment they need." "Won't these potatoes taste delicious this winter when we take them hot out of the oven and put melted butter on them?" She was so enthusiastic and happy about what she was doing that she even made me want to get those nasty weeds away from our delicious winter dinners-to-be.

Rebecca never once commented on what the rest of the children were doing, but by the time she got to the end of her row, they were working like happy beavers and loving it. My faith was restored in the possibility that they might actually want to come out and work in the garden again.

As Albert Schweitzer noted, "Example is not the main thing in influencing others. It is the only thing." If we want children to love their work—and we do—then we must learn to love ours. As we do, the tone of our comments about work changes, and that rising tide raises all the boats in the family, so to speak. There's far less "woe is me!" and much more positive excitement about work in the family culture.

TAKE YOUR CHILDREN TO WORK

If you work outside the home, on occasion take your children with you to work. Help them understand what you do and how it helps. "This is where I work. I fill out this form. It goes over to these people and they do this with it. Then it leaves in big trucks and helps people out there. Sometimes things don't work. My boss gets upset. I feel terrible. But when things go right, I feel great. I know what I do makes a difference."

Too often we only talk about work when things are bad. In consequence, we're raising a generation of children who are afraid to go to work. We can help them understand the good as well as the bad by inviting them into our work world and making them comfortable observers—perhaps even participants—at appropriate times.

One of our daughters-in-law shared this experience:

My dad was great about letting us kids experience his work. As a doctor, he would take us through his exam rooms and show us all the stuff he worked with. He'd let us try out the stethoscope and look through the microscope at a variety of interesting slides. When he taught the residents how to draw blood, he would let us come and watch them practice on each other.

Sometimes, after he had delivered a baby, he would take us up to the hospital nursery to peek at the newborn child. He showed us X rays. He took us to the hospital cafeteria to eat. It was so neat! I felt special and loved. I had a pride in him and in his work.

On career day, my dad would always come and hand out rubber gloves and tongue depressors to my classmates. I would burst with pride, knowing how special my dad was.

I knew my dad was a good doctor. Most of all, I knew that he helped people and really cared about the people he helped.

Because of this, it wasn't as hard for me when he couldn't be at my band concert or softball game. He came when he could, and I knew he loved me. He included me when he could, and made me feel value in myself, in him, and in his work.

Although our daughter-in-law did not choose to become a doctor herself, her life clearly manifests the enormous benefits of this wonderful legacy in the way she approaches her own unique roles in life and interacts in loving and teaching ways with others.

PARTICIPATE IN CAREER DAYS AT SCHOOL

Many schools give children the opportunity to hear from parents and others in the community regarding their professions. The intent is to expose children to a wide variety of career possibilities.

So be a part of it. Make a big deal out of it. Prepare for it. Give it your best effort.

Share not only *what* you do, but *why* and *how*. And reject the temptation to get caught up in comparative thinking. Teaching the joy and excellence of being a great maintenance supervisor is a far greater contribution to a child's future than emphasizing the high profile of a mediocre lawyer's career.

Whatever your job, your *what, why,* and *how* "show and tell" can make a big investment in your child's future, and in your relationship with that child as well.

SHARE POSITIVE WORK EXPERIENCES WITH THE FAMILY

ROGER

Years ago, I remember coming home one day discouraged by the actions of a boss in the company I worked for. When Rebecca asked me about my day, I proceeded to "dump." I told her what this man had done and how unfair I felt he'd been. I told her how hard it was for me to be supportive of him and how other people were also having difficulties. I told her how his particular characteristics were getting in the way and causing problems.

As I heaped this man's shortcomings one on top of another, she listened with increasing amazement and finally replied with some energy, "Roger, do you want me to go punch this guy out?"

Her words stopped me in mid-tirade. Suddenly, I laughed. I put my arms around her and basked in the warmth of someone who loved me and was ready to fly to my defense.

Her response lifted me at the time, but as I thought about it later, I realized that her awareness of my work essentially came from me . . . and I had given her a pretty skewed view. I determined I needed to share more—the good as well as the bad—to give her (and me) a more accurate picture of my work situation.

Certainly there are days when things don't go well at work and you need a loving heart and a listening ear. But if you always share the bad and you never share the good, how will that affect family members' attitudes toward work? How will they think you see your work? How will they see your work? How will they see their own?

Always look for the good and pass it on. When you contribute at work . . . when something happens that makes a difference . . . when the product or the service of the company improves quality of life for someone . . . share it! Talk about it. Celebrate it. You will feel good about it, and others in your family will feel good about it, too, as they better understand the meaning and value of the work you do.

BRING STORIES OF WORK HEROES HOME

Think about someone at work whom you admire. Have you told your family about this person? Have you shared with them experiences when this person went the extra mile, did excellent quality work, or showed great character on the job? Have you talked with them about the contribution this person is making?

Stories of work heroes provide great dinner table conversation, as well as an excellent opportunity to reinforce values in your family and in yourself.

REBECCA

The first time I had the opportunity to help Stephen Covey on one of his books, I did most of the work at home. But the time came when I had to go to the office to help complete, copy, and

send materials to the publisher. Walking into the office environ-
ment as an "outsider," I quickly discovered there was a lot I did-
n't know.

I will never forget one man who immediately welcomed me
warmly and offered any help I might require. He was genuine and
gracious and made me feel very much at home. Although it was
not his job, when I ran into technical problems, he called some-
one to help. If I needed personnel assistance, he made the calls
and got people there. Without even being asked, he smoothed
the way at almost every turn, and I was deeply appreciative of
his efforts.

This man and his wife have since become wonderful friends,
and I always take pleasure in sharing the story of his kindness with
our family. It gives me the opportunity to sincerely acknowledge a
noble human being and to teach my children the importance of
being sensitive to and meeting the needs of others.

BE AWARE AND KEEP IN TOUCH

Do you know what the other members of your family are doing most
of the time? Do you take advantage of opportunities to encourage
them in their work, to help them see their work in the bigger context
of *our* work?

What if just before your spouse's major presentation, an e-mail
from you appears on the screen: "Good luck, hon—I'm thinking of
you." Or if your child finds a note on her desk on the morning of a
big test: "Good luck on your test today—I'm pulling for you!"

REBECCA
Following the publication of First Things First, *I accompanied*
Roger on a couple of international trips where we co-presented. I
enjoyed traveling with him—which was something I hadn't done
much of over the years—but each time, after a few days, I really
missed the family at home.

Before we left on one particular trip, the children handed us an
envelope with some notes in it. We were instructed to read one note

*each day we were gone. What a neat experience it was to open the
envelope from thousands of miles away and read:*

*"If you ever feel down or alone on the trip, remember how
much we love you!—Dan"*

*"How is the weather? How is the wildlife in Asia? I hope the
programs are rewarding and that you feel good about the contributions you are making. I pray for you and love you both.—
Mary"*

*"Dear Mom and Dad, Have you boughten my souveneers
yet? JUST KIDDING! HEE! HEE!—Debbie"*

*Those notes brought smiles to our faces and joy to our hearts.
They warmed our souls and helped us stay connected to the people who meant the most to us in all the world.*

Sometimes just keeping track of where family members are and
sending little communications can make a huge difference in retain-
ing the context of how each family member's work contributes to the
welfare of the whole. And that context creates a sense of unity that
gives hope, encouragement, and connection.

INVOLVE YOUR FAMILY IN WORK PROJECTS

Occasionally, and when it's appropriate, you may want to involve family members in work projects. If you need a dozen booklets for a presentation, for example, you may want to bring the materials home and
have the children help you put them together. It might only take a few
minutes, but you could help the children take pleasure in contributing
in a meaningful way. When you come back from the presentation, you
could tell them, "Thank you so much for your help! It really made a
difference. Everyone loved the booklets. They were so neat."

You may also want to find ways to involve your spouse. You may
even choose to select work based on a common interest and opportunity for shared involvement.

One thing the two of us particularly love in our relationship is
the opportunity to work together on projects we both feel passion-
ate about. Writing, parenting, and being involved in church service
together have given us great opportunities to build our companion-

ship and to experience the tremendous joy of shared accomplishment. It's exciting! It's fun!

The two of us think very differently—one is more abstract and holistic; the other more concrete and linear. And those differences at first created some frustration. But as we've learned to work with our differences, particularly in the context of our deeper shared values, we've found that those differences are the key to the better "whole" we create when we're together. It's precisely *because* we think differently, for example, that we're able to write together. Despite our differences—perhaps because of our differences—work is better because we're involved in it together.

There are also other ways to involve family members—even indirectly.

REBECCA
During most of the 18 months we worked on First Things First, *I was able to write when the children were in school and focus the rest of the time on being a mom.*

But during the last few months, we reached a point where a much greater investment was required. To meet publishing deadlines, I would sometimes need to work until one or two in the morning, sleep, and be at it again by 6:00 a.m. It was definitely a season of imbalance.

One of the most important factors that made it work for us was having everyone in the family "on board." Knowing that the more intense schedule would significantly affect our family life, we called the family together and reviewed our family mission statement.

As we involved the children, we found they were willing to work together and help in countless ways that made the project possible. The younger children agreed to handle laundry and other responsibilities. A teenage daughter volunteered to take on management of the home instead of getting an outside summer job. Some of our married children became involved in the project itself. One Saturday several of our married children and their spouses showed up to help with outdoor projects that had been preempted by our writing.

*Directly or indirectly, that book was the result of the effort of
every member of the family.*

Even though family members may not be able to directly contribute to a work project, they can do so indirectly and still feel the sense
of shared victory that accompanies a "together" project well done.

REMEMBER: BOTH WORK AND BALANCE ARE PRINCIPLES

In order for our work to truly become our love made visible, we need
to see work itself as the noble, edifying, character-building, family
bonding principle it can be.

We need to align our work—in both its nature and its seasonal
emphasis—with what truly matters most.

We need to leverage our work for maximum effectiveness.

We need to develop the discernment to appropriately decide
what, when, and how we will work to best provide for our families
and to contribute in the workplace and in society as a whole.

We need to recognize that, whether our work is in the workplace
or at home, we can do it with excellence and joy, and that the more
we appropriately share and involve our family in the positive aspects
of work, the more "work" can become unifying rather than divisive.

We also need to remember that both work *and* balance are timeless principles. We can't allow ourselves to labor under the illusion
that the ones who really get ahead in life are the "pizza under the
door," long-hours-on-the-job fanatics, and that we're somehow at a
disadvantage if we try to create balance in our lives.

Research shows that "workaholics" often create significant problems at work as well as at home,[16] and investing in life balance creates huge benefits for both the individual and the corporation.
According to a recent article in the *Harvard Business Review*:

> *A small but growing number of managers . . . operate under the
> assumption that work and personal life are not competing priori-
> ties but complementary ones. In essence, they've adopted a win-*

win philosophy. And it appears they are right: In the cases we have studied, the new approach has yielded tangible payoffs both for organizations and for individual employees . . . [17]

Further:

When a manager helps employees balance their work lives with the rest of their lives, they feel a stronger commitment to the organization. Their trust redoubles, and so do their loyalty and the energy they invest in work. Not surprisingly, their performance improves, and the organization benefits. Strong results allow the manager to continue practicing the principles that help employees strike this work-life balance. [18]

The reality is that when you learn how to create balance through the various seasons of your life, it's a win for everyone involved— your boss, your family, and yourself.

CHAPTER

$$4$$

FAMILY MATTERS

Your success as a family, our success as a society,
depends not on what happens in the White House,
but on what happens inside your house.

—Barbara Bush

In seminars, we often have fun asking people if they would like to increase the happiness in their homes by as much as 70 to 80 percent with one single idea. The overwhelming response is "Absolutely! If there's one thing I could do that would make that much of a difference, you bet I want to know about it!" Then we divide them into smaller groups and ask them to go through the following experiment. We invite you to give it a try.

Part One: *List six or seven ordinary, everyday behaviors at home—things family members tend to do—the results of which are generally* not *positive.*

1.

2.

3.

4.

5.

6.

7.

You may want to compare your responses to some typical responses from others who have attended the seminars:

- Leaving stuff out (hair spray, clothing, etc.)
- Finishing off someone else's treat that was saved in the fridge
- Leaving the toilet seat up (or down)
- Not communicating feelings or concerns
- Being sarcastic or complaining
- Not really listening
- Interrupting someone when they're talking
- Having to ask someone repeatedly to do something
- Second guessing family members
- Channel surfing when someone else is trying to watch TV
- Turning on the light when someone is asleep
- Breaking promises
- Leaving cracker crumbs in bed

Review your list and make sure you've identified the behaviors that "nail" what's happening in your family. In the seminar, it's fun to hear the laughter as the different groups share some of these all-too-familiar behaviors that seem to "tick family members off."

Part Two: *List six or seven ordinary, everyday behaviors at home, the results of which* are *generally positive—they usually tend to make people happy.*

1.

2.

3.

4.

5.

6.

7.

Some of our seminar responses include:

- Doing something unexpected to surprise someone (such as bringing flowers or serving breakfast in bed)

- Giving foot rubs or back rubs

- Leaving the toilet seat down (or up)

- Listening

- Respecting each other's space

- Being interested in each other's activities

- Keeping promises

- Saying "Thank you!"

- Doing household chores without being asked

- Doing someone else's jobs or chores for them

- Having quality time with the family—with the television off

- Unexpectedly coming home early from work

As we go through this exercise with a group, we encourage each individual to keep a personal list of the "happy" and "unhappy" things in their own family.

Then, when we've finished sharing, we tell them the one "biggie" that is guaranteed to dramatically change the quality of family life in just a few weeks and most likely solve 70 to 80 percent of problems at home. We ask them to look at their own personal list and commit to:

Stop doing the unhappy stuff!
Start doing the happy stuff!

In other words . . .

Stop doing things like:

- Not really listening

- Interrupting someone when they're talking

- Being sarcastic or complaining

- Having to be asked repeatedly to do something

- Breaking promises

- Leaving stuff out (hair spray, clothing, etc.)

Start doing things like:

- Listening

- Respecting each other's space

- Keeping promises

- Saying "Thank you!"

- Doing household chores without being asked

- Doing something unexpected to surprise someone (such as bringing flowers or serving breakfast in bed)

After an instant of surprised silence, people start to laugh. I can tell some of them are thinking, "You mean I paid to have you tell me this?" But then they start to realize, "Yeah, I did. And it's just what I needed to hear."

It's simple.
But it's not simplistic.

In relationships, the little things *are* the big things. They show caring and commitment. They say, "I care more about you than I care about my own habits or convenience." And, "These things are important to me because *you* are important to me."

In reality, it's not so much the little things themselves that matter, but the attitude, paradigms, and character you show in choosing to give priority to those things.

Take a look at your own personal list of "happy" things. *Could* you do those things? Is there anything on that list that's really too hard or impossible to do?

In performance analysis, a consultant will sometimes ask a manager: "If I held a gun to this employee's head, could he do the task?" If the answer is no, the problem is training. If the answer is yes, the problem is motivation. So, if someone held a gun to your head, *could* you do the things you listed in Part Two?

Our guess is you could.

So why don't you do them? And what would happen if you *did* do them? What if you were really serious about doing those things for even 30 days? Would it make a difference?

We're confident that it would. Experience itself teaches us that understanding and doing the happy stuff, consistently and over time, makes a *huge* difference in the quality of family life. And whether you're a spouse, a parent, a grandparent, a son or daughter, aunt, uncle, or cousin, there are "little things" you can do to improve your family life.

Before moving on, we want to assure you that while the focus in this chapter is on the nuclear family, the principles involved are just as important to those who may be single or do not have children. Applications, such as the one we've just discussed are vital in extended family relationships and in all relationships you might have, both now and in the future.

So don't necessarily limit your thinking to your current nuclear family status. Consider all your close relationships. Think of the family you might want to have in the future. At the end of the "optimizer" section, we'll suggest ways to apply these high leverage ideas in a variety of situations.

FAMILY IS TOP PRIORITY

We all know family is important. In seminars, when we ask people to identify what's most important to them, almost everyone puts family at or near the top of the list. But most report they do not feel satisfied with the quantity or quality of the time they're investing in their families—or with the results.

So how can we more effectively prioritize the family? What can we do to ensure that we're doing the things that will really bring quality family life results?

We hope that by now you are convinced that how you *see* family will determine what you *do* in your family, and what you *do* will determine the results you *get*. By far, then, the most high leverage way to create change and invest in your family is to begin with how you *see* family.

In this chapter, we'll ask you to take a look at:

* How you *see* family

* How you see *your* family

* How you see *your role* as a family member

* How *family leadership* can empower you to create joy at home

HOW DO YOU SEE FAMILY

Years ago we came across a cartoon showing what was going on inside the minds of various family members when one of them suggested, "Let's get a dog." As we recall, in the mom's mind there was a tiny Chihuahua sitting on a pillow. In the dad's it was a Great Dane walking nobly by his side. In the daughter's mind there was a cute French poodle sitting quietly in her lap as she did her homework. In the son's it was a Saint Bernard rolling and tumbling with him in the backyard. To each family member, the word "dog" meant something different. Thus, the decision to "get a dog" had different implications to each.

In today's world the word *family* is often met with the same variety of mental images. From the Brady Bunch to the Simpsons, the Cosbys to the Sopranos, people's media- and experience-created images of family vary widely.

So where does your *seeing* about family come from?

- From your own growing-up experience—good or bad?

- From your own experience as an adult—good or bad?

- From social statistics, newscasts, movies, and television programs that create a sense of cynicism or resignation about family life?

- From TV sitcoms and comedy routines that model abrasive and mocking family interaction?

- From your perceptions of the family life of your neighbors or friends?

How extensively do these or other influences impact the way you *see* family . . . what you expect with regard to family . . . the way you interact with family members . . . the quality of your family life?

We live in a time when social messages about family are incredibly mixed and confusing. Even the purpose of family itself seems muddled. While in the past, the family was generally seen as a sacred institution that was necessary for physical survival, procreation, intergenerational character and skill training, and emotional and spiritual strength, for many today it is seen as optional and essentially social and recreational.

We also live in a time when we're fragmented and diverted by many other things in our lives, making it hard to take the time to think deeply about the quality of our family life and the impact it has on us and on future generations.

But if we really want the richly satisfying and incomparable joy that comes from quality family life, we must make time to think about how we think about family.

As thousands of years of civilization attest, family is the very DNA of society.

*The strength of a nation derives from the integrity of
the home.*
—Confucius

The family is the nucleus of civilization.
—William J. Durant

As Allan Carlson, general secretary of the World Congress of
Families II, observed in his opening address to that body:

*Our very identity as human beings impels us toward family life;
toward marriage and children. A religious person would probably
explain this as a consequence of Divine intent, in the Creation. The
person of science could explain this as a consequence of 10,000
generations of human evolution. The conclusion, though, would
be the same: to be human is to be familial.*[1]

As we look at today's disturbing family statistics, it's easy to get
discouraged. Consider the following:
Over the past 30 years . . .

- Teenage suicide has increased almost 300 percent.

- One-fourth of all adolescents contract a sexually transmitted
disease before they graduate from high school.

- Out-of-wedlock births have increased more than 400 percent.

- The divorce rate has more than doubled.

- The percentage of families headed by a single parent has more
than tripled.

- Scholastic Aptitude Test scores among all students have dropped
73 points.[2]

In addition, the number one health problem for American
women today is domestic violence. Four million women are beaten
each year by their partners.[3] And more and more children have no
functioning fathers. One of three American children go to bed each
night in a home where his or her father does not live.[4]

Perhaps one benefit of such statistics is that they bring to our awareness—in dramatic and unforgettable ways—the foundational and essential nature of family. With strong, stable family life as an almost given in the past, perhaps many of us have been blind to the fact that it was the primary thread around which all other threads in society were woven. But as the threads have begun to unravel, the vital necessity of those primary threads has become unmistakable.

George Haley, former United States ambassador to Gambia— and brother of Alex Haley, who wrote the stirring intergenerational family saga *Roots*—has observed:

> *Much like protons, neutrons, and other subatomic particles consti-tute the building blocks of our physical world, the family is the cornerstone for both our social existence and individual develop-ment. It has been said it takes a village to raise a child, but I tell you it takes strong families to make a true village.*[5]

Clearly, strong families nurture a strong society. A strong society nurtures strong families. Thus, happy, healthy families are both the roots and fruits of a stable and enduring civilization.

And what makes a happy, healthy family? Extensive research explores a variety of factors, but almost everyone who takes a seri-ous look at family issues will agree that:

- A strong, loving marriage tends to create a strong family.

- Families are generally happy and successful to the degree that family members:
    - trust each other
    - love each other
    - believe in each other
    - help each other
    - comfort each other
    - forgive each other
    - work together
    - serve together

- ○ worship together
- ○ play together
- ○ celebrate together

- Families who have healthy relationships with their extended families are generally happier and more resilient to the challenges of life.[6]

Despite some media images to the contrary, research shows that married couples usually live longer,[7] exhibit fewer risk-taking behaviors—such as drunk driving, smoking, and drug abuse—have lower rates of suicide and alcoholism,[8] suffer less from illness and disease, and recover more quickly when they do fall ill.[9] They have less depression and fewer psychiatric disorders.[10] They're better off financially, and tend to save more and invest greater amounts for education and retirement.[11] And faithfully married people report being more satisfied with the physical intimacy in their relationships than all other sexually active people combined.[12] In the words of one researcher, "No part of the unmarried population—separated, divorced, widowed, or never married—describes itself as being so happy and contented with life as the married."[13]

Research also shows that children from strong, stable families are more likely to be successful and happy in every way—physically, mentally, spiritually, economically, and socially—and that those with a strong extended family support system are better able to successfully cope with the challenges of life.[14]

Research aside, consult your own navigational intelligence. Can you honestly imagine anything that would tend to create greater personal happiness and contribute more to societal stability than a family made up of parents who genuinely love each other . . . who welcome children into the family and team well to provide for their physical, emotional, social, and spiritual needs . . . who teach their children to love and serve each other . . . who pass on a wonderful heritage of the principles, such as honesty and integrity, that create quality of life . . . and who are supported in their efforts by a loving network of grandparents, cousins, nieces, nephews, uncles, and aunts?

One of the fundamental characteristics of a principle is that it is self-evident—that its opposite appears absurd. Could anyone imagine that the opposite of what we've just described would serve individuals or society better: parents who despise or are indifferent to each other; who resent children; who act selfishly and independently; who fail to meet their children's physical, emotional, social, and spiritual needs; who fight and quarrel and don't seem to care when their children do the same; who teach dishonesty, slovenliness, and indulgence; and who are critical of and distance themselves from aunts, uncles, cousins, or other extended family members?

Whether you consider it self-evident or you validate it through sociology, biology, theology, or your own navigational intelligence, the reality is that quality family life is essential and foundational to personal and societal well-being and happiness. Even with the enormous challenges of marriage and parenting, the essential ingredients of the family ideal are—and have been—the foundational life experience for many people around the globe and throughout history. Even in the face of significant political, economic, and social problems, "family" has been the strength in the midst of the challenge.

Bottom line, there is simply no better, stronger, more deeply satisfying, richly rewarding, productive, and effective way of life.

HOW DO YOU SEE YOUR FAMILY

When we consider our own families, few if any of us would totally identify with the ideal we just described. In fact, it's more likely that most of us would point out our family's weaknesses and faults and firmly assert that there's no way we will ever reach the ideal. Some— perhaps "burned" by their own damaging experience—would even be bitter or cynical in response to this description of the ideal.

But we suggest that you seriously examine your expectations in this area, and as you do, that you consider three things:

First, whatever our family situation, "ideal" does not mean "without challenge." By its very nature, family life is *filled* with challenge. After 35 years of struggling with health challenges, economic challenges, and the daily scraped knee bandaging, runny nose wiping, teenage trauma solving, and deadline-meeting problems of daily life, we *know* even the best of family life has its challenges!

One of the great benefits of family life is the incomparable interdependence and strength of character that come as a result of working through the challenges together. In fact, our ability to *see* the "ideal" as *strength to handle the challenge*—rather than the absence of challenge—is what gives birth to the thoughts and actions that create the enduring family strength implied in the ideal.

Second, even the ideal family life is a saga of "becoming." The birth and growth of a child is the perfect metaphor for the birth and growth of a family. There are awkward stages, times of learning to walk and falling down, times of learning to meet needs and interact with others in meaningful ways. There's no such thing as a "perfect" family. There's a growing family, a learning family, a becoming family. And the direction in which you're headed as a family is far more important than wherever you happen to be at any given time because, over time, the direction will make all the difference!

Third, whatever your own experience may have been, can you honestly imagine anything that could have a greater impact on the happiness of the people in your family now and the happiness of future generations than to nurture them in the principles of joyful family living? Even if your own situation is far from the ideal . . . even if you were married to an abusive spouse . . . even if you have children who have gone far astray . . . even if you have a legacy of alcoholism, trouble with your in-laws, or a history of choices you'd rather not have made—still, is there anything that would be of greater benefit to your children than to embrace and teach the principles of the ideal family?

There is no greater legacy you could pass on than to prepare your children to fulfill their own family roles with excellence and joy. And what could be more meaningful than transforming your own negative experiences and heritage of dysfunction from a stumbling block into a stepping-stone, a foundation upon which more solid families of the future can be built?

Consider the alternative: How could it be better for our families to sustain the bitterness, nurture the pain, repeat the mistakes, and pass on a legacy of dysfunction?

REBECCA

My mother grew up in a family that could be considered somewhat dysfunctional. My grandmother had been orphaned at five and married at fifteen. She was emotionally dependent on the approval of my grandfather—a man who, at the time, was very strict. When people did something he didn't like, he would cut them off emotionally—sometimes not even speaking to them for years. After giving birth to five children, Grandmom was devastated when Granddad told her he had decided to call it quits.

Although my father grew up in a more stable family, working with his six brothers and sisters on the family farm, he has told me that never once in all his growing up years did he ever hear the words, "I love you." His first birthday that was ever even acknowledged was his 22nd—and that was because by that time, he was engaged to my mother who loved him and thought it natural that his birthday should be celebrated.

As a child, I wasn't really aware of all of this. All I knew was the warm and wonderful security of growing up in a home that was filled with love. In my home, there were "I love you's" every day and birthday celebrations every year. Dad sang to me, read to me and helped me with homework. Mom spent countless hours teaching me songs and making costumes so that I could perform. My parents often asked for my opinion, included me in almost everything, and lovingly supported me in developing my talents and in any other worthwhile project I wanted to do.

As an adult now with more than three decades of experience in raising my own family, the more I think about it, the more I am amazed. Where did my parents get the vision to create something that was so far removed from their own experience? In the midst of daily living, did they realize how profoundly the choices they made would impact my own efforts to raise a family? Did they have any idea they were creating a heritage of security, love and life learning that would impact generations to come?

Whenever I've talked with my parents about it, they've been quick to acknowledge the good things about the families in which they were raised. But it is obvious to me that many of their most important life choices were driven more by their own navigational intelligence than by their environment. Deep inside their hearts was an inner compass that acknowledged and taught the principles of the ideal family. And it was their connection to that compass that enabled them—despite their own experience and scripting— to create such a warm and wonderful legacy of love for me.

Regardless of our current circumstances, each of us has the power and freedom through our own proactivity to teach family members what is both "real" and "realistic" regarding the family and to move toward the ideal. To do so is probably the greatest contribution we can make to our own personal happiness, the happiness and well-being of our children, and the strength of the society in which we live.

HOW DO YOU SEE YOUR ROLE AS A FAMILY MEMBER

ROGER

One night many years ago, I was approaching the door of our home after a challenging day at work, and I was looking forward to just "crashing."

I remember, the moment my hand touched the doorknob, something whispered inside, "You have a house full of people who are waiting for 'Daddy' to come home. They want to be with you. They need you."

My first reaction was to turn around and head the other way. I was so tired, so ready to have everyone else fill my needs. I didn't want to even think about having to do anything for anyone else that day.

But in my heart, I was convinced of the truth of that inner wisdom. I knew that inside those walls were the people I loved most in all the world. Could anything be more important in my life than loving and lifting them?

With a resolve to do that, I squared my shoulders and went inside. I was immediately greeted by my four-year-old daughter with shining eyes and "Daddy!" on her lips. Her enthusiastic hug confirmed my resolution. I spent the rest of the evening finding ways to benefit and bless the members of my family. I listened, fixed broken toys, changed diapers, helped with the dishes, and tucked kids into bed.

What struck me the most about that experience is that later that night, as I was falling into bed exhausted, in the instant before my head hit the pillow, I realized I was smiling.

That night was a turning point for me. My paradigm was changed. I discovered that real joy in family life comes when you see home as a place to give instead of get. And I have found the paradox to be true: The more you give, the more you receive.

All too often we tend to see work as a place to contribute and home as a place to crash. We come home from work exhausted, and we somehow expect that everything should be in order, everyone should be happy, and we should be able to simply recuperate from the efforts of the day.

When we're faced with the impact of the realities that parenting is work, relationships take effort, and maintaining cleanliness and order at home is a significant task, it throws us off balance. It doesn't meet our subconscious, unexamined expectation that somehow the huge benefits of quality home and family life will simply be there for us with little or no real investment on our part. And because that expectation is not met, we begin to blame and accuse and punish those around us in little ways.

While it's true that the greatest joy and satisfaction in life come from family, it's also true that this incomparable fulfillment only comes when we fully give ourselves to the family, work for it, and sacrifice for it. This reality is in harmony with the great governing law of *contribution*—one of the fundamental principles in life.

No one has learned the meaning of living until he has surrendered his ego to the service of his fellow men.
—W. Beran Wolfe

Giving simply because it is right to give, without thought
of return, at a proper time, in proper circumstances, and
to worthy persons, is enlightened giving. Giving with
regrets or in the expectation of receiving some favor or of
getting something in return, is selfish giving.
—Bhagavad Gita

The good news is that once you align your expectations with this overarching principle, you not only open the door to greater personal satisfaction, you open a whole new dimension of life balance. It empowers you to see both work *and* home as avenues of contribution. It empowers you to move beyond competition and compromise by making work and home complementary. It sparks creative third-alternative solutions to traditional work/home dilemmas. It empowers you to recognize that, bottom line, the issue is not *either/or*, but *and*. It's living and contributing in the unifying and encompassing whole of which work and home are both parts. Aligning with the principle of contribution also opens your eyes to ways in which you can contribute that will make a difference. Whether you're a husband, wife, parent, grandparent, son, daughter, niece, nephew, uncle, aunt, or cousin, there are things you can do to make your family better. They may be the "little things" we suggested earlier: remembering to say "Thank you," picking up after yourself, taking the time to listen, or putting the toilet seat up or down. Or they may be bigger things: helping your child with an important school project, taking your spouse on a weekend retreat, apologizing to an extended family member, or making the effort to mend a relationship that's been broken for years.

Keep in mind that *quality family life is never an accident; it is always an achievement.* It is the result of proactive effort and conscious investment in the relationships that matter most.

CREATING AND MAINTAINING THE VISION

So how do you become the kind of proactive, contributing family member who makes a difference?

One high leverage way to begin is by creating and maintaining a clear vision of the kind of family member you want to be. In the midst of the daily challenges of family life, it's far easier to be giving—or honest or courageous or kind—when you've clearly determined and have before you the important values you want to live by.

One way to capture and retain that vision is by incorporating it as part of a personal mission statement.

REBECCA

Many years ago as part of my personal mission statement, I wrote that my goal as a mother was "to welcome into the world and to love, honor, nurture, and empower the special spirits who will be my children and eternal friends." I had no idea when I wrote those words how enormously powerful they would be in shaping my relationship with my children over the years.

Even though my parents set a good example for me—an only child—I had no way of knowing the difficult challenges I would face in trying to parent seven very different children . . . especially in the midst of dealing with my own personal challenges, including chronic fatigue syndrome, severe PMS, and other significant health problems. My personal mission statement often served as an anchor in the midst of the storm.

There were many times when I felt tempted to be authoritative—to insist on my way simply because I thought I was bigger and smarter and I was the MOM! There were times when I wanted to simply solve the problem and get on to other things instead of taking time to teach and explain and build the relationship along with the skill or knowledge base. There were times when it would have been easy to criticize or put down . . . times when I wanted to do my own thing instead of doing for or with them. And there were certainly times when I gave in to those things.

But I kept seeing this vision of mature friendships with wonderful, highly responsible, contributing members of society. And the combination of that vision plus Roger's continuing faith in the future of each child—even when there were problems and chal-

lenges—empowered me most of the time to see beyond simply "raising these children so I can get on with other things in my life." It enabled me to focus on the growth and on my longer-term relationships with some of the most "awesome" people in the world.

We strongly suggest that you capture your vision of the spouse/parent/family member you want to be—either as part of your personal mission statement or in some other way that's helpful for you.

We also suggest that you then be brutally honest with yourself concerning what kind of family member you *are*. Remember the Stockdale Paradox. Remember the need to be both real and realistic. The only way to get to where you want to be is to start where you are. So capture the vision. Recognize the reality. Only then can you effectively chart a course that will get you from one place to the other.

As you move along the path, be sure to review your vision regularly. Keep that vision in sight. It will empower you to stay on a more direct path and to course-correct quickly when you get off.

ROGER

When our children were very young, we moved to a minifarm where we hoped to raise fresh fruits and vegetables and healthy children. I bought an old Case tractor that didn't work, and spent a lot of time that first winter out in an old chicken shed rebuilding it. After investing so much effort, I could hardly wait for the first spring day when the weather would be good enough for me to haul it out and start plowing the rows in which we planned to plant.

I had never plowed with a tractor before, but as I started down the first row and looked behind me, I couldn't believe the great feeling I had watching the earth curl up under that plow. I was absolutely intrigued with the way the rich, black soil kept appearing . . . almost—it seemed—coming to life. In fact, I was so intrigued that I forgot to watch where I was going.

Fortunately, I did look up as I reached the end of the row, but as I turned around and surveyed the entire field, I was sud-

denly dismayed. What I had thought was going to be a beauti-
ful, straight row had turned out to be a horrendously uneven,
zigzag mess.

Much to my chagrin, a longtime farmer and neighbor who
had (unknown to me) been watching with amusement walked
over to where I sat, somewhat dejected. With a twinkle in his eye,
he put his hand on my knee and said, "You know, son, if you want
to keep your rows straight, you've got to keep your eye on the
mark!" He then proceeded to explain how I needed to pick out a
point in the distance, keep my eye on it, keep moving toward it—
and not look back.

That obvious piece of advice has made an enormous differ-
ence in the direction and quality of every other "row" I've plowed
in every area of my life.

Much of success in life comes as a result of that simple strategy.
You raise your sights to a mark and keep moving toward it. Even if
you never fully reach it, simply moving toward it as effectively as you
can will diminish the distance and make a tremendous difference in
the quality of everything you do along the way.

THINK "FAMILY LEADERSHIP"

As you consider your family role, we also recommend that you learn
to think in terms of "family leadership"—in terms of your unique
opportunity to influence and nurture the members of your family in
the principles that have created strong, joyful families and societies
throughout time.

While all family members—spouses, parents, grandparents, siblings, aunts, uncles, cousins—have the opportunity to contribute in
this way, we suggest that the most important ingredient of a successful family is the leadership exercised by parents. Thus:

Family leadership—especially leadership exercised by parents—is
one of the defining activities of the human experience.[15]

Why? Because it powerfully shapes how the next generation *sees* family, what they *do* in their current and future families, and the *results* they will get.

In terms of family leadership, parents have four basic roles:

- *To provide* the basic necessities of life—physical, social, emotional, and spiritual

- *To protect* family members from physical, social, and emotional harm

- *To nurture* family members in love and kindness

- *To teach* family members the principles and values that empower them to have rich, rewarding relationships and joyful, fulfilling lives

In two-parent homes, while one parent may take the prime responsibility for fulfilling one role or another, truly effective parents will fully support each other in their roles as equal partners. Single parents can proactively secure help from close friends, extended family members, or church or community support groups in fulfilling these essential roles.

In Chapter 3, "Work Matters," we focused primarily on the providing role. In the remainder of this chapter we'll focus on eight key optimizers that will help you protect, nurture, and teach family members in ways that create joy at home and prepare children to fulfill their adult roles with balance and peace.

As you consider these ideas, keep in mind that they represent a smorgasbord. Only one or two may be right for you in your current situation. Some may spark other ideas of ways you can even more effectively implement the principles involved. The point is to use your navigational intelligence and focus on the optimizers that will create the best possible results in your situation.

OPTIMIZER 1: CREATE A FAMILY MISSION STATEMENT

One of the most effective family leadership activities is to create a sense of shared vision and values in the minds and hearts of all family members. And one of the best ways to do that is to create a family mission statement.

A family mission statement does the same thing for a family that a personal mission statement does for an individual. It clarifies the fundamental heart-set. It gives a sense of identity and purpose. And from that, almost everything else in the family flows.

When there's no shared vision, family members essentially go their own separate ways, operating out of their individual values and agendas. Work done by parents is unrecognized and unappreciated. Family resources (time and money) are spent arbitrarily, creating resentment and misunderstanding. Individual family members' priorities are not shared with others in the family. There's no understanding of the value of or real agreement concerning family chores.

But when there is shared vision—when the family is of one heart and one mind—the situation is reversed. Family members see and understand the purpose and supreme importance of the family. Each individual sees how his or her role helps to fulfill that shared purpose. Solutions to challenges and concerns engage the creativity and support of all. Decisions concerning time and money—the communicators of value—are agreed upon and made together.

Keep in mind: The way the family sees is at the root of what the family does and the results the family gets. The key is to work together until there's unity in the way the family *sees*. And the process is as important as the product. As family members talk together, share feelings and ideas, work through different concerns and viewpoints, they eventually come up with something everyone buys into.

It sometimes takes weeks—even months—of talking and thinking and talking . . . again and again. But the very process brings family members closer. It opens doors of communication. It touches and draws out the deepest desires and feelings of each family member. It refines and clarifies vision. The final result can take almost any shape: a written document, a poem, a piece of artwork, or a song— whatever captures the essence of your family and enables you to keep it constantly before you.

Over the years, the two of us have made several attempts to capture the vision we wanted to govern our family life. When we were engaged, we ran across some beautiful words of counsel we decided to adopt as a sort of marriage mission statement—though we didn't think of it as such at the time. Since the early months of our married life, those words have hung on our bedroom wall and have helped us to interact in ways that are consistent with the deepest desires of our hearts.

"You two ... build your own quiet world." All things need watching, working at, caring for, and marriage is no exception. Marriage is not something to be treated indifferently or abused, or something that simply takes care of itself. Nothing neglected will remain as it was or is, or will fail to deteriorate. All things need attention, care, and concern, and especially so in this most sensitive of all relationships of life. It isn't difficult to prove that ... none of us is perfect. When we seek to find fault, there is much fault to find. And in marriage as in all else, unkind fault-finding can be destructive. "In the first solitary hour," said an unknown writer, " ... promise each other sacredly, never, not even in jest, to wrangle with each other, never ... indulge in the least ill-humor ... Next, promise each other, sincerely and solemnly, never to keep a secret from each other, under whatever pretext, and whatever excuse it might be. You must continually, and every moment, see clearly into each other's [hearts]. Even when one of you has committed a fault ... confess it. And as you keep nothing from each other, so, on the contrary, preserve the privacies of your house ... [your] marriage ... [your] heart, from ... [all others], from all the world. You two, with God's help, build your own quiet world ... [Let no] party stand between you two ... Promise this to each other ... Your souls will grow . . . to each other, and at last will become as one." Remember to build each other up, to strengthen and sustain, to keep companionship lovely and alive. Remember dignity and respect; understanding; not expecting perfection; a sense of humor and a sense of what is sacred and serious; common purposes, common convictions, and the character to stay with a bargain, to keep a covenant—in these are the makings of a good and solid marriage. Remember "patience, persuasion, gentleness, kindness, and love unfeigned, without hypocrisy and without guile, that you

may know that thy faithfulness is stronger than the cords of death." Every marriage has a right to this. "You two, with God's help, build your own quiet world."

Richard L. Evans[16]

This statement was—and continues to be—a wonderful strength in our marriage.

As our children grew, however, we began to realize that we needed something more—something that captured a vision of the kind of *family* we wanted to be. After several unsuccessful attempts to create such a statement on our own, we finally realized the children needed to be involved.

At that time, some of our children were teenagers, some were quite young, and some were in between. The challenge we faced was figuring out how we could involve each of them in the creation of our family mission.

We decided to begin by asking some simple questions during family dinner and at our weekly family time.

"What do you like best about being a family?"

"When do you think we have the most fun?"

"What do you think our most important family values should be?"

Sometimes, the discussion lasted no more than a few minutes. Sometimes, the children were enthusiastic. Sometimes, nobody said much. But we kept coming back to it and asking the questions.

Finally, we took everyone's ideas, condensed them, edited them, and came up with a statement containing the values and principles we wanted to build our family around.

It's impossible in this book to tap into the power of a family mission statement. But we can tell you that our own statement has been one of the most significant, bonding, unifying, positive factors in our family for many years. It has been the subject of many family discussions. It has provided the foundation for teaching our children many things about character and interdependence. It has served as the standard against which individual and family decisions have been evaluated and made. It has been an anchor for our family in the midst of many storms.

OUR FAMILY MISSION

To love each other . . .

To help each other . . .

To believe in each other . . .

To wisely use our time, talents, and resources
to bless others . . .

To worship together . . .

Forever.

As several of our children have married and created families of their own, this statement has been reexamined by the entire family—including our children's spouses—and still found to express the values we choose to live by as an extended family. At our annual family reunions, we display it on a poster. We renew our understanding of and commitment to it. We teach it to the grandchildren and sing songs together that capture the various points in it. It has become the standard that has pulled all extended family members together in a sense of shared vision.[17]

OPTIMIZER 2: HAVE A WEEKLY "FAMILY TIME"

Many major family-connected organizations today, from churches to government agencies, promote some kind of regular focused "family time." People have begun to realize that when families don't spend quality time together on a consistent basis, things begin to fall apart.

In the past, and in many cultures around the world, the idea of having to make time to be together would be considered ludicrous. Being together as families was and is a huge and natural part of life, and to even suggest otherwise would seem to border on the absurd.

But in today's society—particularly in the Western world—creating time together is a real challenge. Even the traditionally sacred family dinner hour is now subject to fast food establishments, television programming, children's sports activities, and late work assignments. It takes a solid, proactive effort to gather the family to create even a little time together on a regular basis.

There is great wisdom in making dinnertime a high family priority. It's a natural time to talk and share, to provide emotional as well as physical nourishment for family members on a daily basis.

In addition, many families find great value in scheduling a weekly family time. This is something we've felt very strongly about in our own family. Almost without exception, throughout our married life we have scheduled a special time every Monday night to be together. We play games, sing songs, discuss important topics, have a treat, and occasionally enjoy an activity outside the home, such as going bowling, watching a fun family movie or play, or attending a game or concert in which a family member has part. Over the years, we have found this family time to be a significant facilitator of family bonding, communication, coordination, teamwork, and stability.

Now, with four married children and a university student living away from home, we also schedule an extended family time when we can all be together once a month. We have a dinner and a sharing time and have fun watching the grandchildren interact. At the moment, we're fortunate to have everyone in the family living so close. But we realize this may not always be the case. We're grateful that with modern technology it's possible to have quality extended family interaction via phone, the Internet, and, of course, annual family reunions—even when family members live far away.

Consistently having a regular family time is not easy. Scheduling conflicts, fatigue, and preoccupied or grouchy children sometimes create problems that can make you wonder if it's worth the effort. But we're absolutely convinced that it is. Over the years, this high quality time together becomes something family members look forward to. It also produces patterns and values that equip children to live happy, productive, and balanced lives of their own.

Of course, the best time to start is when children are young. Then they grow up enjoying and anticipating a quality weekly time together. If children are older, it's usually best to work into it gently. Sometimes it's enough to just get together to have a treat, and to consider anything else that happens as a bonus.

The most important thing is to keep trying and never give up. Often, it's faith in the positive outcome that makes the positive outcome happen.

OPTIMIZER 3: DATE YOUR MATE

It's been said that the most important thing you can do for your children is to love your spouse. That's because the health of the marriage affects everything else in the family, and the example of the marriage affects marriages and families for generations to come.

In today's world, the responsibilities and pressures associated with jobs, home management and maintenance, professional development, community responsibilities—and, ironically, even the children themselves—often seem to leave little time for real marital togetherness. So in our society, if you want it to happen, you have to be proactive and make it happen.

We've found two ways that seem to work well for many people, including us: weekly dates and semiannual retreats.

Weekly Dates

When we were engaged, we were influenced by a wonderful couple in their 90s who had been happily married for more than 70 years. We learned that one of the things they did to keep their marriage vibrant and growing was to go on a date with each other every week.

We thought that sounded like a great idea . . . and it is! Over the years, our weekly date has been one of the highlights of our married life. We've loved going out to dinner, movies, plays, lectures, or other activities we both enjoy. When the budget's been tight, we've enjoyed going for a walk, sharing a frozen yogurt treat, or just spending uninterrupted time together at home.

Through years of raising children, intense work schedules, and community service, our Friday night dates have been one of the major renewing elements of our relationship. Our married children, who have also adopted this practice, tell us it's proved to be a lifeline for them as well.

In our minds, dating before marriage was okay. But dating each other *after* marriage is an absolute necessity! And when schedules are hectic, money is tight, or problems seem overwhelming is usually when we need it the most.

Weekly mate dates are a great way to renew love and commitment. It's amazing how much better you can face the challenges of the week when you have Friday night together to look forward to.

Semiannual Retreats

Also over the years, we've discovered the power of a semiannual megadate or "retreat." Twice a year we try to take a few days and go someplace where we can have time to ourselves. We usually plan adequate, uninterrupted time to accomplish several important things:

- Have fun. Go fishing or hiking. Go to movies or plays. Enjoy some quiet time together.

- Review the past six months.

- Plan and agree on goals for the next six months.

- Discuss our individual needs and growth and our relationship.

- Talk about the children and determine what we can do to nurture, encourage, and support each one.

This wonderful, renewing time together has significantly increased our sense of unity and shared purpose. And even though we've had to leave our children at home with extended family members to make these quality investments in our relationship, we feel they've made a significant difference in our ability to cope with family problems and give our children a healthy, happy anticipation of what a marriage relationship can be.

OPTIMIZER 4: HAVE "SNEAK-INS" AND "SNEAK-OUTS"

One of the most enjoyable traditions we've had in our family is having "sneak-ins" and "sneak-outs" with our children. We've been doing it for years, and we don't even remember how these occasions came by their name.

A "sneak" time is one-on-one time with a parent and a child. If it's "in," that means it's at home—watching a video, playing a game, or doing a project together. If it's "out," that means it's out of the house. It could be a short activity, such as going out to eat, seeing a movie or a play, going shopping or playing a round of golf. Or it could be an overnighter—camping out in the mountains or enjoying the amenities of staying in a hotel in a nearby city.

We've also created traditions of taking the children on major sneak-outs twice during their growing-up years—during the summer they turn 14 and when they graduate from high school. Sneak-outs for 14-year-olds have included river rafting, backpacking, fishing in Alaska, enjoying the beach in southern California, and seeing Broadway plays and American history sites. Graduation trips have included a university-sponsored travel study program in the United States, a trip to Europe, and a canoe adventure down the Colorado River.

Before you start adding up the cost, you need to understand that most of these trips have been unbelievably inexpensive. Due to special promotions, a week at a California beach condo cost 50 cents (for a phone call), and our son's ticket to Europe was free. By planning ahead and watching for special deals, we've been able to take advantage of frequent flier miles and special promotions.

The one-on-one time between parent and child really says, "I love you. I enjoy spending time with you." It creates pathways of communication and camaraderie that spill over into the whole relationship, eliminating some of the typical parent/child challenges and making others much easier to deal with.

And besides all that, it's fun! You learn a lot about your kids. It's great when your family members are your best friends.

OPTIMIZER 5: HOLD REGULAR "PARENT CHATS"

While sneak-ins and sneak-outs focus on building friendships with our children, "parent chats" focus on strengthening our role and relationship with them as their parent.

Parent chats basically involve interaction around two questions:

- What are you working on?

- What can we do to help?

These questions accomplish some very important things. First, they imply that the child ought to be working on something. And second, they define the role of the parent: "I am not your boss or dictator. I'm here to help."

If you start parent chats when children are small, they will look forward to them as the years go by.

You might ask your five year-old daughter, "What are you working on?"

"Um . . . I dunno."

"Well, what do you think you ought to be working on?"

The very question creates the expectation that we should all always be working on something.

"Um . . . I guess putting my toys away."

"Great! What can I do to help?"

"Put my toys away."

"No, but I can help *you* put your toys away."

"Okay."

So you go put toys away together. Your daughter learns that she is responsible to be working, and that you—her parent—are a source of help.

As she gets older, the conversation changes.

"What are you working on?"

"Getting good grades" or, "Learning how to drive" or, "Getting a job."

"What can I do to help?"

It may be helping her with her homework, taking her to practice driving in the high school parking lot, or going through the "Help Wanted" section of the newspaper together.

As the ability to think longer-term increases, you may find it helpful to use these opportunities to set up and review a parent/ daughter win-win agreement or success plan.[18] In such an agreement, you (the parent) agree to do certain things—provide room, board, health insurance, nutritious meals, a car to drive, lots of "TLC." She (the child) agrees to do certain things—take care of her possessions, fulfill certain home responsibilities, contribute to the family through her attitude and actions.

Weekly or monthly, during your "parent chat," you can review the agreement and let *her* assess how well she and you are doing. Talk over any problems. Work out any issues. If you provide a spending or clothing allowance, you can give it to her during this time, to reinforce the positive nature of these parent chats in her mind. As the years go by, each meeting will reinforce your daughter's responsibility to work on productive, meaningful goals and your role as a source of help.

With the tradition firmly in place, you'll probably find that on more than one occasion you will be surprised as your daughter suddenly opens up and begins to share deep challenges and problems she's trying to solve. Because you've established your role—and particularly if you refrain from being shocked, judgmental, critical, or too quick to give advice—she will, in all probability, turn to you as a source of help.

ROGER

This was brought home forcibly to me one day in a parent chat I was having with one of our daughters. I started out with the usual questions—"What are you working on? How can I help?"—and suddenly she opened up and began talking about a young girl she knew at school who had become pregnant. The girl was scared and talking about getting an abortion through some very risky, illegitimate channels. This was shocking and frightening for our daughter, and she was feeling very burdened and overwhelmed.

As we counseled, we decided together that some action needed to be taken. Calls were made that apparently helped divert what could have been a tragedy. Although it was difficult, our daughter felt right about the action that was taken and grateful for the help in sorting things out.

As I reflected on the situation later, I couldn't help but feel grateful that we had developed the kind of relationship where she felt comfortable in talking with me about it. I was so glad that we had set up the regular chats, and grateful that she felt secure enough in that environment to open up and ask for help.

I know it's important that children see their parents as friends. But that experience taught me it's also important for children to see parents as parents and real sources of help. There's no question in my mind—that one experience was definitely worth all the hours invested in building a relationship of support and trust. Since that time, I have asked myself: "If we hadn't been having these chats on a regular basis, would I have ever even heard about the problem?"

Over time, regular parent chats establish the idea that you are there to help. When the relationship is there, a child's sharing may well come at some other time—not necessarily during the chat. But the chat is one way to build the relationship and lay the foundation so they feel comfortable in sharing and confident in your love and support.

When a child does share, remember that you stand on holy ground. Treat tender feelings and confidences with respect. When your child is really open, sharing, and seeking, you have an incomparable opportunity to influence in positive ways. These "teaching moments"—*not* "preaching" moments—make a profound difference in relationships and in a parent's ability to influence and help.

OPTIMIZER 6: HAVE A DAILY FAMILY WISDOM TIME

What if you and your family were to spend just ten minutes together each day reading and talking about some of the truly great thoughts and ideas throughout time? What would be the impact of such a "wisdom time" on each family member? On relationships between family members? On the way you interact with each other? On the way you spend your individual and family time?

With varying degrees of success, this is something we've tried to do with our family from the beginning. Sometimes we've done it at night, reading to the children and encouraging them to memorize short classic quotes. Most of the time we've done it in the mornings—actually turning it into a family devotional with the addition of a song, a moment of daily planning, and a family prayer.

There have been times when we've wondered if it was worth the effort—mornings when someone was sick or had gone to an early meeting . . . mornings when we started late or were so rushed we could only spend a couple of minutes together . . . mornings when teenagers would drag themselves upstairs, plop down on the couch with blankets over their heads, and utter no more than an unintelligible grunt or a groan during the entire time . . . even mornings when we simply couldn't pull it off.

But for the most part, we've kept working at it. And over the years, the results have been remarkable. In terms of molding character and solidifying family values, this has been one of the most positive and useful things we've done.

And it's had other benefits as well. Family wisdom time is an opportune time to help your children learn how to read. When ours were little, we put books in their hands. They loved to turn the pages and repeat the words after us. Sometimes they held the books upside down. Almost always, they were on the wrong page. But we worked with them and helped them so that eventually they were sounding out the words and doing the reading. At a time when 21 to 23 percent of the adults in this country are functionally illiterate—unable to even fill out a job application, read a food label, or read a simple story to a child[19]—such an investment has a significant impact on the future of a child. One of our married sons, whose elementary age children are currently reading from three to four grade levels ahead of their classes, attributes a good part of their advanced reading skills to a daily investment in family wisdom time.

As with other endeavors, the best time to start is when your children are young. If they grow up with it, it's just part of life. If you have older children, you'll probably want to start gradually. At dinner some night, you might just say, "I ran across this fun quote. Isn't this cool?" Then, another night, you could try reading another quote or a short story. Move into it gently. Eventually you can buy a few little wisdom literature books and leave them on the family room table or in the bathroom. Work up to the point where sharing and discussing great thoughts is a way of life.

OPTIMIZER 7: ESTABLISH CLEAR STEWARDSHIPS

Who pays the bills in your family? Who takes out the garbage? Who does the dishes, makes the financial decisions, prepares the meals, plans vacations, changes the diapers, washes the clothes, or goes to parent-teacher conferences? If you don't talk these things over and come up with clear, agreeable solutions, they can become a source of discontent, smoldering resentment, or even conflict in your home.

Between marriage partners, undiscussed responsibilities typically tend to fall into what we consider "traditional" roles. But what's the tradition? Things can get pretty tricky if you were raised in a family where Dad did the budgeting and your spouse grew up in a situation where Mom did. It becomes even more complex when both spouses are too busy working to really talk, and some of the "traditional" roles just don't cut it anymore. So you need to talk. You need to clarify expectations. You need to have a clear, shared understanding of who does what . . . and when.

Clear stewardships are equally important in working with children. Tasks provide the perfect opportunity for quality parenting. By empowering children to accomplish tasks, you can teach them to work and to love work. You can help them develop skills and qualities of character that will benefit them in whatever they do throughout their lives. You can build your relationship with them as you work side by side. You can reinforce their desire and ability to accomplish something meaningful. You can help them learn to contribute to the family and prepare them to better contribute to the world. All this—from the little family "chores" that all too often are the source of major frustration and disappointment!

So how do you do it?

Throughout our parenting years, we've tried a wide variety of approaches. We've had charts, allowances, and activity rewards. We've had incentives for getting work done and consequences for not getting it done. Probably one of the greatest lessons we've learned from it all is that children—particularly young children—are generally far more motivated when their parents work *with* them rather than expecting them to work alone. Here again we see the power of family work. As you labor side by side with a child, you have a nearly unparalleled opportunity to model, mentor, listen to, express love for, and relate to that child in meaningful ways.

We've also learned that kids appreciate variety. To reinforce their efforts in the same way, year after year for 18 years, would get boring. So try a little variety. Have fun. With young children, posters, stickers, stars, and treats seem to work well. With older children, allowances and privileges tied to performance seems to be a good approach. With teenagers, win-win agreements with built-in consequences provide for self-accountability and eliminate the need for parents to "snoopervise" or nag.

There are some excellent books on organizing home responsibilities and some great tools (charts, schedules, etc.) in the marketplace.[20] But whatever approach you decide to take, you might want to keep a few fundamental guidelines in mind:

- Invite children to participate in decisions concerning what their jobs will be. Involvement breeds commitment. They're much more likely to stick with a task if it was their idea to take it on.

- Remember that an assigned task is a child's responsibility. Never take away from the dignity of the stewardship by taking over and doing it yourself. Teach, train, help, love, encourage, and correct when necessary . . . but don't take over.

- Explain clearly what constitutes a job "well done." Don't assume the words "clean the living room" mean the same thing to your child as they do to you. Go over the desired results. Write them down, and even post necessary steps inside the closet door. Do it with your child a time or two. Make sure the understanding is there before you hold him or her accountable for the results.

- Never "snoopervise." Set up a time for accountability and take the time to go over the job together. Avoid the temptation to correct midstream. Give your child the freedom to succeed—or to fail (with consequences). Only then will the victory truly be the child's.

- When appropriate, celebrate work well done. Praise. Encourage. Have a party. Turn a cartwheel. Set off fireworks. Find joy together in your child's ability to do a job well.

- Instead of focusing on "accomplishing tasks through people," focus on "building people through empowering them to accomplish tasks." This is another example of how the way you *see* a situation has a huge impact on your experience and on the results.

OPTIMIZER 8: BRING HEROES HOME

A young boy saves his father's life by applying first aid techniques he learned in Boy Scouts. A soldier risks his life and military career to stand up for the rights of civilians against the senseless brutality of his own troops. A 75-year-old woman devotes more than 40 hours a week to running a local literacy center to help children and adults learn to read. Someone at your place of work goes the "extra mile" and organizes others to successfully pull off a seemingly impossible task.

Wonderful, often quiet acts of heroism happen daily. Do we celebrate them? Do we find joy in them? Do we even notice them?

Apart from setting a good example and creating opportunities for our children to participate in service, there's really no better way to teach character than by sharing and talking about the acts of real-life heroes. These can become a subject of conversation at any time, but some of the best times we've found are during family dinner—where food and conversation can nourish both body and soul—and during bedtime story time.

REBECCA

A fun variation of bringing heroes home is using your imagination to make your own children heroes. Many of the bedtime stories I've shared with our children over the years have been original adventures with them in the roles of heroes—policemen, firefighters, teachers, dragon slayers, and kind and generous princes and princesses who thwart evil witches and govern kingdoms with wisdom.

Though the stories sometimes got pretty corny when I was tired or lacking in creativity, I tried to repeatedly associate their names with heroic qualities of character in stories that captured their imagination. Some of our children have assured us that these stories had a positive influence on them as they were growing up and have carried on the tradition in their own homes.

In deciding on names for our children, we've tried to choose names associated with historical people of great character—heroes, if you will—both in and out of the family. Over the years, we've shared the stories of these people with our children to help them identify with character traits and values that are heroic in a very personal way. Also, we've tried to have pictures on the walls that exemplify people of character or the manifestation of valuable character traits.

The reality is, you will have heroes in your home—either those you invite or those who show up. Often, the ones who show up are not the ones you'd invite. They are the unsavory characters—often glamorized in the media—who slip into your home through movies, television, music, and posters. Are these really the kinds of heroes you want to enthrone? If you don't take some kind of action, they'll end up being the default heroes in your family members' lives.

Keep in mind that the heroes of today will create the character of tomorrow. So why not invite those heroes you'd like to have in your home? You create the character culture of your home by the heroes you invite in and what you share.

OUTSIDE THE NUCLEAR FAMILY

These eight optimizers clearly provide high leverage intervention for the nuclear family. But at the beginning of this chapter, we said we'd suggest ways you might apply them in other, nonnuclear situations. So if you're looking outside the immediate family—if, for example, you're single or a grandparent, or you don't have children of your own—consider the following application ideas:

CREATE A FAMILY MISSION STATEMENT

Create a personal mission statement, or generate or participate in creating an extended family mission statement. The objective is to create shared vision and values.

HAVE A WEEKLY "FAMILY TIME"

Initiate weekly or monthly extended family get-togethers, set up a family Web site, exchange letters, or schedule regular Internet chats with other members of the extended family. Or get involved in genealogy. Learn about your ancestors and the heritage you've received from them. The objective is to strengthen and reinforce the value of family.

DATE YOUR MATE

Date a prospective mate. Consider your dates in light of the kind of family relationship you someday want to have. The purpose is to learn to nourish a long-term relationship.

HAVE "SNEAK-INS" AND "SNEAK-OUTS"

Have "sneak-ins" and "sneak-outs" with nieces, nephews, and grand-children. The objective is to nurture individual relationships in the family.

> REBECCA
> *One tradition I've started that's really enjoyable for me is taking our grandchildren on sneak-outs for their birthdays. It's wonder-ful to have one-on-one time with them and get to know them bet-ter. Usually, our sneak-outs are shopping trips. I give them a cer-tain amount of money and let them choose whatever they want, as long as I know their parents would approve. But this year, I gave our oldest grandchild the option of seeing a play instead. We had a great time together watching* Peter Pan.

HOLD REGULAR PARENT CHATS

Though you may not have the same authority or responsibility as a parent, you can still let nieces, nephews, younger siblings, or oth-ers know you're there to be a support and help to them. Take occa-sions to be a good listener, to respect confidences, and to offer encouragement and help. The objective is to provide additional adult support.

HAVE A DAILY FAMILY WISDOM TIME

Enjoy your own daily wisdom time. Share inspiration with extended family members via phone, e-mail, "snail mail," or in person. Generate interesting conversation or give family members a lift by sharing wis-dom literature thoughts. The purpose is to celebrate and enjoy the nurturing value of wisdom.

ESTABLISH CLEAR STEWARDSHIPS

Help create some organizational structure in the extended family. Get the family thinking about who could be in charge of a family reunion, who could be responsible for the food or arrange for the accommodations. Help set up ongoing responsibilities, such as organizing family Internet chats, sending out monthly family newsletters, or keeping everyone up to date on home addresses, e-mail addresses and phone numbers. The objective is to encourage order, understanding and responsibility in family relationships.

BRING HEROES HOME

Inspire yourself and other family members by noticing and sharing acts of everyday heroism. Read and talk about past or modern-day heroes together. When you talk about family members, focus on the experiences that reflect how they exercised courage or compassion or went the extra mile. Help create heroes in the family. Call a cousin and volunteer to help out at the literacy center. Take your niece or nephew with you to visit residents of a local nursing home. The objective is to celebrate and reinforce positive character traits.

Once again, we remind you that no matter who you are, you're part of a family, and there are things you can do to build and enjoy the principle of family in your life.

BUILDING NAVIGATIONAL INTELLIGENCE

Again, there are two ways to approach these optimizers—to simply do them and get the results, or to do them with awareness and build your navigational intelligence in the process.

We encourage you to consciously build your navigational intelligence. As you work on an optimizer, look for and seek to embrace the principles behind the optimizer—principles such as:

- Contribution
- Creativity
- Stewardship
- Trust

- Responsibility

- Kindness

- Courage

- Sharing

- Respect

- Love

- Work

- Service

- Forgiveness

- Celebration

As you learn to recognize and value these underlying principles, you become empowered to discover other, more personalized ways to apply them in your situation.

Also, evaluate your experience and be open to inspiration for insight and further application. At the beginning of this chapter we went through an exercise in discovering the "little things" that could make a big difference in your family life. Think about those things you identified. It was your navigational intelligence that empowered you to zero in on the specific, personalized things that could make the greatest difference in your unique situation. It is that intelligence that can also help you know when and how to do these things most meaningfully day by day.

As you read through the pages where we examined expectations and suggested optimizers, it was your navigational intelligence that helped you discern which ideas could be particularly meaningful or helpful to you. It can also help you effectively implement, evaluate, and course-correct.

Navigational intelligence can help you move through any season, any day, any moment of your life with confidence that you're doing what matters most in your family—and in the most effective way. We encourage you to strengthen it. We also encourage you to be aware of the beauty and strength of each principle as you discover it, and to enjoy feeling it unfold in your character and in your life. Allow yourself to grow in confidence and trust in these timeless principles. Celebrate your victory every time you choose to live in harmony with them. This openness, this growing, this process of learning and living in harmony with universal principles, is one of life's most satisfying experiences. It is the process of becoming.

ONE STEP AT A TIME

As we suggested earlier, quality family life is a saga of becoming. It's constantly finding ways to love more, learn more, contribute more, nurture more, and interact with greater effectiveness and interdependence.

One of the best ways to do that is to *see* family leadership as an ongoing focus and to always seek to improve your family, as well as the legacy you give to your family of the future. In two-parent families, family leadership can become a great and joyful "co-mission" —the shared interest and focus that unites couples in purpose and brings the greatest happiness in shared fulfillment.

As you exercise leadership in your family, we encourage you to remember, as we've said before: quality family life is not an accident; it is an achievement. And growth is incremental. It usually comes one step at a time.

Remember also that our most important "success" is within the walls of our own homes.[20] In terms of changing the world and making it a better place, parenting is as good as it gets. Of course, it's important to be successful in other things as well. But there is nothing that will have a more lasting effect than the effort we put into building strong marriages and successfully raising the next generation.

Effective partnering and parenting are not easy. They are immense and complex challenges. They require the greatest talent, creativity, and commitment we can muster. They are at the high end of personal challenge as well as social contribution.

But the investment brings the greatest returns in terms of personal happiness. When we learn to see home as a foundation, a vital place where we can contribute most meaningfully, we open up a whole new dimension of life balance and joy.

CHAPTER

$$5$$

TIME MATTERS

Yesterday is history.
Tomorrow is a mystery.
Today is a gift—that's why it's called "the present."

Okay, this is where the rubber meets the road. This is where we face the ongoing challenge of translating what's most important into the decisions we make every day.

Some of these decisions are made in advance, as we organize and schedule the way we plan to spend our time. Other decisions are made in the heat of the moment, when unanticipated problems, opportunities, or enticements to be spontaneous (or even a little lazy) challenge the earlier decisions we made. The objective is to make all of these decisions in a way that contributes to life balance, satisfaction, and joy.

This is no small task. It hasn't been all that easy in recent decades. But today the challenge is dramatically exacerbated by the need to coordinate hundreds of details—including appointments, goals, contacts, information, financial data—in a world of rapidly changing technologies and tools that require time and effort to understand and often don't even communicate with each other.

These technologies open whole new worlds of potential effectiveness, but they also intensify the challenge of satisfying the needs of daily living and the difficulty of finding time to implement the optimizers that could make a huge difference in the quality of our lives.

Traditionally, these kinds of challenges have fallen into the area of "time management"—of figuring out how to spend the 24 hours a day we each have in the most efficient and effective way. Over the past 30 years, this has been an area of prime focus for the two of us. As we have studied, researched, lived, written and taught, we've come to realize it's not so much the "techniques" and "tricks" of *time management*, but the principles of *personal leadership* that truly empower people to identify and keep first things first in their lives. More than "doing things right," it's "doing the right things."

In line with this personal leadership approach, our objectives in this chapter are to help you:

1. Explore your expectations about time

2. Implement high leverage optimizers that will empower you to identify and do what's most important

3. Develop your navigational intelligence so you can make the best choices in the "decision moments" you face every day

HOW DO YOU SEE TIME?

REBECCA

When we were in South Africa a few years ago, some friends told us about one of the problems they were dealing with in their multicultural world. Some business owners (who were primarily of European descent) were concerned about the habits of some of their employees (who were primarily of tribal descent). If there was an event, such as a funeral in the village, many of the workers would show up late for work or not at all. The employers saw this behavior as evidence of laziness and were upset at the apparent lack of commitment of the workers.

The employees, on the other hand, had an entirely different perspective. Because of their tribal culture, they had a deeply ingrained value around funerals. Interestingly, a birth, to them, was not nearly as important. A person coming into the world had no accomplishments, no successes, no victories, no character strengths. But a person leaving the world was a different matter altogether. All the experiences, struggles, victories, and successes were now a part of that person and deserving of the greatest honor and recognition. Too, it was believed that those attending a funeral were endowed with a portion of the departed person's strength. To miss a funeral—to miss the honoring and the receiving— would be unthinkable. And it was assumed that everyone understood.

As we discussed the issue, our friends observed that the two groups of people were looking at time in different ways. The business owners were seeing time from a perspective of chronos, *a Greek word meaning chronological time. Chronos time is linear and sequential. No second is worth any more than any other second, and the clock essentially dictates the rhythm of life. If work started at 8:00 a.m., the business owners reasoned, their employees should be there at 7:59, ready to punch the clock.*

The employees, on the other hand, were seeing time from a kairos *("appropriate" or "quality" time) perspective. For them, time was something to be experienced. The essence of kairos time was in the value you get out of it rather than in the amount of chronos time you put into it. Thus, the funeral of a friend was supremely important, and they would come to work when the funeral was over. Then it would be "time" to go to work.*

In the Western world, the clock reigns supreme. We have clocks on our buildings, clocks on our street signs, clocks around our necks, clocks in our pockets, clocks on our wrists, and clocks in every room of our homes. In fact, because it is such a predominant feature, archaeologists digging up the remnants of our civilization would probably (and perhaps rightly) assume that we worshiped the clock.

As a result, most of us tend to *see* time as a limited resource. We hurry from task to task. We rush to get things done. A fly on the wall observing our society would probably conclude that one of our highest values is *busyness* . . . and he (or she) would be absolutely right! For most of us, busyness has become a status symbol. If we're busy, we must be important. If we're not busy, we're almost embarrassed to admit it. So we talk about being busy. We complain about being busy. We lament all we could do if we weren't so busy. But we keep being busy. We get caught up in the delusion that being busy, overworked, and at least somewhat out of balance is regrettable, but necessary, in order to validate our sense of self-worth.

We also tend to *see* time as the enemy. Whether in pulsing analog seconds or smoothly rolling digital minutes, we see time as relentlessly marching on, unerringly barreling its way through deadlines, appointments, crises, *to do's*, once-in-a-lifetime experiences, and serious decision moments with no regard for person or compassion for circumstance. We feel frustrated. We feel anxious. We'd like to stop time, slow it down, or rush it forward. But we feel helpless. There's nothing we can do to change it. Minute by minute, time marches on.

In a recent issue of *Scientific American* featuring time, the editors observed:

> *Time heals all wounds, but it is also the great destroyer. Time is relative, but also relentless. There is time for every purpose under heaven, but there is never enough. Time flies, crawls, and races. Seconds can be both split and stretched. Like the tide, time waits for no man, but in dramatic moments it also stands still. It is as personal as the pace of one's heartbeat but as public as the clock tower in the town square . . .*
>
> *[Time] is the partner of change, the antagonist of speed, the currency in which we pay attention. It is our most precious, irreplaceable commodity. Yet still we say we don't know where it goes, and we sleep away a third of it, and none of us really can account for how much we have left. We can find 100 ways to save time, but the amount remaining nonetheless diminishes steadily.*[1]

With such a variety of attitudes about time itself, no wonder we struggle to "manage" it—or, more appropriately, manage ourselves in it—with effectiveness and peace.

EXAMINING YOUR EXPECTATIONS ABOUT TIME

Whatever philosophical reasoning we engage in around the issue of time itself, the main issue here is that our perceptions of time help to create expectations that affect our ability to navigate in a balanced, productive, peaceful, and satisfying way. To be effective, we need to ensure that those expectations are both "real" and "realistic."

So at this point we're going to ask you to ask yourself some hard questions about your expectations and thinking patterns. We suggest you take time to think deeply about these questions. The more seriously you approach them and the more deeply you explore your expectations, the more helpful the material in this chapter will be.

1. HOW MUCH OF THE TIME DO I FEEL FRUSTRATED?

As we've noted before, frustration is a function of expectation. So if you spend a lot of time feeling frustrated, take a hard look at your expectations. Do you expect to be able to do more than you can reasonably do? Do you expect more results than are realistic for the effort you're putting in? Is your main frustration at work or at home—or in the conflict you feel in your ability to handle both? Is there a particular part of work or home life that is especially frustrating?

If you want to change the level of frustration, you obviously have two options: change your ability to do (so you can do faster or better), or change the expectation. Or, you could do some of both. Your navigational intelligence can help you to determine which approach is best.

2. DO I CONSTANTLY STRUGGLE WITH WHAT IS "REALISTIC"— WITH WHETHER I EXPECT TOO MUCH OR TOO LITTLE OF MYSELF?

Do you find yourself wondering if the way you see yourself and your situation is really "realistic"—or if it's a limiting view, keeping you from achieving what you could achieve?

To some extent, learning to set and achieve realistic goals is a lot like playing golf. You decide where you want the ball to go. Sometimes you hit it short and sometimes you hit it long. As you watch where your balls land, you learn to estimate how far you can hit the ball with a particular club. And as you practice, you learn which club to select and how to hit the ball the desired distance more and more often.

On the other hand, there are times when you feel inspired to set goals you've never dreamed of before—dreams to survive a POW camp in Vietnam like Admiral Stockdale, to climb Mount Everest like Erik Weihenmayer, or to do things you never imagined you could do.

So what do you do? How do you know when you have the reach that's right for you? How do you know what you can realistically expect of yourself?

Consult your navigational intelligence. Consider carefully: Where are your goals coming from? Are they minimal "get by's," escape daydreams, or inspiration from the best within you? Should you figure out how to increase them, let them go and move on, or focus your energy on developing realistic plans to achieve them? Answering these questions requires pondering, deep personal honesty, and experience. Bottom line, the question is: Am I using my time in the wisest possible way?

3. DO I ALWAYS THINK "LIFE WILL BE BETTER WHEN . . . "?

Do you find yourself living for the weekends or vacations when you can "crash"? Do you tend to think in terms of "when I graduate" or "when this job is over" or "when my children are grown"? You may want to think about what it is that keeps you from completely immersing yourself in and enjoying the present moment. What is it in your thinking that causes you to wish away the richness of experiencing life as it is?

In Thornton Wilder's play *Our Town,* the main character, Emily, is allowed to come back to earth after her death and observe the events of one day in her life. Choosing her 12th birthday, she returns to her past with the added ability not only to live it, but to see herself and others as she does. She is overwhelmed to see how people trudge through their daily routine, blind to the vision she now sees of the value of each moment of time. She laments, "It goes so fast. We don't have time to look at one another . . . Do any human beings ever realize life while they live it?"

You may want to consider what expectations you're living with that may be keeping you from working to create balance in your everyday life and from fully enjoying every moment of time.

4. Do Interruptions Irritate Me?

Are you living with the expectation that life should move smoothly along as you plan it, with no surprises, no interruptions? If so, you may want to ask yourself: Is there any justification for that expectation in the real world?

Think about it. How many times have you actually been able to chart a course or plan a day and simply carry it out—with no interruptions caused by unanticipated challenges or opportunities . . . or no unexpected consequences from ignoring them? Some jobs, such as customer service, emergency medicine, and parenting, primarily consist of responding to interruptions. An acquaintance of ours who was very busy was once handed this note by a friend:

> *When you are exasperated by interruptions, try to remember that their very frequency may indicate the valuableness of your life. Only the people who are full of help and strength are burdened by other people's needs. The interruptions which we chafe at are the credentials of our indispensability. The greatest condemnation that anybody could incur—and it is a danger to guard against—is to be so independent, so unhelpful, that nobody ever interrupts us and we are left comfortably alone.*

Consider carefully: Your attitude toward interruptions may be at the root of much of your frustration in life.

5. Does the Way I Feel About Myself Affect the Number of Things I Check Off My To Do List?

Checking off *to do's* has become a great source of satisfaction in our society. And it's certainly great to get things done. But is it your expectation that those checks that mark off all your *doing* are somehow your validation as a human *being*? What happens if suddenly you can't do what's on your list? What if an accident or age or some unexpected priority keeps you from doing? Or what if you do check everything off that list, but your spouse is upset, your kids are sullen, and your coworkers are offended because of the way you've done it?

Check your expectation. *Doing* may not be all there is—and maybe not even the most important thing there is—in validating your personal worth.

6. Does My Desire to Do a Lot of Things Reflect Lack of Confidence in My Ability to Do a Few Important Things Well?

Are you always trying to do more than is realistic? Are you using a machine-gun approach because you're not confident you can hit the target with a rifle?

Often, we mistake busyness for success. We get a sense of pseudosecurity from running around solving crises. We think if we're incredibly busy, we must be valuable. But that's not necessarily true. Most crisis-oriented running around comes from "urgency addiction" and a lack of clarity around "Job One."

Other such behavior comes from fear.

Perhaps we fear that what we're doing now may not be valued and we may be out of a job, so we get so many backup plans going, there's no way we can keep up with them all. Or maybe we're afraid because we have no margin; if what we're doing now doesn't work, we have no savings, no reserves to see us through until we're able to find something else. Of course, we need backup earning plans. But if we get too many things going and growing, they soon overtake family time, personal time, and life balance. In addition, the fragmentation will probably exacerbate the problem because we won't be able to give Job One the focus it needs for success.

Generally, it's better to focus on a few things and to do them well. Your navigational intelligence can help you decide what those few things should be.

7. DO I FEEL THAT IF I DO ALL I CAN THE BEST I CAN, IT STILL MAY NOT BE ENOUGH?

When you look in the mirror, do you somehow feel that, as hard as you try, your efforts will never be enough? Ask yourself: Enough for what? Enough to immediately change a teenager's behavior? Enough to change your own past? Enough to fix a struggling economy, stop the threat of terrorism, or avoid a war? No, your efforts may never be enough to do those things. And if you live with an unexamined expectation that they will, you're going to be disappointed.

But there are things your efforts are sufficient to accomplish— things within your circle of influence, such as working to become the kind of person you want to be. What are your expectations regarding those things? Do you believe that if you focus your effort on what you can affect, you can have a sense of well-being and joy in the journey?

If you struggle with feelings of inadequacy, you may want to spend some time reflecting on the past. Is there a chance those feelings may stem from parents or others who never approved of or valued you? Perhaps it's time to examine those feelings, to let go of them and move on. Through thoughtful evaluation and effort, change is possible. As you come to clarity and personal responsibility concerning your own potential and worth, you'll be better able to invest time in doing the aligned, high leverage things that will help you fulfill it.

8. DO I HONESTLY BELIEVE IT'S POSSIBLE TO HAVE A SATISFYING WORK/FAMILY BALANCE IN MY LIFE?

Are you so worn-out by "pipe dream" promises or burned out by experience that you don't truly believe it's possible to balance work and family in your life? Or do you believe that somebody else could do it . . . but not you?

Remember Admiral Stockdale and Eric Weihenmayer. If they had given up on what must have seemed at times to be an impossible hope, there would have been no success stories to tell. Also remember that the kind of balancing we're talking about is not an impossible dream; it is a "real" expectation. It's not a "mechanical" balance; it's not running the bases fast enough to touch them all. It's a living dynamic equilibrium. And learning how to create it is a process of doing and becoming. You have to work for it; but it's something you can trust in, believe in. And with good navigational intelligence, you can grow in your ability to create it each day.

Hopefully, these questions have helped you to gain insight into your expectations and some realities around the issue of time. In addition, we suggest you ask yourself two more questions and, again, that you think seriously about your answers:

- If there were a fly on the wall watching how I spend my time today, and his only criteria for judgment is my behavior—he doesn't know my intentions; he can't hear the words I say—what would he say matters most in my life?

- If everything my children know about time management is learned from me, what kind of adults are they going to be?

Your ability to manage your time well is absolutely critical—to your own personal happiness and well-being, to the quality of your contribution at home and on the job, and to those who watch you and learn from you. With that in mind, we'd like to share a basic paradigm, a way of *seeing* that will significantly impact the way you deal with time matters.

███

QUADRANT II

Over the years, we've found that one of the most significant challenges to focusing on what matters most—and to implementing some of the high leverage optimizers we've talked about—is the inability to discern between what is *urgent* (or apparently urgent) and what is truly *important*. For many, reacting to the urgent has become a way of life. It's easy to get caught up in "urgency addiction," getting our "highs" from handling crises. Unconsciously, without knowing it, we frequently make choices that keep us in a self-perpetuating crisis mode.

Aside from the impact of this kind of reactive lifestyle on health, personal productivity, and family relationships, the bottom line is that we waste a lot of time and energy on things that are pressing and proximate instead of working on what really matters most. In addition, we fail to integrate into our lives those things that have the highest quality of life-improving potential. But this all changes dramatically when we're able to *see* life in terms of *importance*.

In previous works, we've shared how the power of this paradigm of importance can be captured in what we've come to call the "Time Management Matrix." This matrix illustrates how we spend time in one of four different ways as defined by *urgency* and *importance*. In this version, we've listed some of the activities at work and at home that would fall into each of the four quadrants.

As we study this matrix, it becomes evident that the real "mother lode" in terms of effectiveness is in Quadrant II. The key is to learn to see life in terms of importance rather than urgency—to act based on principles and values rather than reacting to everything that's coming at us with an "urgency" tag attached.

Many people find this matrix enormously helpful for at least four reasons:

1. It's wonderfully descriptive. Many people say, "That's exactly what happens to me! I get so caught up trying to solve crises and meet other people's priorities (Quadrants I and III), I feel like I have to escape. So I stay up late watching some dumb show on TV or reading some mindless romance novel (Quadrant IV). Obviously, I need to handle the things in my life that are both urgent and important (Quadrant I), but I also see the enormous benefits that could come from investing time in important things like planning, preparing, recreating, and building relationships (Quadrant II) . . . even though they may not seem urgent at the time."

2. It highlights the importance of proactivity. Clearly, the most aligned, high leverage optimizers in all areas of life are in Quadrant II. They are important; but they aren't urgent. They don't act on us.

THE TIME MANAGEMENT MATRIX

	Urgent		Not Urgent	
	Quadrant I		Quadrant II	
	Work	**Home**	**Work**	**Home**
Important	Handling an irate client. Meeting a deadline. Solving a production line breakdown. Handling a cash flow crisis. Responding to a window of opportunity.	Taking an injured child to the emergency room. Resolving a "credit card declined" problem. Picking up a child from school. Helping a late-for-work spouse find lost car keys. Taking advantage of a teaching moment.	Doing long-range planning. Creating preventive maintenance systems. Developing professional skills. Building networks. Anticipating client needs.	Truly recreating. Nurturing relationships. Creating a family mission statement. Having a regular family time. Going on sneak-outs. Improving family health.
	Quadrant III		Quadrant IV	
	Work	**Home**	**Work**	**Home**
Not Important	Handling junk e-mail (spam). Writing unnecessary reports. Responding to some drop-in visitors, phone calls, and voice mail. Attending unnecessary meetings. Organizational politicking.	Being on time for unimportant television shows. Doing some errands. Responding to some tele-marketing and junk mail. Rushing between scheduled, but not highly meaningful, activities and events.	Gossip at the water fountain. Unnecessary Internet surfing. Doing non-aligned hobby-horse activities.	Watching mindless TV. Playing excessive and addictive computer games or reading addictive light novels. Mindlessly surfing the Web. Nervous eating.

As a result, we have to be highly proactive to choose to do them. Of course, we don't have to do Quadrant II things. We don't have to take our spouse on a date or read wisdom literature or go on a sneak-out with a child. We could wait until things move into Quadrant I—maybe our marriage is on the rocks, we're in a severe state of confusion and depression, or we have a son or daughter on drugs—and then handle the crisis. But we could also be proactive and choose to invest in Quadrant II planning, preparation, and prevention instead. There's no absolute guarantee that everything will work out just the way we want it to. But chances are a lot higher when we work to strengthen relationships and prevent crises rather than trying to salvage and repair what's left.

3. It highlights the importance of investment and continuous improvement. It helps us understand the importance of working *on* the system as well as *in* it. It shows the value of *investing* time regularly in Quadrant II—where it will bring huge returns—instead of merely *spending* or *wasting* time in Quadrants III and IV. As we've said, quality family life is an achievement. It takes work. And much of the vital family work is done by investing in "important" but "not urgent" Quadrant II. The same is true of excellence on the job. You may become really good at managing by crisis and putting out fires. But investing in fire prevention will open the door to a whole new level of professional effectiveness.

4. It reveals where we can get the time to invest in Quadrant II. Obviously, we can't neglect Quadrant I. It's both urgent *and* important. But we can move out of Quadrants III and IV. Quadrant III is the biggest time waster at the office. Remember the research we cited in "Work Matters" revealing how much time at work is not focused on achieving the highest priorities. Quadrant IV is the biggest time waster at home. It's an enormous temptation to just "crash" in front of the television instead of doing something worthwhile or truly rejuvenating. By becoming aware of time wasted in these quadrants, we can consciously choose to shift our "spending" habits and invest that time in Quadrant II, where it will bring greater returns. The key is to always live "above the line" that separates Quadrant I and II from Quadrant III and IV.

For these and other reasons, this Time Management Matrix is a valuable tool in helping people effectively handle time matters. (A complimentary Matrix evaluation tool is available at the Web site www.franklincovey.com/lifematters.)

▬▬

OPTIMIZERS

Understanding the "importance" of the *importance* paradigm, let's take a moment now to look at six aligned, high leverage optimizers that help us focus on importance. A few that we've shared in previous works continue to prove extremely valuable. We will share those here in an abbreviated way that specifically deals with work/home balance issues, and we'll provide additional references for those who want to go deeper. Others deal with the more recently developing challenges and opportunities, such as those created by technology. We will address these in greater detail.

While we recognize that there are other important optimizers that impact on our time—such as maintaining good health—the ones we're focusing on here are more process specific. They will help you integrate important goals, such as improving your health, into your life.

OPTIMIZER 1: PLAN WEEKLY

Weekly planning is a process that grows out of the Quadrant II paradigm. It enables you to create a framework of importance to keep in front of you as you execute and make decisions each day.

Basically, it involves choosing a quiet time at the beginning of the week when you can have a few minutes alone, during which you:

1. Connect with what's most important. Review your personal mission statement if you have one. If you don't, just take a few minutes to focus in on the core governing values in your life.

2. Write down your roles. These would be your roles as an individual, spouse, parent, manager, PTA president, etc.

3. Set goals. Engage your navigational intelligence. As you look at each role, ask yourself, "What are the one or two *important* things I could do in this role this week?" (You'll probably discover that many will be Quadrant II goals.)

Roles
Individual
Family
Household
Work: Administration
Work: Team building
Work: Customers
Community: Literacy Center

Roles and Goals
Individual • *Read* • *Exercise (5X/wk)*
Family • *Work on mission statement* • *Date—concert* • *Sneak out with Jane*
Household • *Clean out garage* • *Pay bills*
Work: Administration • *Long-range planning* • *Sales commission report*
Work: Team building • *Goal alignment meeting* • *One-on-one w/Ruth*
Work: Customers • *Potential client study* • *On-site visit—X Corp*
Community: Literacy Center • *Train new tutors*

4. Calendar your goals. Transfer your navigational insights into your calendar *first*—either as an appointment or as a particular day's *to do*. Then fill in other activities as you can.

Time	Sunday	Monday	Tuesday	Wednesday	Thursday	Friday	Saturday
6:00		Exercise	Exercise	Exercise	Exercise	Exercise	
7:00							
8:00							Clean out garage
9:00		One-on-one with Ruth			Long-range planning		
10:00		Sales Commission	Potential client				
11:00		report	analysis				
12:00							
1:00					On-site visit with X Corp		Sneak out with Jane
2:00	Work on family			Goal alignment			
3:00	mission statement			meeting			
4:00							
5:00							
6:00						Date Concert	
7:00			Train tutors		Pay bills		
8:00							
9:00			Read		Read		Read
10:00							

This organizing process goes a long way toward helping you create life balance. It reminds you of what's important overall. It reminds you of your various roles in life. It increases options for synergy and balance by helping you consider the entire week before you focus on a single day. It engages your navigational intelligence in determining goals that are most aligned and leveraged, and it helps you put those things into your week *first*.

It also keeps you focused on importance. By calendaring key activities first—your Job One priorities, professional development time, a weekly family night, a daily dinnertime, a date with your spouse, or a special one-on-one—you create a framework of importance against which you can measure the value of any unexpected opportunity or challenge that may come up.

Finally, it provides an ongoing process for effectively incorporating all other optimizers and Quadrant II activities. Each week, you can use your navigational intelligence to determine which goals provide the highest leverage for you. Over time, this will enable you to implement many of the things we've talked about in this book as well as other high leverage ideas you may come across.

OPTIMIZER 2: USE TIME ZONES

One way to further enhance the effectiveness of your weekly organizing is to use "time zones"—large, interchangeable blocks of time designated for specific kinds of important activities.

During work time, for example, you might create time zones for handling mission-critical e-mail, prospecting for new clients or devel-

Time	Sunday	Monday	Tuesday	Wednesday	Thursday	Friday	Saturday
6:00		PERSONAL					
7:00							
8:00	PLANNING & PREP.	RESPONSE TIME (IMPORTANT E-MAILS AND CALLS)					HOME PROJECTS
9:00		STAFF TIME	NEW BUSINESS FOCUS		PLANNING AND		
10:00					PREPARATION		
11:00							
12:00							
1:00	FAMILY TIME			TEAM MEETINGS			
2:00							
3:00							
4:00							
5:00							
6:00		FAMILY TIME				SPOUSE DATE NIGHT	
7:00				COMMUNITY SERVICE	HOME MANAGEMENT		
8:00							
9:00							
10:00							

oping professional skills. At home you might schedule time zones for having a weekly family time, going on a date with your spouse, or doing home projects.

The objective in creating time zones is not to fill the week, but to create a few blocks of time specifically reserved for certain types of high leverage activities and goals. This enables you to channel activities for maximum effectiveness. It's like building corrals into which horses of different breeds are then placed. When you set up a repeating time zone—like blocking out one specific night a week for family time—the activities within that time zone may vary from week to week, but the nature of the activities would not. In other words, no horse—unless it's a "family" horse—gets through the gate.

Time	Sunday	Monday	Tuesday	Wednesday	Thursday	Friday	Saturday
6:00		PERSONAL Exercise					
7:00							
8:00		PLANNING & PREP.	RESPONSE TIME (IMPORTANT E-MAILS AND CALLS)				HOME PROJECTS
9:00		STAFF TIME	NEW BUSINESS		PLANNING AND		Clean out garage
10:00		One-on-one with Ruth	FOCUS Potential		PREPARA- TION		
11:00		Sales Com- mission rep	client analysis		L-range planning		
12:00							
1:00	FAMILY TIME			TEAM MEETINGS	On-site visit with X Corp		Sneak out with Jane
2:00				Goal alignment			
3:00	Work on family			meeting			
4:00	mission statement						
5:00							
6:00		FAMILY TIME				SPOUSE DATE	
7:00				COMMU- NITY	HOME MANAGE-	NIGHT Concert	
8:00				SERVICE Train	MENT Pay bills		
9:00			Read	tutors	Read		Read
10:00							

Many effective time managers use time zones, whether they call them by that name or something else. Time zones are valuable optimizers for at least four reasons:

First, they enable you to schedule meaningful chunks of time for those aligned, high leverage (often Quadrant II) activities and goals.

Second, they allow you to group similar activities and goals, facilitating greater organization and focus, so you don't get diverted by switching from one thing to another all the time.

Third, they facilitate more effective interdependence. When someone calls for an appointment or wants to consult on a particular project, for example, you can generally channel it into the time zone you've set aside for those things. When work teams agree on time zones, it becomes easier to schedule meetings and protect independent focus time. Family time zones make it easier for family members to plan quality time together without running into scheduling problems, and to say no to other, less important things.

Fourth, time zones are flexible. If something genuinely more important comes up, you can shift a time zone to another time. Be careful, though, when you need to shift time zones that involve others. When family members are counting on a family priority time, for example, it can be a real downer if you don't create awareness of and agreement on the priority need for the change.

OPTIMIZER 3: T-PLAN DAILY

As you begin each day (or on the night before), take a few minutes to plan your day. The most effective way we've found to do this is to use a "T-Planning" structure that allows you to put time sensitive activities and commitments on one side and those that can be done at any time during the day on the other. Many of the current electronic and paper planning systems are set up this way.

After you review or list your *to do's*, prioritize them in terms of importance. One effective way to do this is to first group your *to do's* in terms of general importance—*A* being high, *B* medium, and *C* low, for instance. Then number the items in each group in the order in which you plan to do them.

But watch out! Even with Quadrant II organizing, many people still tend to prioritize *to do's* in terms of what's urgent out of habit.

Tasks		Appointments	
Call Phil about receipt problem	6:00	Exercise	
Complete January report	7:00		
Check on Smith delivery	8:00		
Schedule luncheon with Chris	9:00	One-on-one with Ruth	
Review expense report	10:00	Sales Commission Reports	
Prepare for Wed. team meeting	11:00	↓	
Order materials for Rite project	12:00		
Set up X Corp visit	1:00		
Get concert tickets	2:00		
Pick up shelving for garage	3:00		
	4:00		
	5:00		
	6:00	Family Time	
	7:00	↓	
	8:00	↓	
	9:00		
	10:00		

Tasks			Appointments	
Call Phil about receipt problem	A-2	✓	6:00	Exercise
Complete January report	B-2		7:00	
Check on Smith delivery	A-4		8:00	
Schedule luncheon with Chris	C-1		9:00	One-on-one with Ruth
Review expense report	B-3		10:00	Sales Commission Reports
Prepare for Wed. team meeting	A-3	✓	11:00	↓
Order materials for Rite project	A-5		12:00	
Set up X Corp visit	A-1	✓	1:00	
Order concert tickets	A-6		2:00	
Pick up shelving for garage	B-1		3:00	
			4:00	
			5:00	
			6:00	Family Time
			7:00	↓
			8:00	↓
			9:00	
			10:00	

Take a minute and think about the last time you prioritized a list. Did you put the things that really mattered most at the top, or the things that were most proximate and pressing? Is the way you prioritized your list a pattern in your life? What's happening as a result?

Also, when you prioritize, be sure to consider items on both sides of the "T." Just because something is scheduled at a specific time doesn't necessarily mean it will have priority when that time arrives. You may be involved in something that is genuinely of a higher priority and need to adjust.

As you navigate through the day, this T structure allows you to meet the top priorities on your schedule and to integrate "anytime" priorities most appropriately into the flow of the day.

OPTIMIZER 4: TRACK YOUR TIME

ROGER

When I first began working in the field of time management, I found that one of the best ways to help people manage their time better was to help them see where they were actually spending it. Like others in my field, I recommended that people keep a "time log" and track their time to get a realistic picture.

The results never failed to surprise the time trackers. People were consistently shocked to discover that what was actually happening in their lives often bore little resemblance to what was on their schedules or in their minds. But after they got over the initial surprise, they were amazed at the insights the log provided for improved efficiency and effectiveness.

In more recent years doing a time log has fallen out of vogue—probably because it takes additional time and follow-through. But the reality is that people who are truly good with their time know where their time goes—just like people who are good with their money know where their money goes. And the most effective way to find out where your time goes is to track it.

Time tracking is a high leverage Quadrant II activity. It empowers you to better align and leverage your time and to tighten up and eliminate inefficiency and waste. It alerts you to potential Quadrants III and IV "black holes," including:

- E-mail

- Meetings

- Shopping

- Web surfing

- Addictive and nonrejuvenating diversions

- Inefficient technology

- Technology shopping

- Computer games

- Snacking

- Television

Like keeping track of what you eat when you're trying to lose weight, time tracking shatters whatever illusions you may be living with that muddy the lines between intent, perception, and performance.

One way to discover for yourself the value of time tracking is to keep a time log for two different weeks. Before you start, answer the following questions:

- What are the most important things I should be spending time on (specific relationships, projects, tasks, etc.)?

- What percentage of my time do I think I'm spending on each of these priorities?

Then track your time. As you review the record, ask yourself:

- How much time am I actually spending on these priorities?

- Where is my time going instead?

- How can I create better alignment?

One effective way to track your time is to note the actual time elapsed for each appointment or task on your planning page.

Roles/Key Activities	Estimated hrs/week	Actual hrs/week	Difference
Individual	4	5	+1
Family	20	12	-8
Household	25	32	+7
Administration	12	7	-5
Team Building	10	13	+3
Customers	15	12	-3
Community Service	4	4	0
E-mail/Calls	5	7	+2
Interruptions (work)	6	10	+4
Eating	7	11	+4
Sleeping	49	40	-9
Recreation	6	15	+9
Unaccounted for	5	0	-5
TOTAL	168	168	0

Tasks			Appointments		
Call Phil about receipt problem	A-2	✓	6:00	Exercise	(45 min)
Complete January report	B-2		7:00	Breakfast, shower, etc.	(1 hour)
Check on Smith delivery	A-4	✓	8:00	E-mail, calls	(1 hr +)
Schedule luncheon with Chris	C-1		9:00	One-on-one with Ruth	(1 hour)
Review expense report	B-3		10:00	E-mail, calls cont'd	(45 min)
Prepare for Wed. team meeting	A-3	✓	11:00	Sales Commission Reports	(1 hr+)
Order materials for XYZ project	A-5	✓	12:00	Lunch	(30 min)
Set up X Corp visit	A-1	✓	1:00	A-1/A-2/A-3	(5 min/10 min/45 min)
Order concert tickets	A-6	✓	2:00	Sales Commission Reports cont'd	(1 hr)
Pick up shelving for garage	B-1	✓	3:00	Jones crisis (unplanned)	(45 min)
			4:00	A-4/A-5	(15/45 min)
			5:00	B-1	(45 min)
			6:00	Family Time	(2 hours)
			7:00	↓	
			8:00	Television (unplanned)	(1 hour)
			9:00	A-6	(10 min)
			10:00		

Lawyers, accountants, consultants, and others who bill by the hour become good at time tracking, though many fail to use the information for effective feedback and evaluation. Time tracking can be a powerful feedback tool. There's no way to get a more realistic view of how you're actually spending your time.

OPTIMIZER 5: BUILD RELATIONSHIPS OF TRUST

REBECCA

After working through the drafts of The 7 Habits of Highly Effective People, *there was much editing to do as the manuscript went back and forth between Stephen and the publisher. One of my tasks was to work through the editor's recommendations and then review proposed changes with Stephen.*

As I worked with Stephen, I realized that he was careful and attentive to every detail. I could sense that it was extremely important to him to be aware of and approve any change.

At one point I said, "Stephen, I will not change a comma in this manuscript without your being aware." Suddenly, he seemed to relax. What was important to him was recognized and attended to. In that moment, it seemed a bridge of trust was created that moved our relationship to a new level.

That was a very precious moment to me. I felt the different level of trust, and it was a good feeling. I am convinced it greatly increased our effectiveness on that project, and opened the way to far greater synergy and productivity on future projects as well.

When we hear the phrase "time management," most of us think about how we can *independently* plan and accomplish a project or task. The reality, however, is that life is highly *interdependent.* Our ability to accomplish what's most important is very much tied into the quality of our relationships with the key people in our lives.

This is true of the bigger picture—our ability to work on major projects and make important contributions—as well as on the "front lines" of day-by-day living, where conflicting time demands create some of our most painful life balance decision moments.

Suppose, for example, that you have an appointment scheduled with a key client at four o'clock tomorrow afternoon. Your daughter's soccer team just qualified for the playoffs. The first game? Four o'clock tomorrow afternoon. What do you do?

Let's say you decide to talk with your client to resolve the problem. And let's assume that your mode of operation with this client is one of continual "overpromise and underdeliver." Your credibility is low. What's going to happen when you say, "I have a problem. Is there any way we could work something out?" Likely, you'll encounter inflexibility: "Not on your life!" or "Sure, go ahead. I've just been waiting to go to another supplier anyway!"

On the other hand, if your mode of operation has been to *realistically* promise and *over*deliver—always exceeding expectations, anticipating needs, solving problems even before they become apparent—the response you get will likely be totally different. Your client knows that you have his interest at heart, and so will probably be willing to try to reschedule, solve the issue over the phone, or come up with a viable third alternative to meet the need.

The same scenario will likely be played out if you try to negotiate with your daughter instead. If you never attend her soccer matches—even those you promise to attend—she rarely sees you, and you're always on her case about something, when you tell her you can't come to her game because of your meeting, her response might well be: "Right! Who'd expect you to come anyway?" Any effort you make to explain the situation will only make it worse.

On the other hand, if your daughter knows you're her biggest fan . . . if, even when you can't attend, you always make it a point to ask, "How was the game?" . . . if you know what's going on in her life . . . if you listen to her and spend time with her and she knows that she's one of the most important people in your life . . . then you'll likely get a different response: "I understand. You have to work sometimes. It's okay."

The point is, to a great extent our ability to resolve conflicting time demands effectively is dependent on the quality of our relationships with the people involved. When the relationship is good, there's a trust and willingness to work things out. In fact, the very process of working them out can actually build the relationship. But when the relationship isn't good, conflicts create additional problems. People feel their expectations are in danger of being violated, and even efforts to solve the problem can actually make the situation worse.

So how do we build relationships of trust?

Basically: value the person. Value the relationship. Treat others the way you want to be treated yourself. Keep the promises you make. Do the things we've talked about at work and at home that build relationships of trust. Recognize and respect the fact that other people have their own expectations, their own needs, their own problems and schedules. Interact with them in win-win ways that not only solve the immediate problem but build interdependent problem-solving capacity for the future.

There are many books that contain excellent relationship-building ideas. We encourage you to just make sure that what you read and do is based on solid principles of effectiveness and character and not on manipulative, personality-based "tricks" or "techniques" designed to help people essentially use others to get their own way. Unfortunately, many approaches masquerading as "time management" are simply ways to get other people and their needs and issues out of the way so we can do what we want to do. But rich relationships and the ability to interact and work effectively with others are vital parts of life balance, and any practical approach to life balance must recognize and deal with this essential interdependent dimension.

Genuine trust can only be created when your own heart is right—when you're sincerely trying to build the kind of relationship that will benefit everyone involved, and to facilitate maximum long-term cooperation and contribution. In the end, the greatest benefit may not be in what you get done, but in the relationship you build in the doing.

OPTIMIZER 6: UTILIZE TECHNOLOGY IN YOUR PERSONAL LEADERSHIP SYSTEMS

Now we come to what is potentially one of the most facilitating or debilitating time management issues of our day—technology.

From technophobia to technomania, there's an enormous range in attitudes, awareness, expectations, comfort levels, and competence with all things that beep, click, and manipulate at high speed. But whatever our personal response may be, the reality is that we live in an increasingly technological world. There's no way we're going to abandon cell phones for land lines or computers for typewriters. The ability to navigate in the midst of technological change has become essential.

So how do we do it? How do we spend appropriate time investigating, evaluating, and learning how to use new tools without getting sucked into a black hole that consumes our time and money? How do we tell when some new or different technology will increase our effectiveness ... or when it's simply a "red herring" that will divert our time and resources and derail our efforts to do what matters most?

It is not our intent in this chapter to evaluate every new personal effectiveness technology on the market today. The options are far too numerous. And your needs are unique to you. Even the specific industry you're in may well have its own approach. In addition, whatever may be out there now, you can be guaranteed there will be new options tomorrow.

Instead, our objective, is to equip you to:

1. Wisely select the tools and systems that will help you do what's most important most effectively.

2. Learn to quickly recognize and take advantage of "better" when you see it.

In order to do these things, you'll need to understand systems, tools and options. Empowered with understanding in these areas, most people find it much easier to navigate with confidence through the world of technological change.

Understanding Systems

A "system" is a group of interdependent elements that form a unified whole and interact synergistically to serve a common purpose. There are all kinds of systems, both natural and manmade: ecological, weather, solar, respiratory, digestive, irrigation, political, and school systems, among others. As we suggested earlier, "balance" itself is a system—a highly integrated dynamic equilibrium.

Recognizing the interrelatedness of elements in systems, people have begun to approach solutions in a way that acknowledges that interdependence. *Systems analysis* in business, holistic health care, and environmental ecology are a few examples. To ignore this inter-relatedness and focus on only one element in a system is usually ineffective—often even counterproductive.

With all the demands and complexities of time management and personal leadership, it's time to bring this powerful systems approach to the personal level. We need to explore the systems in our lives that either facilitate or debilitate our efforts to create life balance—our *planning* system, our *information* system, our *communication* system, and our *finance* system. And we need to look at the larger system—our *personal leadership system*—of which each of these smaller systems is an integral and interdependent part.

Your Personal Systems

To one degree or another, you already have personal leadership systems in place.

Planning system. Your planning system deals with how you translate your mission and goals into the way you spend your time. You may use a high-tech electronic planner or online group calendar. You may use a paper planner. You may use sticky notes and a Mo's Mart calendar on the fridge. Or you may simply keep it all in your head. But in some way and to some degree, you plan and schedule your time. With the addition of space for things such as phone numbers, family and client information, expense sheets, and a daily log, your planning system may also be a major component of communication, information, and financial flow.

Information system. Your information system deals with the things you keep track of. You may keep detailed written records, tape recordings, or a secretary's minutes. You may keep birthdays, anniversaries, phone numbers, and clothing sizes in an organizer or on a computer. You may keep newspaper clippings and information on household services in a file drawer. You may rely on your memory and live with the consequences. But in some way and to some degree, you have some kind of system to keep track of information.

Communication system. Your communication system deals with how you communicate with others and how they communicate with you. It may include written letters and memos. It may include e-mails and faxes. It may include land lines, cell phones, and answering machines. Or it may be tom-tom drums across the valley or yelling out the back door. But you have some system of communicating with other people.

Finance system. Your finance system is part planning system and part information system. It deals with how you keep track of your financial strategy and goals, your actual investment and spending, and alignment between the plan and the actual. You may keep your strategy and goals in your planner, on your computer, or as an electronic bank balance that simply shows if you're overdrawn or you have money left in the account. You may keep financial records on a PDA (personal digital assistant), in a checkbook, or in a shoe box, or you may have a bookkeeper do it for you. You may compare planned to actual spending through a budget review, the amount of cash you have in your wallet at the end of the month, or an unexpected overdrawn notice from the bank. But to some degree or another, you have a system that keeps you somewhat aware of the money you spend and what you owe.

Personal leadership system. As we've observed, your personal leadership system is comprised of the four smaller systems. The degree to which these systems interrelate in helpful ways is the degree to which your personal leadership functions effectively. You may have a cell phone that has a built-in contact file but doesn't allow you to transfer contacts from the program on your desktop computer. As a result, you have to enter 200 contacts by hand. You may use a laptop computer, but have frustration trying to sync information to your desktops at the office and at home. How the parts of the larger system work together is at least as important—if not more important—than the way the parts themselves work. The more fully you align and integrate your smaller systems, the more effective your personal leadership system will be.

As we've said, you already have these systems in place. You may have inherited elements of your systems from the family you grew up in, bosses or work associates, friends who found something that worked for them, response to advertising, or, in some cases, wise, conscious choice. Even abdication itself is a system, with accompanying consequences and effects.

The question is: Are your systems working effectively for you?

No matter how many "bells and whistles" the tools in your systems may have, no matter whomever else they may have worked for, no matter what they're advertised to do, the fact remains that your tools are part of a system. *And if your systems don't work for you, they're not effective.*

To paraphrase colleague and systems expert Dave Hanna, "Every system is perfectly aligned to achieve the results it creates."[2] So if you aren't satisfied with the results, back up and look at the system. Effectively working *on* the system as well as *in* or *with* the system is a high leverage Quadrant II investment of time.

Evaluating Tools

In this day and age it's easy to get carried away with the glitzy features of some new tool. But to be effective, we have to learn to look at the tool in the context of the specific system it will be part of, and also to see it in the context of the larger, overall personal leadership system. If a particular tool doesn't do what we need it to do or if it won't interact with other tools in the system, then any way you cut it, it's not going to be an optimally effective investment of time or money.

To decide if a tool is right for you, we suggest that you consider it in light of four factors:

1. General evaluation criteria

2. Distinguishing characteristics

3. Your specific needs

4. Cost/benefit analysis

General evaluation criteria. When you consider a new tool, you may find it helpful to ask yourself four general evaluation questions:

- *Is it effective?* Does it help you do what's most important?

- *It is efficient?* Does it do it in the best possible way?

- *Is it simple?* Is it streamlined, easy to work with, free of complicating "bells and whistles"?

- *Is it synchronous?* Does it work in cooperation with your other tools and systems?

Answering these questions can help you evaluate the tools you're currently using as well as ones you may be considering.

Distinguishing characteristics. There are different ways to categorize devices based on this criteria, and some of them overlap. For example, a PC (personal computer) could identify anything from a desktop computer to a handheld PDA (personal digital assistant). But the distinguishing characteristic that may make a difference to you is the fact that it's handheld or portable. So "handheld" devices may be a category of tools you want to explore. "PC" would also include devices that provide both keyboard and pen entry. But if the characteristic that's important to you is the fact that you can write on it, you may want to explore "pen entry" products, including things such as paper planners that aren't even included in "PC."

Our point is that there are a number of different ways to categorize. Our objective is not to attempt to redefine industry terminology, but to provide a simple way—from a user's point of view—to look at the unique characteristics of a product that might make a difference in your situation.

For the purposes of this chapter, we've identified six categories of tools—paper-based, PC-based, handheld, wireless, Web-based, and pen-based. The distinguishing characteristics of these categories can provide an effective primary filter for decision making. For example, if you're trying to operate in a system that requires fast electronic communication and turnaround, you can quickly determine that a paper-based tool would not be the best choice. On the other hand, if portability is the primary need, it might be ideal. At least it would make it through the primary filtering process for consideration.

As you consider each group of tools, consider the advantages and disadvantages of each. Think about how the distinguishing characteristic might affect your choice with regard to your current circumstances . . . and also with regard to other circumstances, should your work or home situation change.

Paper-based tools include sticky notes, notepads, notebooks, three-by-five file cards, desk or wall calendars, paper-based organizers, or forms printed off a computer. Paper-based tools are generally easy to use, carry, and file.

PC-based tools include anything from a desktop computer to a laptop computer to the new Tablet PC's with digital ink capability. They have a huge capacity to process and store. The function they perform—such as calendaring, word processing, organizing, tracking financial goals and expenses—depends on the software program they're running.

Handheld tools are basically minicomputers. There are various handheld devices; examples include Palm Pilots and Pocket PC's. These tools are highly portable and will run some programs, but they do not offer the full range and complexity of a regular computer.

Wireless devices can communicate with other devices, people, or the Internet without the use of wires. Cell phones, for example, are inherently wireless. They, too, are highly portable. They make it possible to communicate with other people, and have sufficient computing capacity to achieve Internet access and information retrieval. Other devices, such as laptops, can be turned into wireless devices with the addition of a wireless card.

Web-based tools allow you to perform tasks such as planning and financial management online. Because the information resides on the server of the supplier, you can access it from any device that can be connected to the Web.

Pen-based devices—using a pen or stylus for entry—have been around for some time, but with the exception of handheld devices, they have met with limited success. However, recent advances in technology appear to be making a major shift in the pen-based category. Many believe this will open the world of personal computing to those who have felt limited by keyboards, and will encourage computer use in situations—such as business meetings—that are still alien even to laptop keyboards.

With the rapid rate of technological change, new devices will come and go. One major trend today is "convergence"—merging two or more functions into one appliance. Creating a cell phone that is also a PDA, for example, eliminates the need for one device. Another trend is wearable appliances. Currently in development are PDA watches, cell phone watches, and eyeglass computer screens.

The point is, identifying the distinguishing characteristics of any tool will better enable you to understand whether it will fit into your system and meet your needs. It will automatically eliminate many tools from consideration. It will help you avoid becoming distracted by advertising and focus your attention on the tools that have the greatest potential of working well for you.

Keep in mind that, though your personal leadership system may well include tools from some or all of the six groups, it's important that the elements work together effectively. Remember, you're dealing with a *system*. The parts need to work together to create an effective, efficient, simple, synchronous whole. Don't be led astray by "bells and whistles" advertising for some new tool that does not even have the right basic distinguishing characteristic to be compatible with your system.

Your specific needs. In considering a tool, you'll want to carefully identify your own specific needs. You may want to ask questions such as the following. You might even want to rate the questions according to importance.

1. How much of the time will you be in your office versus in other people's offices (a corridor warrior) or traveling (a road warrior)?

2. How much information do you need to have with you?

3. How do the people you work with communicate and process information?

4. What kind of capacity do you need (such as huge amounts of storage capability for large graphic or scientific files)?

5. How often do you connect with the Web, and for what reasons?

6. What systems does your organization offer, and with which ones do you need to interface?

7. How often do you need to look at your daily plan, task list, calendar, e-mail, or other information, and what circumstances are you in when you look at them (in a noisy environment, in an office, a car, etc.)?

8. How comfortable are you with a keyboard?

9. How comfortable are you with learning how to use a new technology tool?

10. Do you do a lot of long distance calling? Do you use a lot of long distance minutes from locations other than your home?

11. How often do you need to access information (and what kinds of information do you need to access) when you would not be near a computer or have one with you?

12. What kinds of information do you want to have at your finger-tips? When and where will you be when you use it, and where is that information now?

This list could be expanded to include far more detail, and for some people, a deeper level of analysis could be very important. Certainly it would be if you were buying systems for 500 employees. But for most of us, these questions bring enough key issues to light to help us get a handle on our needs.

Cost/benefit analysis. To invest in new technology almost always costs money—sometimes a lot. But there are other costs as well. There's the cost of time and effort required to research, acquire, and set it up. There's also the cost of time and effort to learn how to use it. There's the maintenance cost—the money and time required to keep it in functioning condition. And finally, there's the opportunity cost—whatever else you could have done with the money and time you invested in it. So there's a lot to consider when you "count the cost" of investing in new technology.

On the other hand, to stay with what you have may incur an even greater cost in terms of the increased effectiveness and/or efficiency you might have had.

So how do you know if some new technology or tool is worth the price of change?

First, you can reconsider the fundamental evaluation questions with the new technology in mind:

- *Is it* more *effective?* Will it help you do what's most important *better* than your current system?

- *Is it* more *efficient?* Will it help you do what's most important in a way that is *better* than your current system?

- *Is it* more *simple?* Is it more streamlined, easier to work with, freer of complicating "bells and whistles"?

- *Is it* more *synchronous?* Does it work *better* in cooperation with and *better* help facilitate your other systems?

- *Does it* better *meet specific needs* (such as portability)? Which needs? And how important are those needs?

Second, keep in mind that while many new technologies sport advanced features that promise to do nearly everything but clean the kitchen sink, even suppliers acknowledge that many people do not actually use these tools as they were designed to be used. Consider planning tools, for example. Advanced paper-based planners often wind up being used as nothing more than glorified calendars. Consultants report finding organizers being used as fancy appointment books or left virtually unopened in office desk drawers. Few people use or are even aware of all the features of software programs or equipment such as PDAs.

The reality is that many of us don't need and simply won't use many of the "bells and whistles" that constitute "new and improved." So why pay for them? Why spend the time learning how to use them? If some new technology performs one basic function you need and 29 functions you don't need, you'll probably do well to look for a simpler, less expensive alternative.

On the other hand, if the "new and improved" will help you simplify, it usually pays to investigate further. A single new cell phone may genuinely serve you better than your current pager, PDA, and two voice messaging machines. An electronic planning system with a dialable contact file may make it easier to coordinate planning and communication than your current card file or alphabetized list in your planner. A computer-based finance system that helps you align goals and spending, connects your check register to an online bill-paying service, provides online account access, instantly creates charts and graphs to help you track progress and automatically does your checkbook math may save hundreds of hours over time. As a general rule, the more you can combine and simplify, the better off you'll be.

Third, as you consider new alternatives, keep in mind that your own personal leadership system may well be part of a larger system in which interrelatedness is also an issue. If you work in a situation where information is passed through a specific kind of hardware or software program, keeping abreast of that particular technology may be vital to your effectiveness on the job. In addition, you may want to coordinate your personal systems for greater ease in planning and communication. Remember, too, that a change in your work or home situation may also create the need for a change in your system.

Finally, keep in mind that in most circumstances, you're generally better off staying a little behind the cutting edge of new technology. For instance, 1.0 version software often has "bugs" that need to be worked out, and later versions are usually less expensive and simpler and have shorter learning curves. Deciding how long to wait to invest in new technology is a function of weighing the benefits against the inconvenience and risk of dealing with the drawbacks.

So be aware—but also beware! If you're going to catch the wave, generally do it when it's full and solid enough to support you well.

Our Own Personal Leadership Systems

Over the years, the two of us have used a variety of personal leadership tools. Through the following examples, you can see a few specific applications of the principles we've talked about.

ROGER

I've been working with personal systems for years. I helped design organizers and have trained thousands in their use. I have also been an early adopter of new technologies, from computers to cell phones to electronic tablets.

With this in mind, you can probably understand my enthusiasm for some of the tools that are now available.

The major elements to my system include:

- *a Tablet PC*

- *a cell phone/pocket PC combination*

- *a land line phone*

- *a desktop computer*

- *a wireless home network*

- *an office-based network*

The key piece of my system is the Tablet PC. It can run all the programs of a laptop, but in addition you can write on it. In fact, if you can write or draw something on a piece of paper, you can do it on a Tablet. I carry all the key information I need with me on my Tablet PC, including my notes for books and projects. I also have a program that contains the text of over 3000 books and publications that I refer to and search.

For my organizer, I use the Tablet Planner software. I now have what looks like my trusty paper planner on a computer—with all the advantages of both!

One of the things I'm most excited about is my ability to search my notes for a word or phrase and have it pop up. This works whether the note is associated with a task, appointment, contact, or a simple note page. My cell phone/PDA combination is part of a new generation of phones that combines a cell phone and some or all aspects of a handheld computer in one device. The benefits are obvious—I have one less thing to carry, and my wireless, handheld computer can go online with a couple of clicks.

I keep my contacts in my Tablet Planner, which syncs with my pocket PC phone, so I have all my numbers with me when I have the phone. I program my home office phone to my cell phone when I'm away. When I can't answer, my calls go into my cell phone voice mail. I use instant messaging with close associates and family members.

What's really been helpful is how these elements all work together. My phone and computers sync. I back up my Tablet PC with my desktop, so the two provide backup for each other. Rebecca and I share files between our home offices and from various parts of the house without ever leaving our seats. The Tablet has wireless built in, and with the addition of a PCMCIA cell phone card, I can also use it over the new and faster connections made available through cell phone providers.

REBECCA

My personal systems are somewhat simpler than Roger's—I essentially use a desktop computer. I write, do my weekly planning, store contacts and information, manage our finances, plan presentations, and research genealogical records all on my desktop. With our network, Roger and I can shoot files back and forth as we work. During our weekly meeting when we review our shared mission and address issues of planning, calendaring, parenting, writing, and finance, I use my desktop and he brings his Tablet PC.

When most of our children were at home, we planned weekly as a family. We kept two magnetic dry-erase calendars on the fridge—one for the week and one for the month. Each week we would review the events of the past week. Then we'd write down appointments for each family member for the coming week.

In addition to allowing us to coordinate transportation and family events, this gave each of us a chance to know each other's priorities for the week so that we could give encouragement, help, and support. It was also synergistic in that it provided communication as well as planning and scheduling.

The two of us find ourselves moving more toward computer-based rather than paper-based information storage. We also find ourselves keeping less research in our files. With the Internet, reference CDs, and handheld devices that can carry the contents of a number of key reference books, we find we don't need to duplicate and keep personal copies of all the information we used to keep. In this sense, technology has helped us to simplify our lives.

These systems work well for us. We know of others who use different tools that work well for them. But whether your system is paper and pencil or ultimate high tech, as long as it's effective, efficient, simple, and synergistic—and Quadrant II (importance and improvement focused)—you can't go too far wrong.

NEXT STEPS

In deciding how to best implement the six optimizers we've just described, use your navigational intelligence. If one or two seem particularly useful, start there. Or you might find it helpful to evaluate your current situation. Depending on how you see your level of competence in dealing with "time matters," here are some specific "next step" ideas that may prove helpful.

"I'm out of control!" If you see yourself as basically "out of control," the best way to begin to move into Quadrant II may be to simply employ the "Five Minute Rule"—spend five minutes today doing something that will make tomorrow better. Maybe you have a customer at work who *doesn't* have a problem. Use your five minutes to call her. Build the relationship. Get some specific feedback that will help you with your other customers. Or perhaps there's someone you didn't get as a customer. Call him. Find out what you could have done better—what you can do better in the future. If you were to contact one unsatisfied customer a day for five days, you might be able to come up with a consistent thread, with something specific that would make your whole operation more effective. Then you could ask for five minutes at the next team meeting to share what you've learned. Improving your team performance by 10 percent— even 5 percent—would give you a huge gain.

Try the "Five Minute Rule" at home. Invest in relationships. Do some of the "happy things" you identified in the previous chapter. Stop on your way home from work and pick up a special treat for the family or a flower or card for your spouse. Read a story to your three year-old or sit down for five minutes and really focus on listening to your teenager or your spouse. Or use your five minutes to plan a special family time, create menus for the week, organize a cupboard, or order garden seeds. Do something that helps organize and beautify your home or builds relationships of service and love.

Once you get a feeling for the power of Quadrant II investments, you'll want to jump in. The objective is to eventually invest up to 20, 40 or even 60 percent of your time in Quadrant II.

"I'm doing all right, but ... " If you're a fairly good time manager, but you know you have room for improvement, a good "next step" is to track your time. This will enable you to quickly discover the "black holes" and target specific areas for improvement. Another good area of focus is systems and tools. Streamlining and updating your personal systems can increase your ability to get things done.

"I manage my time well, but I want to get to a new level." If you consider yourself a competent time manager, but you want to discover new levels of effectiveness, a good place for you to work is in the upper corner of Quadrant II. This is where you *anticipate* potential opportunities and problems. You deal with *emerging* needs. It's engaging your ability to envision and imagine. It's creating an anticipation/prevention focus that enables you to keep things from moving into Quadrant I.

"I'm a great time manager at work, but not at home" (or vice-versa). If you're competent in one arena of life, but not in another, a good next step is to zero in on the most likely areas of waste. If your problem is at work, analyze the time you're spending in Quadrant III. Look for the "urgent, but not important" things that are drawing you away from a highest priority focus. But discern carefully; the feeling of urgency can fool you into thinking you're in Quadrant I when you're really in Quadrant III. If the problem is at home, take a closer look at "not urgent, not important" Quadrant IV. If you're spending hours on the couch in front of the television set, have the courage to push the "off" button and do something that's truly renewing and relationship-building.

NAVIGATING YOUR WAY THROUGH THE DAY

Hopefully, from weekly organizing, time zones, T-planning, and time tracking, to personal leadership systems, personal effectiveness technology, and "next steps," this chapter has given you some high leverage help in managing your time and leading your life.

But what it all boils down to is to make good decisions in moments of choice. As Richard L. Evans observed:

Life offers you two precious gifts: one is time, the other, freedom of choice, the freedom to buy with your time what you will.[3]

The quality of what we "buy" with our time is a reflection of our ability to remember and act on what's most important in the decision moments of our lives.

So how do you effectively navigate through a day? How do you balance the need to focus and the need to be aware? How do you keep the "urgent" from overpowering the important? How do you discern in decision moments what truly matters most?

As you face the day, keep in mind that if you implement the optimizers we've suggested, you already have in place a powerful perspective of importance. When you organized your week, you connected with your mission. When you set your goals, you consulted your navigational intelligence and you thoughtfully, consciously, determined the most aligned, high leverage things you could think of to do. When you planned the day, you prioritized your *to do's*—both the ones that were time sensitive and the ones you wanted to fit in. So in terms of what matters most, you're starting the day with your best possible planning.

Keep in mind, though, that what you've created is a "flexible framework." It gives you a standard against which you can measure the importance of unanticipated opportunity, while also allowing you the freedom to recognize genuinely higher priorities and to adjust to them. At the end of the day, the question is not, "How many things did I check off my list?" but, "Did I do what was truly most important?"

So as you move into your day, you can feel free to go into a default "focus" mode. Focus on what you've already decided is most important. But be sure to keep your navigational intelligence on constant background scanning. When it sends a signal, tune in immediately and quickly assess. Decide; then focus again—either on your predetermined priority or on the new opportunity or challenge you have now determined is even more important.

As you go through this process repeatedly, day after day, with awareness, you develop the capacity to quickly make better decisions and to shift gears smoothly, swiftly, automatically. Almost in a breath, you can step outside your focus, consult your navigational intelligence, decide on importance, and refocus with confidence. And the process is recursive; the more you do it, the more keenly you calibrate your navigational intelligence and increase your capacity to do it in the future.

Let's look now at three of the most common kinds of events that might challenge your framework of importance during a day . . .

- Other people's urgencies and emergencies

- Opportunities

- "Flaky" inclinations

   ...and see how you can use this process and the optimizers we've shared in this chapter to deal with them effectively.

OTHER PEOPLE'S URGENCIES AND EMERGENCIES

As part of a recent FranklinCovey survey of more than 11,000 employees in key industries nationwide, participants were shown a list of nine factors and asked: "Which of the following is the most significant distraction that prevents you from completing your most important work tasks?" The top two—by quite a bit—were "interruptions" and "other people's urgencies and emergencies."[4] There's a high probability this is also a problem for you.

   So what do you do—at work or at home—when you're focused on a priority task and someone comes in with an "urgent" request? Here's where the shift/evaluate/refocus process we just mentioned comes in handy.

1. Shift focus immediately to the person. This accomplishes two important things: It affirms the importance of the person and your relationship, and it also allows you to quickly get the information you need to make a decision.

2. Evalute whether or not this is a true Quadrant I. Engage your navigational intelligence. If the relationship is one of shared vision and high trust, you can work together to determine:

   - Is this a high priority in our shared value system?

   - Is it a higher priority to us than what I was working on?

   - Is the timing critical—or negotiable? (If the relationship doesn't allow quality partnership interaction, you'll need to make those decisions on your own.)

3. Re-focus. If it is a true Quadrant I—and it's you're A-1 Quadrant I—then do what's necessary to focus your attention on it. If it's not, you have two choices:

- Postpone shifting focus. You might say something like, "I can tell this is really important to you. I want to be able to give it the time and attention it deserves. I'm tied up right now, but I could focus on this in a couple of hours. Would that work for you?" This affirms the value of the person, the relationship, and the issue. And often, a later time works out even better. It gives the person a chance to move beyond the emotion of the moment and to think and prepare. If the person says "No," you can use your navigational intelligence to determine whether responding to that person's perceived needs or staying focused on your current task is the greater priority and act accordingly.

- Say "No." If it's not the genuine priority, have the courage to say "No" and stay focused on what is. Say it kindly, but firmly. Give some explanation if it's helpful and appropriate. But stay focused on what matters most.

The advantage of this kind of approach is that it enables you to competently and quickly engage your best decision-making capacity and focus on what's most important. It also diminishes the tendency to be reactive to or irritated by interruptions. In addition, it builds people and relationships. Keep in mind: you don't have to be a "people pleaser" to preserve relationships. In fact, quality high trust relationships can only be built as people learn to interact authentically and competently in interdependent situations.

As you deal with urgencies and emergencies, it's important to remember that sometimes people are energized by their emotions but they don't really expect you to drop what you're doing, and are actually surprised when you do. You don't need to automatically assume that anything that has high energy behind it is an emergency or that the expectation is that you act immediately. And even if it feels like an "emergency" to someone and there is an expectation for you to respond, it may not be appropriate or best for you to do so. As the saying goes, "Lack of planning on your part does not constitute an emergency on my part." At home, for example, if parents are continually pulling a child out of scrapes created by his lack of planning, that child may never learn to plan.

Also, some "emergencies" are created when people set artificial deadlines—deadlines that often can be changed. For example, suppose a coworker says, "I hate to bother you, but this is an emergency. I've promised a client this report by 5:00 and I really need your help!" You can find out if the promise was your coworker's idea or your client's. Your coworker may have suggested the time, and the report would simply sit on your client's desk until 9:00 the next morning. By arranging to come in an hour early, the two of you might be able to get your important tasks completed today, do a good job on the report in the morning, and still meet the client's needs. Often, people rush unnecessarily to get things done in a crisis mode, only to have them sit on a desk until someone can get to them.

The point is that sometimes things that seem like emergencies are not. So consult your navigational intelligence and quickly determine whether something is really in Quadrant I before you respond.

Also, don't overlook the fact that there is significant Quadrant II work you can do to minimize interruptions and protect your focus time. At the office, for example, you can set up systems to insulate and isolate yourself for high leverage tasks. You can set up and make people aware of time zones. If you have a secretary or an assistant, you can train him or her to screen visitors and calls. You can build high trust networks and create an environment that facilitates respect for focus time and clear communication in times of real need.

At home, you can also create time zones. You can set up times when the family knows you're there and that they can count on you. If you have to spend time on a work project, you can communicate its importance and set up a system to remind family members when you're on task. Here, too, you can work to build relationships of trust so that family members understand and respect an individual's needs for focus time. However, as we've said before, it's important to remember that some jobs, such as parenting, are basically jobs of responding to interruptions. As much as possible, "interruptions" should be viewed as "opportunities" when you're at home.

Keep in mind that the more you invest in Quadrant II—in things like building relationships, long-term planning, and preventive maintenance—the fewer real Quadrant I emergencies you're likely to have, and also that Quadrant II investments in health and true recreation can also increase your reserves to handle emergencies well.

OPPORTUNITIES

Sometimes opportunities come up during the day that are genuinely more important than what you had on the plan. On the other hand, some "opportunities" are diversions in disguise. So how do you tell the difference? How do you seize the opportunities and avoid the diversions?

First and foremost, this is an issue of importance. If it's "above the line" in Quadrant I or II, it's important. If it's "below the line" in III or IV, it's not. So screen it first through the filter of importance. If it can help you nurture a relationship, build your reserves, increase your capacity, contribute in a meaningful, or resolve a crisis, it's definitely worth considering.

Then, it becomes an issue of *relative* importance. You're working on important things; is the opportunity *more* important? Does it *better* enable you to do what matters most than what was on your plan? This is something your navigational intelligence can help you determine. If your intelligence has been calibrated through personal mission statement contemplation, weekly planning, and thoughtfully evaluated decision moments of the past—and if it's open to inspiration—there's a good chance a quiet moment of connecting will give you the answer.

Keep in mind that some of the best opportunities that come up often give you only a split second to decide to respond. This is particularly true of relationship-building opportunities, such as teaching moments with young children, conversations with teenagers, or helping a coworker or neighbor with an immediate need.

That's why it's so important to calibrate your navigational intelligence, keep it constantly on "scan," and develop the habit to use that split second to listen to it. If you're so focused on what you're doing that you miss that split second window, it's gone.

This is another reason to invest in Quadrant II. The more renewed you are—physically, mentally, and spiritually—the more open and responsive you're going to be to opportunity moments. Quadrant II is not passive; it's the key to a dynamic, energetic, responsive approach to life.

"FLAKY" INCLINATIONS

Sometimes, what challenges "importance" the most is simply a subconscious desire to avoid a particular project or task, or a lack of character strength to follow through.

Suppose, for example, that you're a manager, and your day looks like this:

Tasks			Appointments		
Review staff recommendations	B-2		6:00		
Write proposal	B-1		7:00		
Schedule budget meetings	A-3	✓	8:00	E-mail; A-1	(45 min/15 min)
Review agenda for Wednesday	A-1	✓	9:00	A-2; A-3	(30 min/20 min)
Call Max	B-3		10:00	Long-range planning	
Solve Briscoe problem	A-2	✓	11:00		
Read trade journals	C-1		12:00	Lunch with Alex	
			1:00	Preview new film	
			2:00	Ad meeting	
			3:00		
			4:00	Call Sampson	
			5:00		
			6:00		
			7:00	Dinner with Maxwells	
			8:00		
			9:00		
			10:00		

You come into the office at 8:00 and, despite interruptions, you get the first three *to do's* checked off your list. At 9:55 you get up and walk around your desk. In five minutes you have a two-hour appointment scheduled with yourself to do some long-range planning, which you have identified as your most important task of the day.

At the moment, though, you find you're feeling restless. You've already put in two or three hours, and suddenly long-range planning sounds boring. You glance out the hall and see several of your coworkers gathered around the water fountain. Taking a little time to chat with them, responding to your e-mails, or checking off more *to do's* on your "anytime" list suddenly seems far more appealing than long-range planning. You're not consciously thinking, "I won't do what's on my plan"; you're just in danger of letting your priority slip, of getting distracted and losing focus. You don't have the same sense of perspective you had when you planned that time at the beginning of the week.

This is what we call a "moment of truth." This is when you ask yourself, "What's really most important now?"

If you review your week's plan and consult your navigational intelligence, you will probably realize that it's the long-range planning, and that to act with integrity in that moment means keeping your commitment to yourself. You might look for ways to help spending five minutes doing "office aerobics," envisioning the results of having a quality long-range plan, or having a high protein snack that will sustain your blood sugar level. But, bottom line, if you make the decision to follow through with your planning, you will likely feel much better at the end of the day.

Staying with your priorities, even in the midst of temptation to do otherwise, is a function of habit and character. The more you make good decisions when you're tempted to be "flaky," the stronger your character and ability to make similar decisions in the future will be. It's like exercise—if you want to build a muscle, you have to exercise it. If you want to build your character, you have to exercise it. It may be difficult. You may "sweat" a little and experience temporary discomfort.

But the fact remains that you can do it. And the rewards are definitely worth the effort. At the end of the day, you can go to bed knowing that you did what was most important—that your long-range planning (which will affect the quality of every future day) is done . . . and that you have become stronger in the process.

Keep in mind that life is a process of becoming. Navigating well is not something you can expect to do perfectly every day. But it is something you can expect to improve in. Day by day, as you engage your navigational intelligence—as you identify what's important, act on what's important, evaluate your experience, and course-correct—you're going to get better at doing what matters most.

TIME GIFTS

ROGER

One Monday, in the midst of a highly important, time-sensitive writing project, I received a phone call from one of our daughters. Her daughter was having a "Grandparent's Day" at school on Friday. Could I possibly come?

My navigational intelligence told me immediately that this was important, but I knew it would be very difficult to work it in. Nevertheless, on Friday afternoon I was walking in the front door of the school.

When I entered my granddaughter's classroom, I saw her eyes light up with delight. She grabbed my hand and took me to my seat. I watched as she participated in the program that had been carefully prepared. Then, together, we cut her silhouette out of black paper and mounted it on a poster board.

As I sat there beside her, I realized that this Grandparent's Day program was just as important to her as my writing project was to me. My being there was acknowledging that importance— and her importance. It was because this activity was important to her—and she was important to me—that I was there.

As we've said before, time is the commerce of life balance, the communicator of value. And because this is true, one of the greatest gifts we can give others is the gift of time. As we consider the "important" priorities in our lives, we need to always remember that people and relationships are among the most important. Taking time to listen to a coworker or a spouse or to play with a child communicates the value we place on that person and on the relationship.

Also, making time to contribute to the well-being of others in our society is an indicator of the value we place on other people and on the positive aspects and benefits of living in our society. As others have observed:

We make a living by what we get; we make a life by what we give.
—Sir Winston Churchill

You must give some time to your fellow men. Even if it's a little thing, do something for others—something for which you get no pay but the privilege of doing it.
—Albert Schweitzer

The service we render to others is really the rent we pay for our room on this earth.
—Sir Wilfred T. Grenfell

Some things are important because they simply *are* important. Family, work, contribution, and service are all important. They are principles. They are essential to creating quality and balance in our lives. So as we consider how to spend our precious resource of time, we need to make sure that we invest in these principles that create life balance. These things *are* the things that matter most.

CHAPTER

MONEY MATTERS

There are two kinds of people in this world:
those who understand interest and those who don't.
Those who understand it receive it;
those who don't pay it.

Rex and Janie were good friends of ours. We met them when we attended college together. They were frugal, worked hard, and spent little. In fact, our group of friends always teased them because for Rex, a "big date"—even on their anniversary—was taking Janie to McDonald's for a hamburger.

Over the years, Rex and Janie managed their family budget on one income. They lived within their means and contributed regularly to a savings account. They taught their children to be happy with a few nice outfits instead of a closet full of top label designer clothes. For family vacations, they had great times camping out and using their boat, which was very nice, and which Rex had bought used—in cash—for pennies on the dollar. They lived in the same house for years. When they couldn't afford improvements, they decided to live happily with what they had.

At the age of 42, Rex was diagnosed with pancreatic cancer. Within six months he was gone. He left Janie with six children, ages 5 to 19. But he also left her with a sizable insurance policy, a savings account, and no debt.

As a result, Janie was able to spend the next year at home with her children, being with them and comforting them until they felt secure and were all in school. Unlike many single mothers, she did not have to fight with them about "things" they could no longer buy. They had already been taught to be frugal and they were all willing to pitch in and help. Also, she didn't have use her insurance and savings to pay off debts that had been left behind.

After a year, Janie was able to go back to school and get her master's degree—without going into debt. Though she got an excellent job, she did not feel pressured to bring in the same income Rex had brought in, because she still had backup funds.

Rex and Janie's "investment" mentality, provident living, and thoughtful, disciplined preparation provided a great deal of freedom for Janie to focus on what was most important, even in what could have been a terribly difficult situation. And, despite their frugality—or perhaps because of it—she remarked that there was never a time when the family felt they couldn't have a fun, happy, full life.

Now let's compare their experience to that of another couple—unfortunately, us.

When we were first married, we were both university students, struggling to live on a very tight budget. We went through some fairly stringent times. We were careful with our money. We always had insurance, but we didn't really invest. Our basic operational paradigm was that the best way to improve our financial situation was to earn more money.

So we did. Over the next 30 years, our financial situation improved. We moved several times, always lived in fairly modest homes, managed to pay for education, doctor's bills and braces for seven children, to make regular church and charitable contributions, and even to put away a little for retirement. We used credit cards, but our intent was to reach the point where we were completely out of debt—including our home—and could always pay for everything in cash.

After some years, the business we were involved in reached a point where it had significant market value, and suddenly we found ourselves completely out of debt. We no longer had to worry about whether something we wanted was on sale or not. We had the resources to fulfill what we thought were some important family goals.

We started work on a cabin—a beautiful place in the mountains where we could enjoy nature, work on writing projects, and provide relaxation, inspiration, and bonding for family members and guests for generations to come. At the same time, we started to build a new home. The one we'd lived in for 22 years could scarcely accommodate our family gatherings, which now numbered 29. So we invested a good deal of time and money in these projects.

Then the storms hit. Within a period of a few months, one of our contractors went berserk, walking off the job and leaving the project unfinished and suppliers unpaid, and we were out about 250 percent of what we'd agreed on. At the same time, our stock plummeted, the bank panicked and sold it, and we found ourselves with liens, no resources to finish either project, and a huge capital gains tax bill.

In the midst of all this, we had financial problems with a new business enterprise. One business partner—a company—took a 90-degree turn in strategy. Another partner—a major investor—suddenly lost his money in a stock market dive. Then, within a few months, our health insurance company went under . . . *and* our credit card number was stolen. We felt like the dark-cloaked villain had us in his clutches and was ready to tie us to the railroad tracks . . . with the hero nowhere in sight!

There's no doubt about it—this was a very hard time for us. Just as we were looking toward retirement and different avenues of contribution, we were thrown back to where we'd been years before and were essentially starting all over again. It was a humbling, sobering experience. It made even clearer to us something we had known for a long time: There is no security in material things, which are transitory at best. It also helped us realize that just because you may be doing very well in two or three "life matters" doesn't mean you can ignore, other "life matters" without consequence.

The problem was not that we'd been terrible money managers. We'd done a lot of things right. But had we simply been aligned with the fundamental principle of *investing* instead of *consuming*, even the terrible things that happened would not have created such a personal economic disaster.

MONEY AND LIFE BALANCE

As you can probably tell, the material in this chapter is deeply personal to us. It's something we've paid a significant price to come to understand. Our experience has been the crucible out of which have been forged new levels of knowledge, discipline, and unity in our relationship. It has also opened up a whole new world of insight for us into how profoundly money issues impact every dimension of life balance.

Like time, money is a huge communicator of value. *What* we buy with our money reflects what's important to us—at least, at the time. *How* we buy it reflects our character, discipline, and the value we place on our relationships with those who are (or should be) involved in our spending decisions. Both *what* and *how* we spend dramatically impact the quality of our lives, the quality of our relationships, and the legacy we leave to our children—not only in terms of dollars and cents, but also in terms of character, financial intelligence, and the ability to interact in positive ways around money matters.

Money is inseparably connected to each of the life matters we've already discussed—work, family, and time. Just consider: How much time do we spend trying to earn money, spend money, keep track of money, manage money, take care of things we buy with money, deal with problems in relationships caused by money? How much does our dependence on the money we earn on the job determine what time we can spend with our families, restrict our freedom to consider other work, and even affect the quality of our contribution at work when—for economic reasons—we're afraid to "rock the boat"? How much of the controversial "two working parent" issue is basically a matter of economics?

The good news in all of this is that because money is so interrelated with other life matters, improving our ability to manage it will make a significant difference in every other aspect of our lives. Learning to manage our money wisely—to spend less than we earn, put some away for a rainy day, and invest instead of consume—is a huge optimizer in all areas of life balance. It can strengthen our character, strengthen our relationships, increase our effectiveness as employees, and improve the quality of our personal and family life.

And now, more than ever before, there's a critical need to do it. Despite recent decades of unparalleled prosperity and two-income families, research has shown steadily increasing credit card debt, household debt, mortgage and credit card delinquencies, and personal bankruptcy filings.[1] It identifies money problems as an ongoing major cause of divorce.[2] It also shows a significant correlation between financial stress, employee absenteeism, and performance on the job, and reveals that half of all employees have not even started saving for retirement, and that most of those who have are not saving enough.[3] The truth is that many people—even those with six-figure incomes—are still struggling to pay their debts.

With job insecurities, stock market fluctuations, dwindling 401(k)s, and events such as natural disasters, terrorist attacks, or unexpected health challenges that could throw any of us into serious economic straits at any time, wise money management has become a fundamental survival skill. And the reality is that these past decades of unprecedented prosperity and easy credit have *not* prepared us to deal with the growing economic uncertainties we're facing today.

In light of all this, in this chapter we'll ask you to explore:

- How you *see* money

- How the Quadrant II investment paradigm can help you dramatically improve your money management

- High leverage optimizers that empower you to make better financial decisions

- How you can build true wealth

HOW DO YOU SEE MONEY?

Think for a moment about how you feel when you hear the word "money." What is your immediate emotional response? Is it confidence, peace, security, and hope? Or is it anxiety, hopelessness, fear, inadequacy, or guilt? Where are those feelings coming from? What expectations and experiences are creating your level of comfort or discomfort in money matters?

When it comes to money, we live in a world that often promotes illusion rather than reality. Consider for a moment a few of the myths we sometimes fall victim to in the area of money.

MYTH 1: MONEY AND "THINGS" = SUCCESS AND HAPPINESS

Many of us have been programmed to see "success" in terms of symbols—a fat paycheck, a bigger office, a more elaborate home, a BMW, designer clothing, a villa on the Mediterranean. We assume that the people who have these things have the happy, successful, secure lives we'd all love to have. If we're successful, we think, we, too, will have these things. In fact, we *want* to be successful so we *can* have them.

There are three big problems with this assumption.

First, many of the people who own these things also own huge debts and have lives filled with stress. They have a high consumption lifestyle but no real wealth or financial security at all. They have "big incomes, big homes, big debt, but little net worth."[4] In addition, many who truly are successful don't have all the "things."

Second, symbol is not substance. The office, the boat, the BMW may be great, but they do not necessarily bring happiness or represent the kind of contribution in the workplace and in society that gives you the rich, deep sense of life satisfaction that comes from knowing you've made a meaningful difference. In addition, once the novelty wears off, many people find they're no more satisfied with their lives than they were before they acquired the "things."

Third, symbols are often acquired at an enormous cost in terms of broken health and broken relationships both at home and at work—a price that far exceeds their value. Those who acquire symbols at such a price often end up with impaired judgment, depression, and "burnout," creating problems for themselves, their families, and the organizations in which they work.

Just suppose you could have the villa, the clothing, the new home, and so on at the price of no time with your family, huge interest payments, the stress of barely meeting your financial obligations, tension in your marriage, and no security if you were to lose your job. Or you could have a more modest home and fewer toys, but with greater flexibility, quality family time, no consumer debt, money growing in investments, and less stress. Which would you choose?

Studies show that happiness is not a function of money and things. And most of us would probably agree. In truth, "The best things in life are not things." But we *still* get caught up in the "money and things = success and happiness" myth that drives us into long hours and huge debt to acquire things that in the end only exacerbate the problem.

MYTH 2: THE BEST FINANCIAL IMPROVEMENT STRATEGY IS TO INCREASE INCOME

When we're in financial stress or we want to increase our financial freedom, the most obvious solution seems to be to increase income. So we decide to work longer hours, take on a second job, or get both parents into the work force to bring more money in.

At first, some things may seem better. If we've been struggling, we find that now we can pay our bills. We can provide nicer things for our family. We find we can afford a more expensive home, more expensive clothes, more expensive cars—so we buy them.

But we also discover that we have far less time at home, more job-related costs, and a higher tax rate. And with "consumer debt" habits, our spending increases proportionately. Before long we find that while we've been sacrificing vital personal and family time to get on top of things, we're in financial stress all over again—only at a higher level. We're still living in a delicately balanced no reserve situation, thinking, "When I make that next $50,000, then I'll start investing in something that will bring me some return."

As Robert Kiyosaki observes in his book, *Rich Dad, Poor Dad*:

[More] money will often not solve the problem; in fact, it may actually accelerate the problem. Money often makes obvious our tragic human flaws. Money often puts a spotlight on what we do not know. That is why, all too often, a person who comes into a sudden windfall of cash—let's say an inheritance, a pay raise or lottery winnings—soon returns to the same financial mess, if not worse than the mess they were in before they received the money. Money only accentuates the cashflow pattern running around in your head.[5]

More than what we bring in, it's how well we manage what we have that makes the difference. As Thomas Stanley and William Danko point out in *The Millionaire Next Door,* most Americans who actually have the peace of mind of real financial security aren't all that visibly rich. They save and invest and live frugally. Most live in moderate homes, wear inexpensive suits, and drive American-made cars. They own substantial amounts of appreciable assets, but don't display a high-consumption lifestyle. Most are married, and in half the cases, spouses do not have outside jobs. And as we observed in Chapter 2, they didn't inherit their money or win the lottery or a game show prize. They're people who have simply learned to put principles of sound financial management into practice.[6]

MYTH 3: MONEY = PRIVILEGE = CHILDREN'S SUCCESS

With the need to earn money to provide for our families, it's easy to fall into the trap of thinking that the more money we earn and the more privileges we can give our children, the better parents we are. We think that if we can provide the *best* clothes and the *best* cars and send them to the *best* schools, our children will have the opportunity to do more in life. And that means we must be doing a good job.

But providing things and opportunities to *do* is often at the expense of providing the opportunity to *become*. We all want our children to gain character strengths such as, honesty, integrity, and thrift. Will more money and "things" help them develop important qualities such as these? Not necessarily. In fact, there is evidence to indicate that often the relationship is inverse . . . the greater the money and privilege, the less opportunity many children have to learn character traits that are best taught through sacrifice, cooperation, and the need to prioritize and choose.

In addition, the economic need is only one of four basic and vital needs of all family members. At least equally important are their mental, spiritual, and social/emotional needs. If we're always away from home—physically and/or mentally—and focused primarily on earning money, we may not be able to meet those other vitally important needs.

We would do well, both as parents and as partners, to consider the whole spectrum of family needs and determine whether the extra money is worth the opportunity cost. There is a point at which family members need *us* more than they need what our money can provide. *Working with* the family to solve economic concerns may be a far more productive path than *buying for* them.

As a result of these and other myths, many of us tend to see money as a limited resource. It seems there's never enough, and we're always trying to figure out how we can get more. Often, we work long hours. We take on second jobs. We sacrifice irreplaceable time with the family. And frequently, in the end, we discover that getting more money doesn't necessarily solve the problem.

Probably, most of us would say that deep inside, we know that money can't buy happiness, and that real peace of mind comes from financial security and not from an excess of "things." But a fly on the wall would never believe it! What that fly would see is people rushing from store to store or surfing the Internet, charging "wants" as well as perceived "needs," racking up huge credit card debts, paying interest for years, sometimes arguing with a spouse, bemoaning a lack of funds, and trying to get rid of the headache that seems to come up every time they get a bill in the mail or try to balance their bank statement. An observant fly would be forced to conclude that acquiring "things" is a very high—but costly—value to most people in our society.

EXAMINING YOUR EXPECTATIONS CONCERNING MONEY

So where do we get the paradigms that lead us to act in ways that create these kinds of results?

Many come from the numerous advertisers and credit card companies that urge us to "Buy now; pay later." In the year 2000 alone, credit card companies sent out 3.3 billion solicitations (about 30 per household), despite the fact that the average credit card holder already carries nine credit cards in his or her wallet.[7] Combined with the "have it all" version of the American dream and the blitz of advertising, the encouragement to use credit and its ready availability create an almost irresistible pull to live a high consumption (and what some consider hedonistic) lifestyle. As a result of these and other influences, most of us tend to *see* money in ways that cause us to make choices that lead to debt and frustration.

Other paradigms of money come from relatives, friends, associates, and our experiences growing up.

ROGER

As a child, I remember the times my dad would bring home a new car. It was always an event. It was never discussed ahead of time—sometimes not even with Mom. Dad would simply show up with a new car and it was assumed that we would all be happy about it. In Dad's mind, it was one of the ways he showed his love for the family.

On the other hand, though, I also remember accompanying my Dad to a bank one day. He needed money to finance a production project, and the manager gave him what he asked for on his signature. As we were leaving, the manager pulled me aside and said, "You ought to be very grateful for the heritage your Dad has given you. I've watched him go through very difficult situations where other men would have declared bankruptcy. Your Dad held on, paid all his debts, and did the right thing, no

matter what. I'd put my career on the line and give him anything
he'd ask for because I know he would always come through."

REBECCA:
On several occasions, I remember my parents sharing with me
the story of "Nancy's piano." Nancy was an excellent musician.
When she graduated from high school, her parents bought her a
beautiful grand piano. But then she went away to college and
married, and the beautiful piano sat in her parents' living room
unused.

The point my parents would make in telling the story is how
much more useful it would have been to buy the piano while
Nancy was at home taking piano lessons. "Nancy's piano"
became a symbol of the importance of timing and it influenced
many of the decisions we made with regard to providing oppor-
tunities for our own children.

But what that story didn't become—at least in my life—was
a symbol of the importance of economic timing. Though my par-
ents never intended it, that vision scripted a number of decisions
we made in our family to get things when we thought they would
be most useful—not necessarily when we could afford them.

I have since wondered if the real issue was not, "Should
Nancy's parents have bought the piano earlier?" but "If they had
to go into debt to get it, should Nancy's parents have bought the
piano at all?" Nancy seemed to do just fine developing her talent
with the less expensive, but functional piano she had.

Our childhood experiences have a significant impact on the
financial attitudes and habits we bring with us into marriage, and
on the challenges we encounter as we try to merge two financial
philosophies and bank accounts into one. When you combine the
different scripting of two people with possible issues around power
(most often for men), security and self-worth (most often for
women), integrity and trust (for both in the relationship), and the
psychological burden of living in debt, it's easy to see how handling

finances can become a huge challenge in a marriage. In fact, the impact of emotionally laden financial issues, both in marriages and in individual lives, is so significant that today, in addition to financial planners and advisers, we have "money coaches" and "money mentors" who help people explore their scripting and psychological issues around their spending habits.

Our success in dealing with both time and money is not as much about planners and balance sheets as it is about attitudes and paradigms. People who deal effectively with time or money genuinely *see* differently. Most notably, they see in terms of *importance* and *investing* rather than *urgency* and *consuming*. And because they *see* differently, they *do* differently. And they *get* different results.

Take a moment to examine some of your paradigms about money, and ask yourself the following questions:

1. Why is money such an emotional issue for me (if it is)? What experiences have I had—particularly with the important people in my life—that have helped create the way I feel about money?

2. Is my sense of self-worth a function of my net worth?

3. To what extent do money matters affect my choice of work, my feelings about job security, and my performance at work?

4. To what extent do money matters affect my relationships and decisions at home?

5   If someone were to become aware of my economic situation— including my bank account balances, credit card balances, investments, retirement plan, and last six month's spending— would I feel comfortable . . . or embarrassed?

6. Based upon how I spend my money, what would people assume are the most important things in my life?

7. Do I typically wait, save, and pay in cash for the things I want to buy, or do I get them immediately on credit and pay interest as well as cost?

8. Based on my spending habits, which would my spouse think is more important to me: communication and agreement on spending . . . or getting the things I want?

9. Either by what I do or what I say, what am I teaching my children about financial management?

10. How much money do I think I really need to live a balanced, peaceful life?

It takes a deep self-awareness to come to grips with these issues in our lives. We may not want to do it. We may not want to face the possibility of our own incongruency. But there's no way we can validate our expectations without being realistic as well as real.

So we encourage you to ask the questions. Examine your paradigms. And take a hard look at where you are now. Take a personal audit. Look at your assets. Look at your debts. Consider your retirement. Add up what you're currently paying on interest. Ask yourself this question:

If I continue on the path I'm on financially, what will my situation be 5, 10 or 20 years down the road?

As noted previously, people who are truly effective in managing their money *see* differently. And because they *see* differently, they *do* differently. And they *get* different results.

Let's consider now how the Quadrant II paradigm we introduced in the last chapter, "Time Matters," can also make a dramatic difference in the way you *see* and manage money—and in the results you get.

―――

QUADRANT II MONEY MANAGEMENT

Think back to the Time Management Matrix. Consider how appropriately the four quadrants identify the way we spend money as well as time:

THE MONEY MANAGEMENT MATRIX

	Urgent	Not Urgent
Important	**Quadrant I** Bills Payments Immediate needs Tax penalties Legal judgments Emergency medical expenses for self, family members, or friends	**Quadrant II** Savings Investments Insurance Capital investments (e.g., education, training) Business investments and improvements Investments in preventive health Investments in more effective personal systems or tools
Not Important	**Quadrant III** Impulse spending Interest on borrowed money Excessive entertainment Guilt gifts Excessive tools or gadgets Urgency costs (e.g., overnight shipping charges because you want something *now*)	**Quadrant IV** Waste Loss from bad judgment Self-destructive habits Gambling Excess purchases (e.g., a third car) Tools with features you never use More clothes than you could ever wear Shopping sprees Anything that is a waste when compared to values and principles

As you consider the Money Management Matrix, think about your current spending habits. Where do you spend most of your money now?

As with time, many people spend their financial lives in Quadrants I and III—in this case, paying bills, meeting immediate needs, and buying on impulse. And when their wants exceed their resources, they buy on credit. They accumulate debts. They pay interest. They get frustrated. They think the way out is to increase income. So, if they're married, both spouses will work, or one takes on a second job. They make more. They buy more. They get a bigger house, another car. They spend more money on babysitters, work clothes, and fast foods. They get further into debt. They pay more interest. They pay more taxes. They never get ahead. And if some unexpected event comes up causing them to miss a paycheck or two, they're in deep trouble.

Once again, Quadrant II is the key. Quadrant II is not only the quadrant of *importance*, it's also the quadrant of *investment*. It's the quadrant of Financial Freedom. And this is where the truly wealthy people have put their money. As Stanley and Danko point out, most Americans who become "millionaires" invest an average of nearly 20 percent of their taxable income yearly in assets that create wealth.[8] In doing this, they create an "artificial scarcity." Then they practice principles of industry and thrift to live on what's left. As a result, they earn interest instead of pay it.

And what kind of difference does that make? Just contrast the feeling of Quadrant II freedom with the feeling you get when you read former Undersecretary of State J. Reuben Clarke's description of the interest you pay when you're in Quadrant III:

Interest never sleeps nor sickens nor dies; it never goes to the hospital; it works on Sundays and holidays; it never takes a vacation; it never visits nor travels; it takes no pleasure; it is never laid off work nor discharged from employment; it never works on reduced hours; it never has short crops nor droughts; it never pays taxes; it buys no food; it wears no clothes; it is unhoused and without home and so has no repairs, no replacements, no shingling, plumbing, painting, or whitewashing; it has neither wife, children, father, mother, nor kinfolk to watch over and care for; it has no expense of living; it has neither weddings nor births nor deaths; it has no love, no sympathy; it is as hard and soulless as a granite cliff. Once in debt, interest is your companion every minute of the day and night; you cannot shun it or slip away from it; you cannot dismiss it; it yields neither to entreaties, demands, or orders; and whenever you get in its way or cross its course or fail to meet its demands, it crushes you.[9]

So which would you rather be doing—paying interest in Quadrant III or gaining interest in Quadrant II?

Bottom line, the Quadrant II financial management approach is to invest money in things that create growth. When we use the term *invest*, we're not talking about investment in the stock market or any other specific instrument of investment. We're talking about the *principle* of investment—of using the resources you have to create more. Investments that increase financial resources are typically in assets such as your own business, real estate, savings accounts, CDs, stocks, bonds, mutual funds, IRAs, or 401(k)s. Investments that increase human (and, in some cases, long-term financial) resources are typically in things such as education, talent or skill development, or humanitarian efforts. With both kinds of investments, the focus is on *creating* instead of merely consuming.

Where should you invest? With a fluctuating economy, it pays to get good, up-to-date financial counsel. Some investments that would have been considered wise five years ago would not be wise today.

How much should you invest? It depends on your situation. Again, most people who have accumulated wealth invest about 20 percent of their taxable yearly income. However, even if you begin by living the "Five Percent Rule" (like the "Five Minute Rule" we suggested in "Time Matters)—investing just 5 percent of your income in interest-creating assets—you'll start to catch the spirit of Quadrant II investment . . . from the first statement that arrives showing interest you earned instead of interest you have to pay. Month after month, seeing the cumulative interest will encourage you to figure out ways to invest more.

As with time, the best place to get resources to invest in Quadrant II is from Quadrant III, which is filled with high consumption spending. Marketing, advertising agencies, and credit card companies make it feel *urgent* as they use sensory, social, psychological, and economic enticements to urge you to spend. But most high consumption spending is not *important*—it doesn't help you accomplish what matters most. As we noted earlier, Quadrant III is also filled with the interest you pay on borrowed money. This interest is urgent—as bills and every day's accumulation of interest attest—but it certainly doesn't contribute in any way toward your goals, and in fact drains resources from them.

Again, the key principles are *importance* and *investment*. Put your money where it will help you accomplish what matters most to you. And stick to other time-proven principles such as *thrift*, *industry*, and *deferred gratification*. Unfortunately, those words are not "in" now; what is "in" are words like *quick*, *easy*, and *buy now, pay later*. But there's no way those words will ever empower us to get the results—the balance, the peace, the freedom—we want in our lives.

The reality is, most of us will never have enough money to do all the things we might like to do or could think of to do. So we have to choose. The key is to spend and invest in the things that will bring the greatest returns. With both money and time, it's when we learn to *invest* instead of merely *consume* that we generate true wealth—more abundant resources, personal integrity, and rich relationships with the important people in our lives. Over time, this approach makes an enormous difference—not only in our ability to weather the unexpected storms of life, but also in our ability to create balance in daily living.

THE VALUE OF THE MONEY MATRIX

As you can see, with money as with time, the Quadrant Matrix is powerfully descriptive. "I can see it now! I am totally caught up in impulse buying and consumer debt! (Quadrant III) I'm always feeling pressured by payments that are due (Quadrants I and III). There are times when I want to go out and buy something totally frivolous and unnecessary (Quadrant IV) just to preserve my sanity!" Even those who invest time and money in Quadrant II are happy to discover a visual image that captures the wisdom of Quadrant II choices and suggests even greater opportunities for effective investment.

It also shows the importance of proactivity. It gives context to our financial choices and highlights the wisdom of choosing to invest money, as well as time, where it will bring the greatest returns. It empowers us to see through the "buy now, pay later" philosophies that flood our environment.

It also carries with it the spirit of investment and continuous improvement. It helps us understand that rather than spending our future, we can invest in it.

Finally, it shows us where we waste our money "below the line" in Quadrants III and IV—money we could be investing in Quadrant II. In many cases, we don't need to earn more money, we simply need to manage well the money we have.

OPTIMIZERS

As we move into the area of optimizers, let's take a moment to notice some of the similarities and differences between money and time.

As we've said before, time and money are both resources. They are both languages of value. They are highly interrelated, and the way we spend both communicates what's important in our lives.

Also, both have an enormous potential for strengthening relationships. The way you interact with others around time and money issues can make huge deposits or withdrawals in relationships, as well as in bank accounts.

In addition, they both provide wonderful opportunities for self-discovery. The more you learn about the way you spend and invest both time and money, the more you learn about yourself. The more you consciously choose to make better spending and investing decisions, the more you grow in strength of character and develop the capacity to exercise better judgment and more discipline in every area of your life.

But while time and money are both resources, there are differences in the way we can allocate each.

First, when you deal with time, it's like trying to navigate a kayak through the rapids. You're in the flow. Obviously, you need to chart your course. But you have to be able to respond in the moment. When you deal with money, however, you're not in the flow. You may *feel* like you're in the flow with all the pressure to spend; but the reality is that, while time moves independently, money doesn't move until you move it. So you're on land. And—like a farmer needing to get irrigation water to the end of the row—your job is to *channel* the flow where it will produce the greatest growth.

Second, while many time decisions have to be made on the spot, most money decisions can be made in advance. You can't "save" or store time. You can only spend it in the moment. But you can save and store money, and doing so generally causes it to increase in value. Your ability to save and spend money in advance can actually make handling money easier than handling time because it gives you greater control.

With these similarities and differences—and our Quadrant II paradigm—in mind, let's look now at high leverage optimizers in the area of money management.

OPTIMIZER 1: KNOW WHERE YOUR MONEY IS GOING

As we mentioned earlier, people who are good with money know where their money goes. So the first optimizer we suggest is to track where you're currently spending your money. Just like tracking your time, this will put the reality and consequences of your choices right in front of you.

Logically, it might seem more effective to start by setting your financial goals first. But experience shows that most people have at least a few subconscious values around money, and simply tracking where it's going tends to bring them immediately face-to-face with discrepancies. Even without a clear vision of your financial goals, your navigational intelligence—somewhat calibrated by these subconscious values—will immediately begin to pick up on areas of misalignment and waste.

For example, one financial counselor told us of a man—a truck driver—who was concerned about his ability to provide for his young daughter's future college education. Even though he didn't have his financial goals all figured out, the counselor suggested that he start tracking where he was spending his money. He was surprised to discover that he was spending $80 a month on Big Chills. (extra-large convenience store drinks) When this counselor showed him how that $80 a month properly invested over time could pay for his daughter's education, he was moved to tears.

Because it's such a powerful revelatory tool, if you're not already doing it, we suggest you begin tracking immediately. Here are some ways you could do it:

- Turn into a "receipt hog." Get receipts for every transaction and take a few minutes at the end of the day (or the end of the week) to record them.

- Pay for things with a check card and access online banking or get a summary statement from your bank.

- Carry a three-by-five card or use a planner page to note your expenses, or write checks and record them in a register.

However you choose to do it, record your expenses, and at some point sit down and analyze where your money is going. It's likely that you'll immediately spot places where your money is disappearing in Quadrant III and IV black holes—money you could be investing and growing in Quadrant II. Many financial software programs, such as Microsoft Money and Quicken, and online services such as themoneyplanner.com make categorization easy and enable you to quickly recall and organize information—even providing summary graphs and charts—for effective review.

OPTIMIZER 2: KNOW WHERE YOU WANT YOUR MONEY TO GO

A second high leverage optimizer is to create a clear and, if appropriate, shared vision of where you want your money to go. The lack of this kind of vision is at the root of much of the stress we feel about money and work, and also at the root of much of our impulse buying. It's also at the root of much of the financial distress in marriages and families. When family members—particularly spouses—don't take the time to work through their differences to come up with a solid, unified financial vision and strategy, spending decisions often become shocking, divisive, and a source of hidden pain, creating withdrawals from far more than bank accounts.

In order to clarify your financial values and goals, it can be helpful to make a list of possibilities, which might include some of the following:

- Become debt free

- Buy or pay off a home

- Establish an emergency fund (three to six months of living expenses)

- Pay off education loans

- Reduce financial stress

- Establish a fund to care for aging parents

- Have money put away for a well-funded retirement

- Gain control of finances

- Reduce taxes

- Own a business

- Fund a humanitarian project or consistently donate to a charitable cause

- Remodel the house

- Have money for a dream vacation

- Establish a fund for children's weddings

- Own a better car free and clear

- Be able to fund private schooling and/or college education for the children

- Help children with down payments for first homes

- Own a farm, mountain cabin, or vacation retreat

- Own a motor home or boat

- Build a swimming pool or spa

- Save money for the birth of a new baby

- Invest in rental property

- Increase your current standard of living

When you have all the possibilities out on the table, identify your top five and prioritize them according to importance. Then focus on the five. Keep them constantly in front of you. When you're tempted to waste money in Quadrants III and IV, remember your important Quadrant II goals. Look for ways you can grow your money and put them into action.

This kind of activity can be turned into a fun and instructive game for couples, single parents who want to involve older children in financial decision making, or anyone in a situation of shared financial responsibility. The following version of this game was adapted from one created by our friends at themoneyplanner.com.

THE MONEY GAME

1. Transfer the list of possible financial goals to 5 three-by-five cards, putting one goal on a card. Make enough duplicates for each person to have a full set of cards.

2. Set a timer. Without consultation, allow two minutes for each person to select the five cards out of the set that represent his or her top five financial goals.

3. Set the timer again. Allow one more minute to order the five cards in terms of priority.

4. Compare the sets of cards. How unified are you on your financial goals and priorities?

When you play this game with others, you may well discover that you're operating out of completely different expectations. And this unrecognized difference is often a source of a lot of tension and stress.

Continuing exploration may reveal other expectation differences as well. In many marriages, for example, there's a sort of loose assumption, on the part of one spouse or the other, that both should agree on spending. But when that spouse discovers the other has gone out and bought something without talking it over, it creates frustration and disappointment. That action comes across in one of two ways: either as saying, "What I wanted to spend that money for was more important than my commitment to you," or as a rude reminder that vision and values are not shared. Either message can create pain and distress.

So it becomes very high leverage to create—either on your own or with others with whom you have shared financial responsibility—a financial mission/strategy statement. Realistically, this may take a significant investment of time and effort. Marriage partners may need to face and resolve issues around different scripting, paradigms, and habits. Likely, children will initially see finances essentially through the limited view of their own immediate needs.

But keep in mind that this is a high leverage Quadrant II investment of time. It will facilitate high leverage Quadrant II investments of money. It will also facilitate Quadrant II relationship building. And the shared understanding you create will enable you to help family members align their expectations with what is both "real" and "realistic," eliminating many disappointments and arguments and enhancing the quality of all future interactions around finance.

In creating a financial mission/strategy statement, you would first want to identify your goals, the resources you need to accomplish those goals, and the principles, values, and guidelines that would govern the acquisition and management of those resources. You might address questions such as the following, or others more appropriate to your situation:

- What principles will serve as guidelines for our economic decisions and actions?

- What degree of financial security do we want to achieve and how are we going to achieve it?

- What lifestyle parameters do we want to set?

- What should we set aside for future needs, such as retirement, children's education, and caring for aging parents?

- What roles ("provider," "financial manager," etc.) will each of us fulfill?

- What is our strategy to coordinate and account for our spending?

- What are our commitments to each other?

The strategy part of the statement would include your long- and short-range goals and the ways you plan to fulfill them. You can use your navigational intelligence to help you discern the financial goals and strategies that are best for you.

Below is a sample financial mission/strategy statement for a young couple—whom we'll call Tom and Laura—with two children:

Principles	Goals	Financial Strategies	Integrated Life Strategies	Roles
• Live within our means • Set some aside for a "rainy day" • Earn interest rather than pay it	• Generate enough income to cover basic living expenses and savings goals • Pay off school loans (three years) • Own our own home (15 years) • Have $50,000 in college funds for Janie and Tyler (15 years) • Have $2 million in retirement funds (40 years)	• Invest 5 percent of income in emergency savings • Invest 5 percent of income in college accounts • Invest as much as possible in company 401(k) • Manage rental property (inherited from parents); invest profit in annuities • Stay with current job; advance • Refinance home on a 15-year mortgage while rates are low • Do not go into consumer debt • Do not purchase a car that is less than one year old • Have weekly meetings to track expenses and set budget goals	• Live on one full income and rental property income until Janie and Tyler are in school • Stay in current home unless income becomes sufficient to handle higher payment on current percentage level	*Tom:* • Provide primary income • Manage investments • Balance bank and credit card statements *Laura:* • Propose monthly budget • Pay bills • Manage rental property for five years • Provide secondary income when Janie and Tyler are in school.

Developing a statement such as this can provide high leverage optimization not only in your family, but also at work—or in any circumstance where financial responsibilities are involved.

Particularly when there is a shared financial responsibility—people find it strategically wise to invest some Quadrant II time in coming to a clear agreement. Clear, shared vision makes the whole process of money management much easier.

OPTIMIZER 3: PLAN WEEKLY

During the earlier years of our married life, we thought it would be a good idea to meet together weekly to discuss issues around being partners and parents in our home. One of these issues was finance.

Often, we did meet weekly. But financial matters were somewhat low on the list. It seemed there were always so many other things to talk about, so we frequently gave finance a halfhearted gloss-over and moved on to other things. As a result, we didn't have as clear and unified a vision as we should have had, and we were not always unified in our spending decisions.

Because we have one of those absolutely incredible, once-in-a-millennium love affairs and so many deeply shared values, our differences over finances didn't ruin our relationship. But they did cause moments of grief and pain, and they certainly didn't add value to what we had.

It wasn't until our financial disaster that we learned the value of addressing money matters every week. On one of our retreats together, we created a shared financial vision that was truly meaningful. In it, we identified the principles of effective financial management. We agreed on priorities and goals. We committed ourselves to integrity in execution.

Then, in our weekly meetings, we began to:

- Review our financial mission/strategy statement

- Track our expenses from the past week

- Compare actual spending to our spending goals (budget)

- Celebrate victories of the past week—no matter how small

- Discuss what we'd learned and ways to improve

- Plan spending and investment for the coming week and make necessary budget adjustments

As a result, the differences in our values and approaches began to slowly disappear and we gradually became more unified. We knew we were doing better when, after several months of weekly meetings, we came across The Money Game for the first time. When we compared our cards at the end, they were identical! Not only had we chosen the same goals, we'd put them in exactly the same order. (And incidentally, we finished ahead of time!) All the effort we had invested to hammer out the issues had obviously paid off.

We recognize, of course, that individuals, couples, and families handle their finances in many different ways. Some set up separate bank accounts. Some use separate credit cards. Some divide the roles up differently.

But however you choose to handle your finances, we recommend a weekly—or even biweekly or monthly—financial meeting as a high leverage way to ensure that you stay connected and focused on what's important. You could even include it as part of an expanded planning session and consider your investments of time and money at the same time. With both resources, constantly renewing your vision and values helps ensure that what feels urgent or appealing in the short run does not short-circuit what matters in the long run.

OPTIMIZER 4: INCREASE YOUR FINANCIAL INTELLIGENCE

In the words of Robert Kiyosaki, more money seldom solves someone's money problems. Intelligence solves problems. There is a saying a friend of mine says over and over to people in debt: if you find you have dug yourself into a hole . . . stop digging.[10]

According to a recent "financial literacy survey" conducted by Roper ASW, "America isn't flunking financial literacy, but it's close. With a grade of 67 out of 100, Americans get a 'D' in the subject."[11] So what can we do to increase financial intelligence?

In addition to investing *money* in Quadrant II, invest some *time*. Read a book. Attend a seminar. Watch a PBS special on finance. Find out more about effective debt elimination, investments, money markets, annuities, CDs, and 401(k)s. Talk with people who are good at managing their money. Find ways to consciously invest in increasing your financial intelligence. If you're married, do it together. Learn together, talk together, improve together. Make it a date.

One of the great benefits of weekly financial meetings is that they also increase your financial intelligence. Week after week, as you account for, evaluate, and learn from your experience, you get better. You see where your money's going. You compare it to where you want it to go. You start moving out of Quadrants III and IV and investing in Quadrant II. You learn how to "set your standard of living lower than your level of income, even though many of your neighbors and friends set their standard of living at the limit of their credit-worthiness."[12] As you consistently pit performance against principle, you grow in financial intelligence and gradually reduce the distance between the two.

Your financial intelligence is part of your navigational intelligence. The more keenly you calibrate it, the better decisions you're going to make. Even when it's on automatic scan, as you go through the day it will help you avoid traps such as impulse buying, and to stay on your predetermined path of financial security and strength.

OPTIMIZER 5: BUILD MARGIN

Margin is space between resources and immediate needs. If you're living from paycheck to paycheck, you have no margin. If you have $1,000 in a savings account, you have a little margin. If you have six months' worth of income in a money market account, a good supply of canned foods in your basement, and retirement funds in place, you have a lot of margin.

In this day and age, we're beginning to understand more about the importance of margin. With economic uncertainties, downsizing, and layoffs, job security has become a serious concern. With the possibility of natural disasters or terrorist threats in a time when grocery stores are no longer supplied by neighborhood or small regional warehouses but by mega-warehouses typically long distances from the stores, the vulnerability of our food supplies has also become a concern.

To create margin can provide considerable comfort in these troubled times. And it brings other benefits as well. Money in the bank can be earning interest. Bulk-quantity shopping can save money. And margin can give you the freedom to do the important things you need to do.

Consider two fathers. The first puts "family" at the top of his list of priorities. A few years ago his teenage son was having problems, struggling with some important decisions in his life. If there was ever a time he needed guidance and help, this was it.

In his heart, this man knew he needed to spend some quality time with the boy. Because he had margin—not only in his financial affairs, but also in his relationships at work—he was able to arrange to get away for several days He packed up his Jeep, and he and his boy headed for the mountains. The setting was beautiful. They walked and fished and slept out under the stars. After a time, the boy began to talk, sharing his deep concerns with his dad. It was a time of close communication and bonding, of making deep inner connections and good decisions that would impact the rest of a young life. In the process, this man gained tremendous insight into the nature of the challenges his son was facing. He discovered things he could do and changes he could make to better help his boy.

If this man had not had the margin to adjust and meet this critical need in his son's life, those important decisions would have been made under very different circumstances and could well have taken a much different turn.

We contrast this father's situation to that of another father who also puts high priority on his family. He earnestly wants to be there for his children when they need him. But he's holding down two jobs to pay off his debts. He hardly sees his family. Taking time off from work to spend with his son would be out of the realm of possibility.

Your ability to create margin in your life generally has a huge impact on the degree of freedom you have to manage your time and seize opportunity. The more you free yourself from debt and high consumption, credit and impulse spending, and the more you build your resources—not only in terms of money, but also in terms of employability and high trust relationships—the greater freedom you will have to do what's really important—both now and in the future.

OPTIMIZER 6: DEVELOP AN EFFECTIVE FINANCIAL SYSTEM

In the previous chapter, "Time Matters," we discussed the importance of having quality, aligned personal leadership systems, including a system for finance. Such a system would ideally enable you to:

- Know what resources you have (e.g., money in the bank)

- Know what's committed (e.g., payments)

- Spend (e.g., write checks, make electronic payments)

- Track and evaluate spending (i.e., record receipts, summarize spending patterns)

- Plan (i.e., forecast, create budgets)

- Remind you of your purposes and goals

As we've said, you already have some kind of system currently in place that, to one degree or another, performs at least some of these functions. So look at your current system. How effective is it? Does it meet the above criteria? Does it help you set and achieve meaningful financial goals? Does it provide the information you need?

Consider this: Are you ever surprised by what's on your bank or credit card statement? If someone were to ask you right now how much you have in your checking account, what the outstanding balance is on your credit card(s), the amount of your monthly expenses, or what your net worth is . . . could you answer?

You might want to review your current system by using a checklist such as the following:

1. What are the components of your current finance system?

   ☐ A clear statement of financial strategy and goals

   ☐ An online or computer-based finance program

   ☐ A PDA

   ☐ A checkbook

   ☐ A bank card

   ☐ One or more savings accounts

☐ One or more checking accounts

☐ One or more credit card accounts

☐ Personal record-keeping help (e.g., assistant/secretary)

☐ Online banking

☐ Automatic bill pay

☐ An investment counselor

☐ Other (what?)

_____

_____

_____

2. How well does your current system meet your general needs?

☐ Is it effective? Does it help you do what's most important?

☐ Is it efficient? Does it do it in the best possible way?

☐ Is it simple? Is it streamlined, easy to work with, free of complicating "bells and whistles"?

☐ It is synchronous? Does it work in cooperation with your other tools and systems?

3. What are the distinguishing characteristics of the tools in your systems?

☐ Paper-based

☐ PC-based

☐ Handless

☐ Wireless

☐ Web-based

☐ Pen-based

Do these characteristics work well in your situation?

4. What are your specific needs?

_____

_____

_____

_____

_____

_____

How well does your system meet those needs?

5. What could you do to augment, improve, or replace elements of your current system to create greater alignment?

If you determine that your current system is not meeting your needs, explore the alternatives. In today's competitive market, financial institutions are investing a lot of time and money in creating user-friendly system components, including:

- Online banking

- Online bill pay

- Telephone access to account balances and transfers

- Credit card statement options, including categorization for business and other expenses

- Credit report access and monitoring

- Credit card aggregation, where all your accounts and transactions are listed in one place on the Web

There are even Web sites designed to educate consumers on the different options and compare product and service providers.[13]

If you decide to improve your financial system, the first step is to be clear about exactly what you want your system to do. Then contact your current financial institution. See what products and services they offer. Keep abreast of new changes and developments.

If you're not satisfied, check out the competition. Check the Internet. Identify options that could meet your needs. Then do a cost/benefit analysis. Ask yourself:

- Is this option *more* effective? Will it help me do what's most important *better* than my current system?

- Is it *more* efficient? Will it help me do what's most important in a way that is *better* than my current system?)

- Is it *more* simple? Is it *more* streamlined, easier to work with, freer of complicating "bells and whistles"?

- Is it *more* synchronous? Does it work *better* in cooperation with and *better* help facilitate my other systems?)

- Does it *better* meet specific needs? Which needs? And how important are those needs?

Considering these questions will help you determine which options will work for you.

ROGER

We keep most of our financial records on Rebecca's desktop computer. We're currently using a computer software program to track and plan, and an online program to pay our bills. We also use separate credit cards for home and business expenses, which we pay off monthly to avoid interest.

When I'm not at home, I can access our records through the Internet. With my Tablet Planner or Pocket PC, I can check balances, record expenses, and transfer funds.

This system allows us to coordinate our spending and fulfill our roles wherever we are.

As we consider financial systems, we sometimes think it might be a lot easier if we could all just do all our business in cash, or even barter: "You give me so much of your product, I'll give you so much of mine, and we'll both be happy."

But the reality is that we live in a high-tech financial world, and computers are fast becoming the almost exclusive mode of financial transaction. In fact, at a recent seminar in Stockholm, Sweden, when the word "checks" came up, participants laughed. They said, "We don't even use checks anymore!"

So we encourage you to give serious thought to your financial system. Evaluate it. Investigate options. Make sure you have the system that will work best for you.

This is a high leverage Quadrant II activity. As you do it, you will not only enhance your own financial management effectiveness, but also expand your awareness and increase your ability to navigate in systems at work and in other interdependent situations.

NAVIGATION

Some people might think it's hard to spend time in Quadrant II on money matters doing things such as creating shared vision, having weekly meetings, or increasing your financial intelligence. But the reality is, if you don't spend it in Quadrant II now, you'll definitely spend it in other quadrants later—working longer hours, paying more bills, and handling financial crises.

As you make and live with your money decisions day by day—particularly if you're having your weekly meetings—you're learning and becoming more effective as you go. You're discovering principles that empower you to make effective decisions with both your money and your time—principles such as:

- Importance

- Investment

- Margin

- Alignment

- Leverage

- Choice

- Trust

- Deferred gratification

- Integrity

- Discipline

- Synchronization

- Accountability

- Simplicity

As you interact with these principles and consciously use them to calibrate your navigational intelligence, you become better at dealing with money matters. You also discover that as much as *deciding* what's most important, successful navigation is *remembering* what's most important. And the optimizers we examined earlier can help.

As you track your spending, create and regularly review a vision of your goals, and plan and evaluate weekly, you develop the navigational intelligence to avoid major money traps such as reacting unwisely to the "urgency" pressure of advertising, or becoming impatient to get what you want *now*. You create *context* for your decisions. You develop *character* to defer gratification and to act with integrity in decision moments. The strength of what you *are* doing overpowers what you should *not* be doing and creates that deeper "Yes!" that empowers you to say "No!" to the less important.

Also, as you develop the Quadrant II paradigm and habits of managing money, it actually strengthens your ability to handle your time. Once you catch the vision of Quadrant II, you realize that each decision you make to invest instead of consume in one area strengthens your ability to do so in both.

Best of all, investing in Quadrant II enables you to create a legacy of *importance* and *investment* that will bless your children's lives for generations. Can you honestly imagine a greater inheritance you could give your posterity than a 24/7 example of a lifestyle based on the principles and values that lead to balance and peace?

TRUE WEALTH

The greatest value of Quadrant II as it applies to both money and time is in the wealth it generates—not just in terms of financial security and growth, but also in terms of inner wealth and fulfillment.

Each time you act in ways that demonstrate that your commitment to your goals, your future, your spouse, and yourself is stronger than your moods or whatever is pushing you at the moment, you make deposits in your own "Personal Integrity Account."[14] This is your most important "trust" account. It reflects the amount of trust you have in your relationship with yourself. The higher the balance, the greater your reservoir of personal strength and the greater your ability to do what matters most on a regular basis.

In addition, the more you act with integrity to the value you place on your family, the more you build the "family trust," or the "Emotional Bank Accounts,"[15] you have with the members of your family. As we observed before, time and money are the language of value. Where we spend our time and money—and how we make time/money decisions—communicate what's important to us. That's why time/money issues and decisions are often so frustrating and emotionally charged.

In a marriage, they become symbolic of the importance we place on shared vision, unity and communication, on our spouses' needs and desires, on the true degree of equality and partnership in the marriage, and on our own integrity and trustworthiness in making commitments and following through. In the family, they become symbolic of the relationship between parents and children and the value given to children's needs, desires, and input. That's why the way we deal with time/money issues on a day-in and day-out basis has such a significant impact on the quality of marriage and family life. It tends to either build or destroy the most important "family trust" in which we can invest.

CHAPTER

7

WISDOM MATTERS

Don't squat with your spurs on.
Never kick a cow chip on a hot day.
Never slap a man who's chewing tobacco.

A Cowboy's Guide to Life

We've taken an in-depth look now at work, family, time, and money. In each of these areas, we've looked at ways to validate expectations, optimize efforts, and navigate effectively. We've also opened some doors to create synergy between the four—to make work and home complementary instead of competitive, and to see time and money in ways that empower us to invest both in what truly matters most.

Now we'll take a step back and look at all these life elements as one, synergistic whole. We need to examine how all four elements interrelate and create the integrated life balance questions—both large and small—that we face every day . . . questions such as:

- Do I work late on this project, or do I quit now and go home?

- Do I stay with my current job, or do I take time out to get an advanced degree that will increase my earning capacity in the future?

225

- With 20 things on my task list today that all feel like A-1 priorities, which should I work on first?

- Should I take a second job and try to get out of debt, even though it means more time away from the family?

- Do I stay at home with my new baby or go back to work?

- Which is more important: spending more time with my family or getting involved in a community service project that would make a difference to others?

- Should we move to a newer home that would better meet our family's needs or stay where we are and keep the payments down?

- Should we stretch our resources to pay for nursing home care for my parents or try to figure out a way to take them into our home?

- Should I invest in private school education for my children, or should I send them to public school?

- Do I keep working on this deadline-driven project or take time to exercise?

These are the kinds of life questions that come at us day in and day out. And they will never be resolved with "balance the scale" or "run between the bases fast enough to touch them all" approaches to life. Believing they will can only create frustration.

As we've said, balance is a dynamic equilibrium in which work, family, time, and money are all essential parts. And the discomfort that often masquerades as "imbalance" is usually not created by a lack of mechanical "balance" at all; it is created by lack of alignment with principles and with what our navigational intelligence tells us is "wise."

There are times in our lives when seasonal imbalance is absolutely vital to overall life balance. There are times when the best decision in one situation is not right in another. So how do we know what's right? What empowers us to access and to act on the best answers? What enables us to create this dynamic equilibrium every day?

The answer, we suggest, is *wisdom*.

WHAT IS WISDOM?

Basically, wisdom is navigational intelligence. It's the capacity we've worked to build in each of the chapters in this book. It's the ability to make the choices that create the positive consequences we want to have in our lives.

Think about the excerpts from *A Cowboy's Guide to Life* at the beginning of this chapter. What would happen if you *did* squat with your spurs on . . . or kick a cow chip on a hot day . . . or slap a man who's chewing tobacco? You probably wouldn't like the results. So you avoid doing the things that bring those negative results. That's wisdom.

On the other hand, what would happen if you decided to go to college instead of skateboarding your way through life . . . or put 10 percent of your income into a savings account every month . . . or invest time and effort in creating a great marriage or raising good kids? You'd probably like those results . . . particularly over time. You'd be making decisions that bring positive results. That's wisdom.

Something or someone who is "wise" is "characterized by wisdom; marked by deep understanding, keen discernment, and a capacity for sound judgment." Synonyms include sage, sapient, judicious, prudent, and sensible. Can you imagine a better characteristic to have as you try to make the daily decisions that will create satisfaction, life balance, and peace?

To one degree or another, we're all aware of wisdom. It's reflected in the way we speak:

- "It's not smart to 'burn the candle at both ends.'"

- "Those people are really wise with their money."

- "It's dumb to spend too much time on the Web."

- "It would be foolish to buy that on credit—with interest, we'd end up paying for it twice."

- "They're a nice young couple, but they spend their money as fast as they get it. That doesn't seem very smart."

- "I didn't say anything at the time; it wouldn't have been wise."

As we suggested in Chapter 2, the more we learn to value principles, evaluate experience and invite inspiration, the stronger our navigational intelligence, or "wisdom," will be.

Having considered how to best navigate in each of the four areas—work, family, time, and money independently—let's now revisit the three wisdom builders we identified in Chapter 2 and consider some high leverage ways to increase your navigational intelligence in life as a whole.

1. VALUE PRINCIPLES

Once you truly understand that success, happiness, and life balance come from living in harmony with timeless principles—and you determine that you want those things—you can decide to make the search for principles a life quest. You can seek to discover the wisdom of the ages and apply it to the challenges of today.

Consciously making the decision to seek and live by wisdom puts you on the path. It gives you the openness that comes with being a seeker of wisdom and truth. Faced in the direction of wisdom, then, there are several things you can do to move along the path.

As we mentioned in Chapter 2, one of the most high leverage things you can do is make a daily commitment to study the "wisdom literature" created by poets, philosophers, leaders and other wise men and women involved in this quest throughout the ages. This will center you and put you in tune with wisdom. It will increase the quality of your decision making throughout the day.

What we're suggesting is that you spend a few minutes every day with some of the best books, stories, thoughts and ideas from around the globe and throughout time. But don't just read them; engage with them. Ponder over them. Look beyond the ideas themselves and into the values they reflect. Consider how you might apply them in your own life. Begin to collect and focus on passages or thoughts that are particularly meaningful to you.

We encourage you to take a few minutes now and read the "wisdom literature" excerpts on the following pages. Ask yourself: "If I were to spend even a few minutes each morning interacting with such ideas, what kind of difference would it make in the quality of my decisions throughout the day?"

THOUGHTS FROM WISDOM LITERATURE

*There are more things to do than we ever shall get done;
there are more books to read than we ever can look at;
there are more avenues to enjoyment than we ever shall
find time to travel. Life appeals to us from innumerable
directions, crying, "Attend to me here!" In consequence,
we litter up our lives with indiscriminate preoccupation.
We let first come be first served, forgetting that the finest
things do not crowd. We let the loudest voices fill our
ears, forgetting that asses bray, but gentlemen speak low.
Multitudes of people are living not bad but frittered
lives—split, scattered, uncoordinated. They are like
pictures into which a would-be artist has put, in messy
disarray, everything that he has chanced to see; like
music into which has been hurled, helter-skelter, every
vagrant melody that strayed into the composer's mind.
Preoccupation is the most common form of failure.*

—Harry Emerson Fosdick[1]

*Besides the noble art of getting things done, there is the
noble art of leaving things undone. The wisdom of life
consists in the elimination of nonessentials.*

—Lin Yutang

*The consumption society has made us feel that happiness
lies in having things, and has failed to teach us the happiness of not having things.*

—Elise Boulding

*One going to take a pointed stick to pinch a baby bird
should first try it on himself to feel how it hurts.*

—Yoruba Proverb (Nigeria)

Continued

Thou shalt love thy neighbor as thyself.
—The Holy Bible

Tsekung asked, "Is there one word that can serve as a principle of conduct for life? Confucius replied, "It is the word shu—*reciprocity: Do not do to others what you do not want them to do to you."*
— The Analects of
Confucius 15.23

Into the hands of every individual is given a marvelous power for good or evil—the silent, unconscious, unseen influence of his life. This is simply the constant radiation of what man really is, not what he pretends to be.
—William George Jordan

Parents can only give good advice or put children on the right paths. The final forming of a person's character lies in their own hands.
—Anne Frank

The world is not a playground; it is a schoolroom. Life is not a holiday, but an education. And the one eternal lesson for us all is how better we can love. What makes a man a good cricketer? Practice. What makes a man a good artist, a good sculptor, a good musician? Practice. What makes a man a good linguist, a good stenographer? Practice. What makes a man a good man? Practice. Nothing else ... We do not get the soul in different ways, under different laws, from those in which we get the body and the mind. If a man does not exercise his arm he develops no biceps muscle; and if a man does not exercise his soul, he requires no muscle in his soul, no strength of character, no vigor of moral fibre, nor beauty of spiritual growth. Love is not a thing of enthusiastic

Continued

emotion. It is a rich, strong, manly, vigorous expression of the whole round ... character ... in its fullest development. And the constituents of this great character are only to be built up by ceaseless practice.

—Henry Drummond[2]

We who lived in concentration camps can remember the men who walked through the huts comforting others, giving away their last piece of bread. They may have been few in number, but they offer sufficient proof that everything can be taken from a man but one thing: the last of the human freedoms—to choose one's attitude in any given set of circumstances, to choose one's own way.

—Viktor Frankl[3]

If you love others, but they do not love you in return, reexamine your own love. If you would bring peace and order to men, but disorder ensure, reexamine your own wisdom. If you are ceremonious with others and they do not return it, reexamine your own reverence. If your deeds are unsuccessful, seek for the reason in yourself. When your own person is correct, the whole world will turn to you.

—Mencius[4]

A lot of people learned during the war how scarcity can sharpen perceptions and heighten enthusiasm. Once, flying home from blacked-out Britain, my plane landed briefly in Iceland, and somebody handed me an orange. I hadn't seen an orange for over a year, much less tasted one; but for a long time I couldn't bring myself to eat it. As we roared on to Greenland over the steel-gray sea, I sat there and stroked that orange and smelled it and held it up to the light to admire its color. In the end, I did eat

Continued

it. It was sensational; I've never had an orange like that one since. I really loved that orange, and perhaps because I loved it I learned something from it.

I learned that sometimes, when you're feeling jaded or blasé, you can revive your sense of wonder by saying to yourself: suppose this were the only time. Suppose this sunset, this moonrise, this symphony, this buttered toast, this sleeping child, this flag against the sky . . . suppose you would never experience these things again . . .
　　　　　　　　　　　　　—Arthur Gordon[5]

To be elated at success and disappointed at failure is to be the child of circumstances; how can such a one be called master of himself?
　　　　　　　　　　　　　—Chinese Proverb

Your pain is the breaking of the shell that encloses your understanding.
　　　　　　　　　　　　　—Kahlil Gibran

I do not believe that sheer suffering teaches. If suffering alone taught, all the world would be wise, since everyone suffers. To suffering must be added mourning, under-standing, patience, love, openness and the willingness to remain vulnerable.
　　　　　　　　　　　　　—Anne Morrow Lindbergh

A blind man, being stopped in a bad piece of road, meets with a lame man, and entreats him to guide him through the difficulty he got into. How can I do that, replied the lame man, since I am scarce able to drag myself along? But as you appear to be very strong, if you will carry me, we will seek our fortunes together. It will then be my

Continued

*interest to warn you of anything that may obstruct your
way; your feet shall be my feet, and my eyes yours. With
all my heart, returned the blind man; let us render each
other our mutual services. So taking his lame companion
on his back, they by means of their union traveled on
with safety and pleasure.*

—Aesop[6]

*Observe how all God's creations borrow from each
other: day borrows from night and night from day, but
they do not go to law one with another as mortals do . . .
The moon borrows from the stars and the stars from the
moon . . . the sky borrows from the earth and the earth
from the sky . . . All God's creatures borrow from the
other, yet make peace with one another without lawsuits;
but if man borrows from his friend, he seeks to swallow
him up with usury and robbery.*

—Midrash, Exodus Rabbah 31.15

*What I like about experience is that it is such an honest
thing. You may take any number of wrong turnings, but
keep your eyes open and you will not be allowed to go
very far before the warning signs appear. You may have
deceived yourself, but experience is not trying to deceive
you. The universe rings true wherever you fairly test it.*

—C. S. Lewis[7]

*It is a trite saying that one half the world knows not how
the other half lives. Who can say what sores might be
healed, what hurts solved, were the doings of each half of
the world's inhabitants understood and appreciated by
the other?*

—Gandhi

Continued

*What a man dislikes in those above him, he must not
bring to bear on those beneath him. What he dislikes in
those beneath him, he must not bring to the service of
those above him. The treatment which he dislikes from
his neighbours on the right, he must not give to those
on the left. The treatment which he dislikes from his
neighbours on the left, he must not give to those on
the right. This is what is meant by the Way of the
Measuring Square.*

—The Great Learning, x, 2
(Chinese)

*The diameter of each day is measured by the stretch of
thought—not by the rising and setting of the sun.*
—Henry Ward Beecher

*I don't know who, or what, put the question. I don't
know when it was put. I don't even remember answering.
But at some moment I did answer "Yes" to someone or
something. And from that hour I was certain that existence is meaningful and that, therefore, my life, in self-
surrender, had a goal.*

—Dag Hammarskjöld

*If I had only . . .
forgotten future greatness
and looked at the green things and the buildings
and reached out to those around me
and smelled the air
and ignored the forms and the self-styled obligations
and heard the rain on the roof
and put my arms around my wife
. . . and it's not too late!*

—Hugh Prather[8]

Continued

Most people measure their happiness in terms of physical pleasure and material possession. Could they win some visible goal which they have set on the horizon, how happy they would be! Lacking this gift or that circumstance, they would be miserable.

If happiness is to be so measured, I who cannot hear or see have every reason to sit in a corner with folded hands and weep. If I am happy in spite of my deprivations, if my happiness is so deep that it is a faith, so thoughtful that it becomes a philosophy of life—if, in short, I am an optimist, my testimony to the creed of optimism is worth hearing.

—Helen Keller

The human soul is like a mountain reservoir. Quietly and slowly, away from the multitude, it fills and renews itself with strength, purpose, faith, courage, energy, speed, initiative. Then it pours down through the world and moves the mills of trade like a Niagara!

—Edward Earle Purinton

We think in secret; it comes to pass.
Environment is but our looking-glass.

—James Allen

Now stop and consider: How do you feel after reading these timeless thoughts and reflections? A little stronger? A little more "together"? Think about it: If you were to read and digest material such as this for a few minutes every morning, would it improve the quality of your decision making throughout the day?

We believe it would. After sharing this experience with people in seminars around the globe, we've seen how it can significantly reduce levels of stress. People feel "calmer," "more peaceful," "more connected." They often make comments such as:

- "I can't believe how long it's been since I read something like this."
- "I can't believe the difference I felt."
- "I feel reminded of what's really important in life."

Reading wisdom literature is a high leverage Quadrant II activity. It has great benefits. And it doesn't take that much time. In fact, it's like spending a few minutes at the gas pump—it gives you the fuel you need to travel effectively another 300 miles down the road.

REBECCA

One of the most treasured practices of my life is the daily study of wisdom literature—most often, the sacred literature of my own faith. Each time the circumstances in my life have changed— another baby, another writing project, another move—I've had to fight to create sufficient order in my life to allow it. But it has been one of my greatest sources of peace. It's empowered me to be more patient, more kind, more loving, more focused, more capable in handling the challenges of the day.

I remember one morning when I had an important project that had to be done by 8:00 a.m. As I walked into my study at 6:00, I looked at the project on my computer desk and then at my reading for the day on my writing desk. I was sorely tempted to dispense with the reading and get right into the project. But deep inside, I felt I really needed to put my reading first. So I did. I spent about 20 minutes "centering" for the day, then I attacked the project with gusto. I forced myself to work quickly and I didn't even look at the clock until I was nearly through. When I did look, I couldn't believe it! It was only 7:30! What had seemed like a good two or three hours of work had been done in one hour and ten minutes.

ROGER

Due to the travel that comes with my work, I spend many hours driving in cars and flying in planes. Over the years, I've learned to use this time to listen to some of the many classic and inspirational works that are available on cassette tape and CD. This enables me to transform what would otherwise be less useful time into a quality investment in learning. In addition, I find there's a different flow, an added perspective, that comes from listening instead of reading. I've been amazed at the influence these things have had on my thinking over time.

Taking even a few minutes a day to expose our minds and hearts to the great thoughts of civilizations throughout time gives powerful perspective to the challenges of the day. To find wisdom literature, you can check your local library, bookstores, or the Internet for titles that represent the best thinking over the centuries. We've included a concise bibliography for further study.

2. EVALUATE EXPERIENCE

Because our search for wisdom must be conducted in an "information age," it's important to distinguish between information, knowledge, and wisdom.

Information is essentially organized data. It's important, but no amount of information by itself will create knowledge. To move from information to knowledge requires *experience.*

ROGER

I have a business degree with a triple minor in statistics, economics, and accounting. In working toward that degree, I took several courses on financial management. In other words, I had a lot of information *about money and some experience in the business world.*

But I must admit, our "financial adventures" of the last few years have taught me more about money than I ever learned in the classroom or the business world. It seems I had to experience *some of the challenges on a deep personal level before I really understood—even though I didn't gain much information I didn't already know.*

Of course, we don't have to experience everything in life to know there are paths we should avoid. And the more we learn to observe choice and consequence in our own lives as well as in the lives of others, the better we can identify paths that are productive or destructive.

But it is experience—good and bad—that gives us knowledge to make good choices. It might be our experience with the pain of sickness or the "high" that comes from exercise that causes us to value health. It might be our experience with the grief of difficult relationships or the joy of strong ones that causes us to value relationships of high trust. It might be our experience with the anguish of debt or the satisfaction of accruing interest that causes us to value financial intelligence. In each case, it's experience that helps us to know which path is best.

So how do we gain the most from experience? As we pointed out in Chapter 2, life is a process of learning, growing and course-correcting. To expect that we will *not* need to course-correct only leads to frustration. To make the same mistakes over and over also leads to frustration and creates enormous waste of energy and time. Instead of moving ahead, we're simply spinning our wheels.

Thus, we need to process our experience. We need to ponder over it, reflect on it, and gain insight and understanding from our encounters with the affairs—large and small—of everyday life. Our ability to live with awareness and to evaluate and learn from our experience is one of the best ways we move toward wisdom and engage the gears that get us moving most effectively ahead.

Three "to do's" we've found especially helpful in this area are:

1. Keep a personal learning journal

2. Learn from the experience of others

3. Share experience with others

KEEP A PERSONAL LEARNING JOURNAL

One powerful way we've found to process experience is by keeping a personal learning journal. Aside from the therapeutic, documentation, and other values in keeping such a record, there is profound wisdom that comes from capturing your insights and thoughtfully processing the experiences of everyday living. As you do this, you become actively involved in observing and processing your own experience. You become much more aware of your navigational intelligence. You begin to notice the consequences that come when you follow it and when you don't. And you can use that awareness, even in the midst of challenge, to recognize and seize wisdom-building capacity.

REBECCA

I remember one particular time when I was feeling a little burned out and unclear on my goals. Roger arranged to spend a few days with the children so that I could have a few days of personal time. I went to a nearby inn, where I enjoyed resting and relaxing, and that was very helpful. But what helped me the most is the fact that I took my journal with me and reviewed the past year. As I looked at my life from a larger perspective, I was able to see patterns that were not visible day-to-day. Experiences and insights began fitting together in ways I hadn't even imagined. As a result, I was able to get a clear sense of what I needed to do, and I returned home energized and refreshed.

Journaling can take as little as five minutes a day, or it can be done on a weekly basis instead. It can be done on paper or electronically.

Advantages of a handwritten journal include portability and unlimited access—during a power outage, for instance—as well as a healthy slowing of thought processes, blood pressure, and heart rate. In addition, it constitutes a more personalized legacy for children or grandchildren who may someday read it.

Advantages of an electronic journal include quick entry, easy correction and editing, fast electronic or hard-copy backup to ensure against loss, and the ability to perform a word search when you want to look something up.

But however you do it, we encourage you to do it, and to periodically review what you've written to widen your perspective.

LEARN FROM THE EXPERIENCE OF OTHERS

In addition to learning from our own experience, we can also learn from the experiences of others. We can enjoy biographies and quality films, plays and documentaries—anything that puts us in touch with real human experience that shows *real* consequences. Although the popular media presents abundant "life images," we know deep inside that many of these images don't represent what's "real." As a result, they create illusions and unreal expectations that can lead to frustration. Thus, it is "wise" to seriously examine media-created expectations instead of simply absorbing them unaware.

Another valuable source of wisdom and influence is people who are living in the world today. Many religious, political, business, educational, and humanitarian leaders are people of talent, experience, and inspiration who have something worthwhile to say. We can learn from their lives, their choices, their perspectives. Your navigational intelligence can help you bypass charismatic personalities or popular philosophies that are not principle-centered. Test what people say and do against the common themes written in the wisdom literature throughout time.

Also, we can learn to more carefully observe and value the example of choice and consequence in the lives of the people around us. A great advantage of this source—particularly when we learn from family members, friends, or neighbors who are willing to share openly—is that we are invited into the hearts and minds of others, so the learning goes well beyond behavior and into motive and meaning. One of the great benefits of rich relationships is shared learning.

SHARE EXPERIENCE WITH OTHERS

This leads us to another wisdom path: sharing what we have learned with others. As you consider this path, we suggest you try the following experiment:

Stop for a minute and think about one person who has significantly influenced your life. Who is this person? What was it that enabled him or her to influence you in such a powerful way? Before you read further, take a moment and reflect on the influence that person has had on your life.

If your experience is like many, you've probably identified someone:

1. Who has strength of character
2. With whom you've had some kind of personal connection
3. Who had valuable wisdom to share

Maybe it was a parent or a grandparent. Maybe it was a teacher or a coach. Maybe it was a friend who believed in you when nobody else did. Whoever it was, this person made a difference in your life— most likely through his or her example and willingness to share.

The point is that *you* are a parent, a grandparent, a teacher, a coach, or a friend to someone else. And your example and sharing could make a profound difference in the quality of that someone else's life. Of course, you never want to share in a way that's perceived as being nosy or giving unsolicited or unwelcome advice. But if you're focused on genuinely contributing to the well-being of others and you're sensitive to "teaching moments," you can invest in others in ways that will bring great returns—in their lives and also in your own.

By sharing in this way, you align your life with the principle of contribution. In addition, you open a dialogue that creates a bridge between your own experiences with principles and the experiences of others. As you interact back and forth across that bridge, you create a larger, shared vision, and understanding for both is increased.

This is one reason why marriage provides an incomparable opportunity for learning and growth. When two people with different backgrounds, experiences, and perspectives come together in an intimate, loving, caring relationship, life learning is significantly enhanced as they interact and share experience and insight with each other on important issues of life. They can become wiser together than they could ever be alone.

3. INVITE INSPIRATION

In addition to valuing principles and evaluating experience, there is one more important way we suggest to increase your wisdom, and that is to "invite inspiration."

Historically, there are two general approaches to wisdom. One suggests that wisdom is the pinnacle to which you ascend through knowledge, experience, and maturity. The other agrees that such ascension is vital, but adds that real wisdom is achieved through a higher source, a divine intervention. In this latter case, wisdom is seen as a gift.

In the first approach, the gate to the path of wisdom is *wonder*—curiosity, excited amazed admiration. In the second, the gate is *humility*—being open to guidance from a higher, more all-knowing, source.

However you may see the source of inspiration in your own life, the fact remains that we all experience flashes of insight that are definitely beyond our experience. And the degree to which we pay attention to these insights makes a profound difference in the direction and quality of our lives.

In the wisdom literature, this kind of personal inspiration is often connected with the word *conscience*. Classically, conscience is attributed with the ability to help us discern principles and the degree to which we are living in accordance with them. But it is also attributed with the ability to provide specific, personal life direction. And the observation has been made that the more heed and diligence we give to what we perceive through inspired experience, the more active it becomes.

> *Every human being has a work to do, duties to perform, influence to exert, which are peculiarly his, and which no conscience but his own can teach.*
> —William Ellery Channing

> *There are moments in your life when you must act, even though you cannot carry your best friends with you. The "still small voice" within you must always be the final arbiter when there is a conflict of duty.*
> —Mahatma Gandhi

> *Clear conscience never fears midnight knocking.*
> —Chinese Proverb

*Nothing is more powerful than an individual acting out
of his conscience, thus helping to bring the collective conscience to life.*

—Norman Cousins

*I feel within me
A peace above all earthly dignities
A still and quiet conscience.*

—William Shakespeare

*The voice of conscience is so delicate that it is easy to
stifle it; but it is also so clear that it is impossible to
mistake it.*

—Madame Anne Louise
Germaine de Stael

*Labor to keep alive in your breast that little spark of
celestial fire, called conscience.*

—George Washington

The existence of this "inner voice" of conscience is one of the
most validated truths in all of wisdom literature. As we nurture and
engage it in our decision making, we access a powerful wisdom far
beyond our own.

One way to grow in our ability to receive and effectively use
inspiration is to record it in our personal learning journal. As
we record it, review it, act on it, and evaluate the results, we become more aware of the role and the great benefit of inspiration in
our lives.

THE POWER OF SOLITUDE

In our search for wisdom, we need to recognize the value
of solitude. In fact, one of the things that valuing principles, evaluating experience, and inviting inspiration all have in common
is that they are enhanced by times of solitude. It is often in

quiet, uninterrupted times alone that we can most effectively increase our connection to timeless truths, awareness, and inspiration.

In today's fast-paced world, it's a challenge to take time to stop and think deeply about our lives. But as Plato once said, "The unexamined life is not worth living." That's a strong statement! But think about it: When we're operating out of inaccurate or incomplete paradigms, running around doing things that are not aligned or high leverage, and making the same mistakes again and again—how much satisfaction are we going to get out of life? How balanced and peaceful are we going to feel?

In the Middle East, Bedouin families often send their children out with their herds for extended periods of time as part of their basic education. They consider quiet times of solitude and meditation to be critical to a child's development. Certainly, we don't want to get caught in the trap of "analysis paralysis," spending so much time in introspection that we never get anything done. But, for the most part in our society, we're in far more danger of never spending any truly introspective time at all.

REBECCA

One of the things I've really appreciated about Roger over the years is the way he has provided personal retreat time for me— time when I could just get away from everything and reconnect with myself. About once a year, he's arranged to be at home with the children for a few days so I could be alone. I think this time has been important for him as well as for me. It's given him the opportunity to interact with the children and build relationships, and in the earlier days of our marriage, it gave him a better perspective of the challenges I faced as a full-time homemaker and parent.

As philosopher and mathematician Blaise Pascal observed: "All of our ills stem from our inability to sit quietly in a room." When we do take time to mediate and ponder over our lives, we open the door to enriched perspective and wisdom.

CHARACTER IS THE KEY

Earlier in this chapter we observed that the difference between information and knowledge is *experience.* The difference between knowledge and wisdom, then, is *character.* It's not only *knowing* the things that bring positive results or even *knowing how* to do them; it's also *doing* them—for the right reasons, at the right time, and in the right way.

According to a recent survey conducted by bankrate.com, "When it comes to personal finances, most people generally know what they should do, but a lot of them don't do it . . . Like an overweight person who perpetually vows to start dieting next week, the typical American plans to whip those finances into shape, *just as soon as there is time.*"[9] (Emphasis added.)

Yet, the average American watches over four hours of television a day.

Probably we all *know* more than we *do* in almost every area of life. So what's the solution? It's character. It's having the moral or ethical strength to subordinate our immediate desires to our longer term values and commitments and to do what will bring the positive results we want—even if we are tempted to procrastinate or be distracted by paths that appear to be easier or more pleasant in the short run. It's having the integrity to be true to the best within.

And how do you develop character? You seek it. You grow it. You exercise it in the decisions you make every day. Every time you choose to spend time on what's important instead of what's merely urgent, every time you decide to invest instead of merely consume, every time you decide to avoid a time trap, get out of a financial "black hole," or contribute at work or at home, you're building character strength. Character is forged in the crucible of daily living.

That's why living with awareness and processing our own experience are so vital. You can learn about principles. You can read about the experience of others. But the place you really develop navigational intelligence is on the water. That's where cognitive learning becomes experiential. That's where experiential learning—properly processed—becomes wisdom. It is as you confront the challenges of daily living with awareness that you learn to set your compass and your course based on "true north."

LIFE MATTERS

As we navigate our way through life, it becomes apparent that we all have strengths in some areas and weaknesses in others. We may be great at managing our money but poor at managing our time. We may be effective at work, but not very good at home.

And that's okay. That's "realistic." That's where we are.

But we need to also understand what's "real." We need to recognize that work matters, family matters, time matters, and money matters . . . and in order to create life balance, we need to invest in developing at least a basic level of competence and wisdom in all four.

We also need to remember that life itself matters. As Emily cried out in *Our Town*: "Do any human beings ever realize life while they live it? Every, every minute?"

Almost universally, the answer to that question is: "No." Most of the time we don't realize how short life is and how foolish we are to waste time, live with grudges, close our hearts to others, and refuse to forgive. We don't realize how precious each moment of life is and how much good each of us can do.

There are times when we look at the Helen Kellers, the Mother Teresas, the Mahatma Gandhis, and the Nelson Mandelas of this world and realize that one life can make a difference. But if we are wise, we discover that often we don't have to look any further than our own backyard.

Rebecca

About a year ago, my father—who had just turned 80—passed away. As I prepared to speak at his funeral, I had some wonderful moments thinking about his life.

My dad was not famous in a popular, public sense. But he was a successful man. More importantly, he was a good man. Many times, after a full day's work, he would drive Mom and me to hospitals, prisons, USO dances, and other places where we put on variety shows that brought laughter and enjoyment to people who had significant struggles in their lives.

One day toward the end of Dad's life, when he was very ill, I sat by his bedside and together we began counting the neighbors he'd helped by tilling gardens and doing other such projects. As we mentally went down the street in both directions, there was hardly a home where he hadn't helped somebody. As I thought about all the friends and neighbors he'd helped, all the people whose lives were better because of his work, and the influence he'd had in the lives of three generations of family, I realized that you don't have to be a Mahatma Gandhi or a Mother Teresa to make a difference in this world. All you have to do is act within your circle of influence—no matter how large or small—and do and be the best you can. And that will make a difference!

Each life matters. Your life matters. Our lives matter. And it is often in the quiet daily doing that they matter most.

In our busy, entertainment- and media-saturated world, it's easy to get so focused on *events* that we forget that the real joys and contributions in life are in day-to-day living. But the truth is, while events are like punctuation in writing—and great events may even be the exclamation points—the meaning is not in the punctuation. It is the crucible of day-to-day life that renders knowledge, experience, and wisdom. And most often it is in the crucible of day-to-day living that our greatest contributions—often unknowingly—are made.

As we've said before, it's a process of becoming. We're going to make mistakes. The key is to keep living, keep loving, keep trying.

ROGER
When our three oldest sons were young, I spent a great deal of time taking them camping and fishing. We were good buddies and our relationships were a source of joy to us all.

But as these boys got older, we went through a period of time when I was very busy at work. One day, I discovered that my old-

est son—then a senior in high school—was beginning to get testy about several things, including curfews and being home on time. "What's the matter?" he'd demand. "Don't you trust me?" Frequently, he would come home late.

Behind the words and the actions, I could sense that our relationship was beginning to weaken. I realized that I had unintentionally allowed my life to get out of balance, and I hadn't been spending the time I needed to spend with him. I felt that what I really needed to do was take him camping.

I went to great lengths to rearrange my schedule to create the time. But when I approached him, expecting the same excited "Camping? Great!" response I'd gotten when he was 13 or 14, I was disappointed when instead he hemmed and hawed about parties and girls and basically didn't want to go.

So I laid a guilt trip on him. I told him I had created this time for him at great sacrifice and reminded him of all his mother and I had done for him throughout his life (Parenting Mistake 2a). He still didn't want to go. Finally, I resorted to parental authority. "We're going. Get your bag packed." Resigned, he finally complied.

As we headed out, he apparently decided to test me. He asked if he could turn on the radio—to his station preference. I gritted my teeth as the loud, obnoxious music filled the air. But after a few minutes he reached over and switched to a quieter, more pleasant sound. I guessed I'd passed the test. "Wasn't that awful?" he said with a grin.

A few minutes later I decided to pull out my new "wounded rabbit" call. (In attempting to come up with an activity for us to do, I'd talked with a friend who assured me that hunting coyotes would be an exciting and environmentally positive thing to do ... and that this "wounded rabbit" call was the very thing to entice them out into the open.) So I blew on the call. Before long the horrible, mournful sound had us both choked up, so I put it away.

When we arrived at the place to set up camp, we decided it was too late to hunt coyotes, so we went for steaks grilled on an open

fire. After dinner we started making "stick bread"—our tradition-
al family camping treat. (It's made by sticking a wad of biscuit
dough on the end of a stick—about two inches in diameter and
carved clean at the end—and cooking it slowly over low burning
coals. The end product is a biscuit shaped like a cup, which you
can then fill with butter and honey or jam.)

The great thing about stick bread is that it takes a long time to
make, so it gives you a lot of time to talk. So we did. Huddled by
the campfire, with the Milky Way overhead and miles from any
electrical lights, we talked. And before long he began to open up.
To my surprise, I discovered that he had been "going" with a girl
for months, and it appeared that everybody knew about it except
me. One of the reasons he hadn't said anything to me was because
he knew I disapproved of "going steady." Evidently, this girl had
started talking about getting a lot more serious than he wanted to,
and he'd broken up with her just the night before.

I felt terrible. Here was my son, going through a major event
in his life, and I didn't have a clue. As we continued to talk, he
began to share other deep concerns about his future—about grad-
uating, going to college, and facing some of the responsibilities
of adult life. We talked long into the night before finally going
to sleep.

In the morning when we got up, we decided it was too late to
go after coyotes, so I packed up my "wounded rabbit" call and we
cooked up some bacon and eggs. I guess we never were any real
threat to the coyote population—which is fine with me, as I much
prefer to do my "shooting" with a camera. After breakfast we
hiked, did some target practice and enjoyed just "hanging out"
together. Eventually, we made our way, happily, companionably,
toward home.

As meaningful as that time with my son turned out to be,
the real payoff came a few weeks later. Some of the senior boys
were getting together for a night of fun—a dance, games, movies,
and bowling—and our son wanted to go. I didn't feel it was wise
for him to be out all night, so I asked him to set a reasonable

time to be back. He suggested 2:00 a.m., which I thought was plenty late.

When the clock struck two (I just "happened" to be up reading at the time), he walked through the door. Considering his recent attitude toward curfews, I was pleasantly surprised.

As he headed toward his room, I said, "I just have to ask—I honestly thought you'd be late. I thought you agreed to the time because you figured it would be easier to get forgiveness than permission. What's happening?"

He looked at me for a moment, then said, "Well, Dad, I decided our relationship means more to me than staying out."

This son is now married and has a beautiful family of his own. Once, when I asked him if there was anything I had done right during those years, he replied, "The thing I appreciated most is that you just kept trying."

What matters?

Life matters.

And each day of life is an unknown, unwritten page.

But if we value principles, learn from our experience, and invite and live in harmony with inspiration in our lives—and we keep trying—we can develop the wisdom to live joyfully and well.

We hope our sharing will help you on your journey . . . because we know that your life matters.

NOTES

CHAPTER 1: What Matters

1. This information is from a study conducted by the Profiles Department at FranklinCovey. A complimentary copy of this report is available at www.franklincovey.com/lifematters.

2. Covey, Stephen R. *The 7 Habits of Highly Effective Families.* Golden Books, New York, 1997, p. 17.

CHAPTER 2: The Three "Gotta Do's"

1. This story was shared by a colleague. We also became aware of a similar story printed in *Reader's Digest*, July 1980, p. 21.

2. Weihenmayer, Erik. *Touch the Top of the World: A Blind Man's Journey to Climb Farther Than the Eye Can See.* Plume, New York, reprint edition, March 26, 2002. This is Erik's biography. Erik shared this story at the FranklinCovey Symposium in 2002.

3. Collins, Jim. *Good to Great. Why Some Companies Make the Leap . . . and Others Don't.* Harper Business, New York, 2001, pp. 83–87. While we shared the story in this book as Jim shared it in a program for executives in Arizona, we took the quotes directly from his subsequently released book.

4. Peck, M. Scott. *The Road Less Traveled.* Touchstone, New York, 1978, p. 15.

5. Ibid., p. 16.

6. This summary of the work of Kathleen S. Bahr and Cheri A. Loveless is used with their permission. Portions are available in Bahr, Kathleen S. "The Power of the Home Economy," World Congress of Families II, Geneva, Switzerland, November 1417, 1999. See also note 8.

7. Demos, John. "The Changing Faces of Fatherhood." *In Past, Present, Personal: The Family and the Life Course in American History.* Oxford University Press, New York, 1986. Also quoted in Bahr and Loveless (1998), see note 8.

8. Bahr, Kathleen S., and Loveless, Cheri A., "Family Work in the 21st Century." In *Charting a New Millennium*, edited by Maurine Proctor and Scot Proctor, Aspen Books, Salt Lake City, UT, 1998, p. 184.

9. Ibid., pp. 185–187.

10. Ibid., p. 187.

11. Ibid., pp. 188–189.

12. Ibid., p. 177.

13. Stanley, Thomas J., and Danko, William D. *The Millionaire Next Door.* Longstreet Press, Marietta, GA, 1997.

14. Thanks to Marci and Ken Redding at www.themoneyplanner.com for their help with this example.

15. Covey, Stephen R.; Merrill, A. Roger; and Merrill, Rebecca R. *First Things First: to Live, to Learn, to Love, to Leave a Legacy*. Simon and Schuster, New York, 1994. See Chapter 5, "The Passion of Vision" and Appendix A, "Mission Statement Workshop."

16. Garfield, Charles. *Peak Performers: The New Heroes of American Business*. Avon Books, New York, reprint edition, 1991, p. 102.

17. Whittier, John Greenleaf. "The Grave by the Lake." *The Complete Poetical Works of John Greenleaf Whittier*. Houghton, Mifflin, Boston, 1904.

CHAPTER 3: Work Matters

1. Brown, Bettina Lankard. "Changing Career Patterns." *ERIC Digest* 219, ERIC Clearing House on Adult Career and Vocational Education, Columbus, OH, October 2000. Although definitive research in this area is difficult, due to varying definitions of "career," it is a topic addressed by many career counselors, all of whom agree it is increasing dramatically. This article provides a good overview.

2. Stanley, Thomas J., and Danko, William D. *The Millionaire Next Door*. Longstreet Press, Marietta, GA, 1997, p. 9.

3. Christiansen, Shawn L., and Palkovitz, Rob. "Why the 'Good Provider' Role Still Matters." *Journal of Family Issues*, Vol. 22, No. 1 (January 2001): 84–106; as quoted in *The Family in America*, New Research Supplement, March 2001.

4. Levine, James A. and Pittinsky, Todd L. *Working Fathers: New Strategies for Balancing Work and Family*, Addison-Wesley, Reading, MA, 1997, pp. 20–33.

5. www.workandfamily.org. Center for Work Family Balance. Research tables of collected data. Table 15, Composition of Working Households.

6. Kelley, Linda. *Two Incomes and Still Broke?* Random House, New York, 1996; Dappen, Andy. *Shattering the Two-Income Myth*, Brier Books, Brier, WA, 1997. See also the Motley Fool Website (www.fool.com), which offers an online calculator, Should My Spouse Work?"

7. Hochschild, Arlie R. *The Time Bind*. Metropolitan Books, New York, 1997.

8. Astorga, Henry. "Asian Work Ethic—Fact or Fluff?" *Today's Asian Business Strategy Ezine*, September 19, 2001; see also Kotkin, Joel. *Tribes*. Random House, New York, 1993, see esp. Chapters 5–6.

9. Bruch, H. and Ghoshal, S. "Beware the Busy Manger." *Harvard Business Review*. February 2002.

10. FranklinCovey/Harris Interactive "xQ™" (Execution Quotient) Survey of 11,045 U.S. workers, representing executives, managers, and

front-line workers across 11 major industries, including banking and finance, retail trade, healthcare, public administration and government, military, technology services, telecommunications, education, automotive, accommodation and food services, and communications. Survey results are accessible at www.franklincovey.com.

11. Virginia Tech's National Institute for Personal Finance Employee Education, presentation to the AICCA Mid-Winter Meeting, San Diego, CA, January 14, 2000.

12. Covey, Stephen R. *The 7 Habits of Highly Effective People.* Simon and Schuster, New York, 1989, pp. 65–94.

13. Drucker, Peter. *The Effective Executive.* HarperCollins, New York, New York, 2002, p. 52.

14. Ibid., p. 98.

15. Alcott, Louisa May. *Little Women.* Grosset and Dunlap, New York. Reprint of 1915 Little, Brown edition, p. 281.

16. Killinger, Barbara. *Workaholics: The Respectable Addicts.* Simon and Schuster, New York, 1991; also Robinson, Bryan E. *Chained to the Desk: A Guidebook for Workaholics, Their Partners and Children, and the Clinicians Who Treat Them.* New York University Press, New York, 2001.

17. Friedman, Stewart D., Christensen, Perry, and DeGroot, Jessica. "Work and Life: The End of the Zero-Sum Game." *Harvard Business Review,* November–December 1998, pp. 119—120.

18. Ibid., pp. 120—121.

CHAPTER 4: Family Matters

1. Carlson, Allan. "The Natural Family is the Fundamental Social Unit: A Summons to Create Social Engineering," Speech given at the World Congress of Families II, Geneva, Switzerland, November 15, 1999.

2. From references cited in Covey, Stephen R. *The 7 Habits of Highly Effective Families.* Golden Books, New York, 1997, p. 17.

3. Ibid., p. 17.

4. Horn, Wade F., and Sylvester, Tom. *Father Facts,* 4th edition. National Fatherhood Initiative, Gaithersburg, MD, 2002. Statistic in the text is from the 1997 Fatherhood Initiative Study, also accessible at www.fatherhood.org.

5. Haley, George. "Family." Speech given at the World Congress of Families II, Geneva, Switzerland, November 17, 1999.

6. Used by permission of Family Leadership International, LLC.

(Notes 7–13 and information referenced in the text were taken from the following source: VanDenBerghe, Elizabeth, "Happiness, Health and Marriage," *Ensign Magazine,* August 2001, pp. 28–35.)

7. Lillard, L.A., and White, L.J. "'Til Death Do Us Part: Marital Disruption and Mortality." *American Journal of Sociology,* March 1995, pp. 1131, 1143.

8. Burr, J.A.; McCall, P.L.; and Powell-Griner, E. "Catholic Religion and Suicide: The Mediating Effect of Divorce." *Social Science Quarterly,* June 1994, 300–318; Robins, L.N., and Regier, D.A. *Psychiatric Disorders in America: The Epidemiologic Catchment Area Study* (1991).

9. Waite, L.J. "Does Marriage Matter?" *Demography,* November 1995, pp. 483–507; Gove, W.R. "Sex, Marital Status, and Mortality." *American Journal of Sociology,* July 1973, pp. 45–67.

10. Robins, L.N., and Regier, D.A. *Psychiatric Disorders in America: The Epidemiologic Catchment Area Study* (1991).

11. Rindfuss, R.R., and VandenHeuvel, A. "Cohabitation: A Precursor to Marriage or an Alternative to Being Single?" *Population and Development Review,* December 1990, 703–26.

12. Michael, R.T.; Gagnon, J.H.; Laumann, E.O.; and Kolata, G. *Sex in America: A Definitive Survey* (1994).

13. Coombs, R.H. "Marital Status and Personal Well-Being: A Literature Review." *Family Relations,* January 1991, p. 100; Gove, W.R.; Style, C.B.; and Hughes, M. "The Effect of Marriage on the Well-Being of Adults: A Theoretical Analysis" *Journal of Family Issues,* March 1990, pp. 4–35; Wood, W.; Rhodes, N.; and Whelan, M. "Sex Differences in Positive Well-Being: A Consideration of Emotional Style and Marital Status." *Psychological Bulletin,* vol. 106, no. 2 (1989), pp. 249–64.

14. The Family and Society Data Base—a component of the John L. Swan Library on Family and Culture. See www.profam.org.

15. Used by permission of Family Leadership International, LLC.

16. Evans, Richard L. . . . *An Open Road.* Vol. 3. *Thoughts for 100 Days.* Publishers Press, Salt Lake City, 1968. Used by permission.

17. For more information on how to write a family mission statement, refer to: Covey, Stephen R. *The 7 Habits of Highly Effective Families,* Golden Books, New York, New York, 1997, pp. 70–109.

18. For more information on how to create win-win agreements in the family, refer to Ibid., pp. 188–195

19. Statistics on Adult Literacy, Orange County Register, Santa Anna, CA, September 22, 2002.

20. Lee, Harold B. *Strengthening the Home.* Pamphlet. The Church of Jesus Christ of Latter-day Saints, 1973, p. 7.

CHAPTER 5: Time Matters

1. "The Chronic Complaint." *Scientific American,* September 2002, p. 10.

2. Hanna, David P. *Leadership for the Ages,* Executive Excellence Publishing, Provo, UT, 2001, pp. 163, 170.

3. Evans, Richard L., taken from our personal notes after seeing an inspirational film, *Man's Search for Happiness*, in the 1960s.

4. FranklinCovey/Harris Interactive "xQ™" (Execution Quotient)
Survey. Survey results are accessible at www.franklincovey.com.

CHAPTER 6: Money Matters

1. This and quality information on many related economic issues is available at www.economy.com. Specific information regarding credit card
usage is available at cardweb.com.

2. "Making Marriage Last," published by the American Academy of
Matrimonial Lawyers, www.aaml.org/Marriage_Last/MarriageLast
Text.htm.

3. Virginia Tech's National Institute for Personal Finance Employee
Education, presentation to the AICCA Mid-Winter Meeting, San
Diego, CA, January 14, 2000.

4. Stanley, Thomas J. *The Millionaire Mind*. Andrews McMeel Publishing,
Kansas City, 2000, p. 4.

5. Kiyosaki, Robert T. *Rich Dad, Poor Dad* Warner Books, New York,
New York, 1997, p. 65.

6. Stanley, Thomas J., and Danko, William D. *The Millionaire Next Door*.
Longstreet Press, Atlanta, 1996, pp. 8–11.

7. www.cardweb.com; see also "Credit Crunch" by Dayana Yochim at
www.fool.com.

8. Stanley, Thomas J., and Danko, William D. *The Millionaire Next Door*.
Longstreet Press, Atlanta, 1996, p. 10.

9. Clarke, J. Reuben *One Hundred Eighth Annual Conference*, The
Church of Jesus Christ of Latter-day Saints, Salt Lake City, UT, April
1938, p. 103.

10. Kiyosaki, Robert T. *Rich Dad, Poor Dad*. Warner Books, New York,
1997, p. 69.

11. "Financial Literacy in America," posted on www.bankrate.com, March
16, 2003.

12. Harris, Blaine, and Coonradt, Charles. *The Four Laws of Debt Free
Prosperity*. Chequemate International, Bountiful, UT, 1996, 2001,
p. 59.

13. www.bankrate.com; www.cardweb.com; www.fool.com; www.credit-
cardsusa.com.

14. Covey, Stephen R.; Merrill, A. Roger; and Merrill, Rebecca R. *First
Things First*, Simon and Schuster, New York, 1994, see esp. pp. 137–138.

15. Covey, Stephen R. *The 7 Habits of Highly Effective People*. Simon and
Schuster, New York, 1989, pp. 188–203.

CHAPTER 7: Wisdom Matters

1. Fosdick, Harry Emerson. *Twelve Tests of Character.* Harper and Brothers, New York and London, 1923.

2. Drummond, Henry. *The Greatest Thing in the World and Pax Vobiscum.* The Gold Medal Library, London and Calcutta, pp. 29–30.

3. Frankl, Viktor E.. *Man's Search for Meaning,* First Washington Square Press Printing, Simon and Schuster, New York, 1985, p. 86.

4. Mencius. *The Sayings of Mencius.* Translated by James R. Ware. New American Library, New York, 1960, p. 100.

5. Gordon, Arthur. *A Touch of Wonder: A Book to Help People Stay in Love With Life,* Jove Edition, Jove Publications, New York, 1978, p. 171.

6. *Aesop's Fables.* Illustrated by Ernest Griset, with text based on Croxall, LaFontaine, and L'Estrange. London: Cassell, Petter, Galpin, p. 372.

7. Lewis, C. S. *Surprised by Joy.* Harcourt Brace Jovanovich, 1955, p. 177.

8. Prather, Hugh, *Notes to Myself,* reprint edition, Bantam Books, New York, 1983.

9. "Financial Literacy in America," www.bankrate.com, March, 2003.

10. www.tvturnoff.org.

ABOUT THE AUTHORS

Roger Merrill has had over 36 years of experience as a senior executive, writer, teacher, and consultant. He was a cofounder of the Covey Leadership Center—now The FranklinCovey Company—and is a principal of Agilix Labs, which is involved in the creation of software applications for the new Tablet PCs.

In addition to her primary focus on home and family over the years, **Rebecca Merrill** has assisted Stephen R. Covey in writing *The 7 Habits of Highly Effective People* and *The 7 Habits of Highly Effective Families.* She also assisted Roger, Stephen, and DeWitt Jones with *The Nature of Leadership.*

Together, Roger and Rebecca wrote *Connections Quadrant II Time Management* and, with Stephen Covey, coauthored *First Things First*—the best-selling time management book of all time. They have seven children and fifteen grandchildren, and live in Lehi, Utah. E-mail the authors at lifematters@armerrill.com.

A BRIEF BIBLIOGRAPHY

For a more complete list, log on to www.Franklincovey.lifematters.

Bennett, William J. *The Broken Hearth: Reversing the Moral Collapse of the American Family.* Random House/WaterBrook Press, 2001.

Blankenhorn, David, *Fatherless America: Confronting Our Most Urgent Social Problem.* Basic Books, 1995.

Carlson, Allan C. *From Cottage to Workstation: The Family's Search for Social Harmony in the Industrial Age.* Ignatius Press, 1993.

Cherrington, David J. *The Work Ethic, Working Values and Values That Work.* Amacom, 1980.

Chilton, David. *The Wealthy Barber: Everyone's Commonsense Guide to Becoming Financially Independent.* Prima Publishing, 1998.

Ciulla, Joanne B. *The Working Life: The Promise and Betrayal of Modern Work.* Times Books, 2000.

Dappen, Andy. *Shattering the Two-Income Myth: Daily Secrets for Living Well on One Income.* Brier Books, 1997.

Desert Wisdom: Sacred Middle Eastern Writings From the Goddess Through the Sufis, trans. and commentary by Neil Douglas-Klotz. HarperCollins, 1995.

Eyre, Linda and Richard. *Teaching Your Children Responsibility.* Simon and Schuster, 1994.

Fraser, J.T. *Time, the Familiar Stranger.* Microsoft Press, 1987.

Friedman, Stewart D., and Greenhaus, Jeffrey. *Work and Family—Allies or Enemies? What Happens When Business Professionals Confront Life Choices.* Oxford University Press, 2000.

Gies, Frances and Joseph. *Marriage and the Family in the Middle Ages.* Harper and Row, 1987.

Hunnicutt, Benjamin Kline. *Work Without End. Abandoning Shorter Hours for the Right to Work.* Temple University Press, 1988.

Kelley, Linda. *Two Incomes and Still Broke? It's Not How Much You Make, but How Much You Keep.* Times Books, 1996.

Levine, James A., and Pittinsky, Todd L. *Working Fathers: New Strategies for Balancing Work and Family.* Addison-Wesley, 1997.

Nemeth, Maria. *The Energy of Money: A Spiritual Guide to Financial and Personal Fullfillment.* Ballantine, 2000.

Orman, Suze. *The 9 Steps to Financial Freedom: Practical and Spiritual Steps So You Can Stop Worrying.* Three Rivers Press, 2000.

Peel, Kathy. *The Family Manager's Guide for Working Moms.* Ballantine, 1997.

Popenoe, David. *Life Without Father: Compelling New Evidence That Fatherhood and Marriage Are Indispensable for the Good of Children and Society.* Harvard University Press, 1999.

Robinson, John P., and Godbey, Geoffrey. *Time for Life: The Surprising Ways Americans Use Their Time,* 2nd ed., Pennsylvania State University Press, 1999.

Smith, Steve, ed. *Ways of Wisdom: Readings on the Good Life.* University Press of America, 1983.

Sternberg, Robert J. *Wisdom: Its Nature, Origins, and Development.* Cambridge University Press, 1990.

Telishkin, Rabbi Joseph. *Jewish Wisdom: Ethical, Spiritual, and Historical Lessons from the Great Works and Thinkers.* Morrow, 1994.

Thomas, Keith, ed. *The Oxford Book of Work.* Oxford University Press, 1999.

Thorpe, Douglas, ed. *Work and the Life of the Spirit.* Mercury House, 1998.

World Scripture: A Comparative Anthology of Sacred Texts. Paragon House, 1991.

INDEX

258

About FranklinCovey.

FranklinCovey (NYSE:FC) is a global leader in effectiveness training, productivity tools, and assessment services for organizations and individuals. Our clients include 90 percent of the Fortune 100, more than 75 percent of the Fortune 500, thousands of small and mid-sized businesses, as well as numerous government and educational institutions. FranklinCovey provides professional services and products in 39 offices and in 95 countries worldwide.

FranklinCovey's purpose is to help organizations succeed by unleashing the power of their workforce to focus and execute on organizational priorities. We do this through a series of assessments, work sessions, and tools designed to get everyone focused on the few "wildly important"goals that, if achieved, make all the difference.

Our core products and services include:
xQTM Survey and Debrief
(to help leaders assess their organization's
"Execution Quotient")
Workshops
> Aligning Goals for Results
> FOCUS: Achieving Your Highest Priorities
> The 7 Habits of Highly Effective People©
> The 4 Roles of Leadership

Planning Systems
> Tablet Planner for the Tablet PC
> PlanPlus for Microsoft Outlook
> FranklinCovey Planning Software
> Palm OS and Pocket PC Software

For free trial versions:
Tablet PlannerTM software, www.franklincovey.com/tabletplanner.
PlanPlusTM for Microsoft Outlook, www.franklincovey.com/planplus.

For speaking engagements with Roger and Rebecca Merrill:
FranklinCovey Speakers Bureau, www.franklincovey.com/speakers
or call 1-800-240-1706.

For information on all other products and services:
www.franklincovey.com/forbusiness
2200 West Parkway Blvd., Salt Lake City, Utah, 84119-2331, USA
1-800-868-1776 (International callers: 001-801-817-1776)
Fax: 001-801-342-6664